PARANORMAL & THE OCCULT

PARANORMAL & THE OCCULT

The Interviews: Volume 6

ALAN R. WARREN

Copyright

Paranormal & The Occult: The Interviews
Written by Alan R. Warren
Published by House of Mystery

Cover design, formatting, layout, and editing by Evening Sky Publishing Services

Published in United States of America
ISBN (Paperback): 978-1-989980-30-9
ISBN (eBook): 978-1-989980-29-3

CONTENTS

MIND OVER MATTER

PARANORMAL TOOLS

RELIGION & THE OCCULT

Introduction

The *House of Mystery Radio Show* has been on the air for ten years now, broadcasting in over a dozen cities in the United States, including KKNW 1150 A.M. Seattle/Tacoma, KCAA 106.5 F.M. Los Angeles/102.3 F.M. Riverside/1050 A.M. Palm Springs. I started the show to find out as much information on the world's mysteries in areas of crime, science, religion, history, paranormal, and more.

Like most people, I have heard stories and rumors and read books or watched documentaries on television, but I would seldom hear one direct answer to a question. Throughout my time recording interviews, I sought out people who had themselves researched a subject enough to have written a book or created a documentary, or even people involved in the event or topic that would have first-hand knowledge.

In most cases, the strange thing was that there was a popular or mainstream idea about what happened; one reported at the time of the event, but then there was an alternative idea. Most writers who had books or shows that did well quite often disagreed with the current theory and would accuse the media of faking the story and hiding the truth from everyone. An example would be "Who shot JFK?" Different government agencies and news media have reported a well-known theory that most people in America have come to accept as the truth. But since the original Warren Report on JFK's assassination, there have been hundreds of theories promoted by many authors and lots of research completed.

In this series, we review the most accepted explanation on the topic. Then, we follow up with each of the alternative theories presented during our interviews with the person or people reporting them. There will be no committed answer at the end of the book. Our goal is to provide a concise review of the extraordinary things we learned during the show's interviews.

Each book in this series lays out the topic's details and then follows up with what we've learned from each guest. Like the others in the *House of Mystery Radio Show Interviews Series,* this book does not attempt to solve the case but only reviews it. It is an excellent reference for researchers and a good overview for people who don't know the topic well.

Similar to the other volumes in this series, only the highlights of each interview will be included. All of these interviews, and more, are available to listen to on my website: www.alanrwarren.com/hom-podcast-episodes.

In this book, Volume 6, the subject of the Paranormal will be covered. During the show's first ten years, the paranormal was a very popular topic. In society, several television series were airing that covered themes such as ghost hunting, haunted houses, mediums communicating with the dead, and witchcraft. Even Satanism or spirituality was often covered since religion was often given the power to either protect or attack the person doing the investigating.

One thing to mention is that I selected some of the most known personalities working in each paranormal field mentioned. If you would like to hear the complete interviews, you can go to my website or follow the links listed at the end of each chapter or under the Reference section of this book. There are several more interviews on my website than what is included here in this book, as I tried to include the guest that I found to be the most reliable and honest in their particular field. That doesn't mean that I didn't enjoy or appreciate the interviews not placed in this book, but I had to curate them in the best way possible.

Another thing to note is that for the most part, I kept all of the television, radio, and movie guests of the paranormal field that I interviewed out of the book as well. I found that sometimes their brand came through during their interviews. They were sometimes under contract or felt obligated to speak of only what they were allowed. Again, I'm not saying that I don't like guests in the spotlight through different media forms, but I found they often had something to sell or spoke in a particular formula. This book isn't the proper forum for those interviews. All interviews are available on my website.

PARAPSYCHOLOGY

School of Parapsychology

INTERVIEW WITH DR. CIARAN O'KEEFE

Throughout my life, I often found myself up watching T.V. late into the night, unable to sleep for various reasons, usually because of how I dealt with stress. I remember coming across a show out of the U.K. called *Most Haunted*, which starred Yvette Fielding as the host and usually a medium that changed throughout the series. During my time watching the series, I saw Derek Acorah, David Wells, and Chris Conway as the mediums on the show.

Another team member of the show was who I became most interested in, Dr. Ciaran O'Keefe. He had the role of a parapsychologist. O'Keefe was an open-minded skeptic who would try to explain any logical or scientific answer on any reported paranormal activity in the location where the *Most Haunted* team would travel to and investigate.

The *Most Haunted* series ran on television from 2002 until 2010. I was living in Canada or the United States during those years, and in both countries, the series was on late at night, usually after midnight, and it was a rerun, and never the current episode that was airing in the U.K. at the same time.

O'Keefe works at Bucks New University and has held a research associate position at the University of Toulouse II–Le Mirail. He is also an online tutor at Derby University. O'Keefe is a Society for Psychical Research member and a senior advisor to the Ghost Club. He completed his Ph.D. at the University of Hertfordshire under the supervision of Richard Wiseman and Julia Buckroyd.

O'Keefe started the School of Parapsychology to provide a gateway to scientific inquiry into the world of the paranormal. The online course lasted several weeks, whereby all the students met once a week with O'Keefe. He gave a class and administered homework to be accomplished before the next class.

I'm usually not one to join such a thing, especially back in the early 2000s when the internet was new and not always reliable. But O'Keefe's performance on the *Most Haunted* series and his educational history intrigued me. I ended up taking two courses, Foundations of Parapsychology and Intermediate Parapsychology. In fact, after completing the courses, I traveled to London, U.K., and met O'Keefe and everyone else with who I had been in the courses.

Looking back at it now, I realize that it had a rather significant impact upon life at the time, but all without me knowing it. Before my *House of Mystery Radio Show* had made it to the NBC talk radio network in Los Angeles, I produced other people's podcasts and radio shows. Knowing that I had wanted to be a radio host myself, I used the podcast platform to practice doing interviews to get ready for radio.

O'Keefe was the first interview I did for a recording, and when I listen to it now to produce this interview series of books, it's embarrassing on how bad I was. I have heard this from some of the greatest radio hosts of our time, and I am okay with it. I have thankfully gotten better and good enough to be on network radio.

I am honored to have had O'Keefe as my first interview, someone as intelligent and good at what he does, but very thankful that he didn't completely ghost me from his life after listening to the interview! Yes, it was that awful!

O'Keefe's online classes can be found at https://www.ecwid.com/store/theschoolofparapsychology/ABOUT-DR-CIARAN-OKEEFFE-c24458005

This interview was recorded on July 18, 2014, and these are the highlights of the show.

A: How are you doing tonight?

C: Hello Alan, how are you?

Q. Parapsychology seems to have a lot of different meanings, especially on T.V., which lead people to believe that it's something that it's not really, correct?

A. Yes! Yes definitely. Even asking members of the public what their perception of a parapsychologist is, and a lot of people think it's just a ghostbuster, and that's it. The media is to blame for that, and I say that even being part of the media, ghost hunting campaign.

Unfortunately, academia, universities, and mainstream science, generally listen to what the media does and how the media portrays these things.

Q. But why is that? Certainly, they have to know that there are educated people like yourself working in this field. But there are not a lot of parapsychologists in the world?

A. No, and it wouldn't be wrong for me to say that probably in the world today, we're talking about parapsychologists educated up to Ph.D.. level and doing a Ph.D. within parapsychology. We're probably talking about 50 or 60. When you compare that to a hard science, physics, chemistry, or biology, for example, you can add any number of zeroes onto that figure in terms of the number of scientists employed in those disciplines. For that reason, there isn't a great representation of parapsychology.

And as to answering your question, "Why do I think there's this perception? Or misperception of what parapsychology is?" Partly it's the history of parapsychology, which you know all too well. There's accusations and instances of fraud throughout its history of certain scientists being caught at cheating their data. But also, psychics being caught cheating as well, and that means that parapsychology has a reputation that it has to constantly fight to get away from.

Mainstream science looks at parapsychology and still considers it to be related to the psychic at the end of the pier or the ghostbusters going into a house. As soon as my colleagues see that there are peer-review journals, there are conferences, and there is good science going on, then, of course, it changes their minds instantly.

Q. It does seem strange.

A. There's a huge kind of philosophical and world-changing aspect to it as well, which is if you're talking to physicists and mainstream scientists, there's the idea that if any of this stuff is true from their perspective. So, things like telepathy, precognition, and even ghosts as being true, it means that the laws of physics would have to change. Parapsychology can come across as a little bit of a threat to the laws of mainstream science. For that reason, you're dealing with scientists that have a huge belief system in psychics and their own belief system, and therefore it's a threat to their belief system that this stuff could be true. It's easier to come from a very cynical point of view and say, "It's not true at all, and I don't even know why you're researching this stuff?"

Q. I noticed that your degree covers criminal behaviors and wondered how that connects with parapsychology?

A. It is very different, apart from the interesting cross-over you get within an area I like to call psychic criminology, where there's an aspect of the paranormal involved in investigations. A prime example is psychic detectives – these people who claim that, on the one hand, they have psychic abilities and can use those abilities to aid in a criminal investigation. So, that's one side. Then there's the other side which is the quite common claim you get from some police officers or investigators when they have a sense that something is going to happen. So, it's the sense that when they go into a particular building that there's danger around the corner.

Q. Would you consider that sense from the detectives' something that's in their DNA or with which we are born?

A. Yes. I think there's a lot of merit to thinking about it from an evolutionary perspective. There are some evolutionary parapsychologists that say this predictive ability is something that we all had thousands and thousands of years ago when it was something that we needed. We needed to know if there were dangerous animals around the corner. We needed to have that sixth sense, as it were. As the world has become more developed and there are fewer of those dangers around, we have lost that ability, and it's only fleeting in a certain number of people.

But there's been some recent research only in the last five or so years about something called "Presentiment," which is a professed ability to sense something in the future, but it's an unconscious sense. Several researchers have set up experiments where they show people random photographs. Within those photographs, there'll be a random picture of a spider or snake – something people are phobic about or fearful of. In measuring people's physiology when they're presented with those photos, what tends to happen is people's physiology reacts fearfully immediately before they're shown the spider or the snake. Even though they are not aware that it's going to happen and they are not consciously aware of becoming fearful, their physiology changes: their heart rate goes up, and they sweat more because they are just about to be shown quite a scary photo. That's good laboratory evidence for this idea that there might be something sort of inherent, predictive abilities, some inherent sixth sense like I said we once had, but now perhaps we've lost it. It's buried somewhere in our conscience.

Q. It must be very difficult to test this scientifically? You know, to have a closed environment.

A. Yes, very difficult. It's the reason why the word "PSI" exists, or "Sci" in parapsychology because very early on, parapsychologists realized that if you're trying to differentiate between telepathy, precognition, and clairvoyant – clairvoyance being the action of the mind on an object. So, if you draw an object on paper, and put it in an envelope, how can I work out what's on that piece of paper in the envelope? I might use a form of clairvoyance. Parapsychologists realized very quickly that if I get that particular drawing correct, am I using telepathy, so mind to mind contact? Did I have a dream about it last night? Then remember the dream today? Therefore, it's a form of precognition. Or am I interacting with the drawing in some way?

So, essentially I'm saying that it's all very confusing, and we can't work out exactly what the ability is. That ties into what you're saying that as parapsychologists, it's very difficult to work out that if somebody has some form of paranormal communication, what is that process? What is actually going on? But also, yes, you're right, how can you set up experiments to specifically test a specific ability?

I know Caroline Watt, in Edinburgh, has been doing some good work on dream telepathy. She calls it "Dream Cognition" or "Dream Precognition." But it's getting groups of people to dream about a randomly selected clip that's selected by a computer at random the following day - then getting people to review their dream from the night before. So, there you have a prime example of something that, if they're correct, can only be precognition. It can't be telepathy. It can't be some other form.

Q. Have you yourself done any tests on mediums or psychics?

A. Yes, I've done lots of tests. In fact, my Ph.D. was focused on testing mediums and finding a way of testing mediums in a very controlled environment. So that if they were successful, the only explanation that you could say is that it was mediumship. Since then, at Buxton University, I have been involved in mediumship research as well.

You can do it. You work with mediums to make sure that they are comfortable in the environment because as soon as you start to get too clinical, there's the worry that they could lose their ability. So, you need to really work in collaboration.

The other aspect of it is, I think that one of the main findings that I've come up with is that you can't actually test mediumship communication in the lab. All you can test is paranormal communication. By that, I mean if you had a medium in a lab, and you ask them to come up with a reading for somebody in a highly controlled way, there has to be some verification of the information that the medium came up with. There has to be some way down the line.

In order for that to happen, if they are accurate, it means that maybe what happened in that particular scenario was that maybe there was some form of telepathy. Or maybe they accessed some record somewhere in an ethereal plane. What I'm trying to get at is, maybe a medium might say that they are getting the message directly from spirit. There's no way that we, as researchers, can verify that. All we can verify is that the medium came up with the information, and it has to be some form of paranormal communication. That in itself would be fantastic, but I'm just saying that I don't think we can test mediumship in a lab.

Q. That brings us to "Suggestion." When you are out on a ghost hunt and walking through a haunted place and knowing a lot of facts about the place, is that going to create some sort of image in your mind?

A. Yes, absolutely! As soon as you tell people that the place is haunted, forget any information. Just telling them the place is haunted, you suffer from a situation where they can interpret any natural environmental changes as being a result of ghosts or a ghostly presence. It can be something as simple as a change in temperature. If there's a change of temperature and somebody knows the location is haunted, they may actually say that it is a ghost. Whereas, if you put them in an office building and don't tell them anything about the building, don't tell them it's haunted, but just have them in there working. Then, if the temperature drops, they might put the heating on or check to see if the window is open. So, suggestion plays a huge factor in paranormal hauntings.

Q. What do you think the advantage is to having a parapsychologist with you during a ghost hunt or on one of those paranormal shows you see on television?

A. The advantage is because of our training and knowledge. It's taking a very skeptical position of anything paranormal. By that, I don't mean cynical. I mean skeptical in the true sense of the word, which means we question the evidence.

We're not expert physicists. We're not expert environmentalists. But by the same token, we have knowledge about psychology. Most of us have psychology training in our background, so we are aware of these things like "suggestion." But also, things like hypnagogic experiences, sleep paralysis, stuff like this which can occur. We are also aware of the environmental explanations for what's going on.

But I think a team of solely parapsychologists investigating would be rubbish. You need paranormal investigators that have field experience. Parapsychologist lends that alternative explanation and that knowledge to what's going on.

Q. Ciaran, being a parapsychologist and skeptical when you are on a ghost hunt, do you ever get out of that mode and become scared?

A. It's interesting. Walking around the bunker myself (Nazi wartime bunker), in the pitch dark, with just a camera to light the way, I didn't feel remotely scared. I felt excited about the possibility that I might come across something. I think that for the majority of locations, it's simply that. It's excitement because I've devoted my life to investigating this sort of thing, so I'm not going to run away or be scared if anything should appear. If anything, if a ghost should appear in front of me, it would get bored from the battery of questions I'd ask it or photos I'd take.

There is a caveat with that. I can go to the most awful location, such as Eastern State Penitentiary in North America is a great example, or Waverly Hills Sanatorium. I've been in both of those locations, and I haven't felt the slightest bit scared.

S.S. Great Britain, which is a ship docked in Bristol, a ship that used to often take criminals, and also members of the public, over to America and Australia over one hundred years ago. Walking into a particular area on that ship and I felt spooked. I wished there was a better word for it. But I did feel spooked, I just didn't like it, and I'm glad I had that experience because it gives me empathy for the sorts of experiences Anna (Ciaran's wife) has had. It makes me realize that this is the sort of feeling that she's talking about. This sense that you don't like it.

Q. What kinds of data do you as a parapsychologist collect?

A. It's led by eyewitness testimony, initially research, speaking to people working in the location, the staff, but also speaking to eyewitnesses about their experiences. I use a cognitive interview, which is used by the police to get the most accurate information from witnesses. You get that information, and from that, you can pinpoint exact areas within that location. Those are the areas that you should focus the investigation on. Essentially there's no reason to investigate other areas where people haven't reported anything. For me, it doesn't make a lot of logic.

The first thing we do as a ghost-hunting team is to pinpoint those areas, then measure environmental variables in those areas. You can also focus as well, so if there's particular experiences that people or having, for example, if they're all reporting hairs going up on the back of their necks, then you might focus on infrasound.

If they are all talking about temperature drops, then you would look for temperature anomalies or humidity aspects, that sort of thing. But you focus all the equipment and measure as many environmental variables as you can, which includes infrasound, electromagnetic feels, humidity, air pressure, temperature, and have that recording for as close to 24 hours as you can.

You would also focus on times when people have had those experiences. If there's a repeatable time, then it would be interesting data from those particular times.

The next thing would be to send in individual members of the team. The preference is that some of the investigators would know the location and the stories, and some of the investigators wouldn't. Then you'd get them to record their experiences; a camera is the preferred method. The hope is that their experiences would tally up with what the eyewitnesses reported. That's why it's quite important not to have "suggestion" for everybody and to have some investigators going into the location blind.

The next step is to go from individuals to groups to see if that makes any difference. Constantly whilst this is going on, the environmental variables are being recorded. The logic behind that is if you are recording temperature, humidity in a particular area of the location, then it might vary if somebody goes into that location, and you need to be able to have that information.

Q. I noticed that in the investigation you did, you used the medium Chris Conway.

Do you use a medium in your investigations all the time?

A. No. We used Chris in a couple of episodes on two locations mainly because we work very well with Chris and have a lot of respect for him. But his involvement in the team is just like any other of the investigators. So, if we do use a medium, we don't use them in the way that you find some other teams do. They'll listen to what the medium says, and then suddenly, they'll follow exactly what the medium says.

So, if the medium says, "I'm getting the impression that there's a spirit of a little girl in the corner," suddenly the investigation turns into, "Right, let's have people sitting in the corner," or "Let's do a Ouija Board and try and contact this little girl." They're reacting to what the medium said. So, we might have mediums on investigations sometime, but it's not a medium-led investigation like you see with other teams.

Q. To a parapsychologist, what's the difference between a haunting and a poltergeist?

A. Hauntings are particularly spirits, whereas poltergeist cases are centered around individuals, and that's either because they have consciously or unconsciously created the phenomena. It is actually not a ghost at all. The individual is actually creating the phenomena. Therefore, some parapsychologists call poltergeists "RSPK," which is Recurrent Spontaneous Psycho Kinesis. It's almost as if the individual is using some sort of PK to move objects and create noises.

Q. What's your personal take on that?

A. It's very interesting. Quite early in my career, I bought into the idea of RSPK and that it was the individual causing it. Now I'm not so sure. Certainly, there's a book by Alan Gauld and Tony Cornell called *Poltergeist*, in which they do a survey of poltergeist and haunting cases, and they actually show that you cannot distinguish between the two so easily.

You will get some haunting cases where there's occasionally a noise that occurs, or when an object is moved, or there's a spontaneous fire, that sort of thing. Or you'll get a situation that's described as a poltergeist case, and yet the family moves away, and people in that location still experience the phenomena.

Well, if it is RSPK, then there's no way that the phenomenon should continue if the family leaves. The phenomenon should follow them. So, I'm of the opinion that I don't think we should be too quick to distinguish between the two, and I don't think we should be too quick to say that if there is a poltergeist phenomenon, it's because of a particular individual. The other thing is that William Roll, the parapsychologist that came up with this idea, said that the phenomena are normally focused around, or the majority of cases, about 70%, are focused around adolescent girls because of the emotional turmoil that they are going through. Now, if that's the case, it's genuinely because of adolescent turmoil, then we should be seeing poltergeist cases all over the place.

Q. Do you find there's a difference in the way that paranormal is investigated in the U.S. as compared to the U.K.?

A. Yes. Very, very different. There are two camps in North America. There is one camp that is focused on gadgets, focused on the scientific side. Who would basically like to go into an investigation armed to the teeth with as many gadgets as they can get? I think that same camp exists here in the U.K. as well.

But there are also investigators in the States who, I think, follow too much what the medium says. Even if the medium is speaking with vagueness and ambiguity, not picking up on anything specific, they'll often follow what the medium says and focus the investigation on that.

I don't want to make it sound arrogant that I have the only way of investigating, and I think it's the right way. I think that's far too arrogant. I think there is a number of ways of investigating. There's the spiritualism route, there's the use of seances, Ouija Boards, the use of equipment, or just back to the basics and not using any equipment at all, and just using the human senses. Of all of those, who is to say which one is the right one, and which one is the wrong one? It's just quite interesting that in North America, there seems to be a little bit more of an emphasis on having mediums involved in the investigations.

I think the word "science" is misused in investigations. Even the process that I was explaining earlier isn't necessarily a scientific approach. It's scientifically-minded but not necessarily scientific as we know it in laboratory research.

Q. What do you think of all the paranormal shows on the air?

A. I think the shows create a warped sense that every time you go out for an investigation, something happens. It's nothing like that at all.

Q. But they're cutting out the dead time, correct?

A. Yes, absolutely. Excuse the pun!

Q. Do you think that there's more of a belief in the paranormal in the United States or the U.K.?

A. That's a tough one. That's a really tough one. I think there's more of a belief in North America.

Q. Well, there's certainly more shows on the subject in the U.S.

A. Yes, there's more shows. They're more in the mainstream. People always ask me if I think the shows on ghost hunting have created a bad situation – kind of given ghost hunting a bad reputation. There's two sides to it. The advantage to all of the media stuff or the T.V. shows is they made discussion. They've made things like this, us doing this radio show, people going out on an investigation every weekend, stuff like that. They've made it more acceptable to believe in this sort of thing. That's a really good thing.

Q. If there are ghosts, do you think us investigating it will affect it in a negative way?

A. That's interesting. I've spoken to colleagues at particular locations who have said, "Wow, if you had only been here five years ago, stuff was happening five years ago. But unfortunately, now, every weekend, we have had ghost groups come in, ghost events come in, and it's almost as though them coming in have tired the ghosts out. They have got bored."

The constant groups kind of trudging through the location has almost killed the ghosts if that's the right expression. Sent them on their way, as it were. Without specifically saying, "They've gone to the light." But you're right. Having human agents, having people in a location can affect what's happening in that location too.

Q. Can it disturb the atmosphere?

A. Yes. I think it possibly could. It could really disturb it. Also, we're just talking about human beings in general. The emotion, feeling, and personalities of the people involved in those investigations can alter the atmosphere of the location in a particular way. If you have people in a particular mood, or highly negative, or people with aggressive personalities, that can have a different effect than somebody who is more positive.

Listen to the full interview with Dr. Ciaran O'Keefe on my website:

www.alanrwarren.com/hom-podcast-episodes/episode/80e4656a/ciaran-o-keefe-parapsychology-2014

Ghost Hunter

INTERVIEW WITH STEVE PARSONS

Steve Parsons has been a paranormal investigator for over 25 years, with several published articles and books out on the subject. He has been a consultant for several television networks covering ghost hunting as well, including the Discovery Channel and cohost of the BBC radio program *Ghost Chronicles*.

Parsons is also the co-founder of the U.K.-based paranormal research group "Para-Science," which is committed to moving forward quality investigations of the paranormal without any exaggerated claims. They are well known for being the best and most trustworthy of paranormal researchers in the world.

The *House of Mystery Radio Show* interviewed Steve Parsons three times over ten years because he was one of the best explainers of the attributes of a true parapsychologist. These are the highlights of all three interviews held in 2015, 2015, and 2018.

Q. Can you tell the listeners, in a snapshot, what you think the ideal way to investigate is?

A. In a snapshot. You are only there to investigate because somebody is having an experience. This idea of just going somewhere because it looks old and damp and haunted, or a murder has taken place, is the wrong way to be considering an investigation. If somebody is having an experience that they believe or claim to be paranormal, then the role of the investigator is to test that claim and understand the nature of the experience.

That is the starting point for every investigation. As it's a human experience, the last thing you would take out of the box is the ghost toys because you don't need them at this stage because you have nothing to measure. The only thing that you have to deal with is the account, the testimony of a human being who has had the experience.

The first stage has to be you go alone to examine the location, to spend time at the location, and to see if you, another human being at the same place, at the same sort of time, under the same sort of general conditions, will have the same similar sort of experience, and try and understand it.

Ghost investigators are a bit like Ufologists (one who studies UFOs) because they are never there when the original witness has their experience. So, you're always playing catch-up. You're always behind the curb. You are totally reliant on what you are being told by the witnesses. You have to put your beliefs, your own expectations, and agendas; you have to leave them behind.

If you're a skeptic, you're going to be naturally dismissive of somebody's account. They saw a ghost. There's no such thing as ghosts. So, you're already biased in your objectivity. Likewise, if you're a believer, if you're inclined to believe and somebody says they saw a ghost, "Oh wow! You saw a ghost!" Again, you're biased in the experiences you have.

All you have to go on is the information that you're given by the person. You know where there were, you know when they were, so you can try and be there on a similar sort of time. If people are watching this idea of turning the lights off and wandering around buildings in the dark, well, that applies if the building was dark, to begin with, and there's no electricity. But if somebody had been watching their favorite soap opera at 8 o'clock in the evening, sipping a glass of their favorite red wine, and they saw an apparition, why are they (ghost hunters) there at 3 o'clock in the morning, looking through a full spectrum camera, and trying to talk to the ghosts with an EVP. You're completely wasting your time.

You're going to find things that were never meant to be found anyway, and you're going to spend time misleading yourself and everyone else. You wait until 3 o'clock in the morning, turn off the lights, and you start saying, "Is there anybody there," and "I've got an EVP saying you're going to hell," and "I've got these shadow people on my infrared camera," well, that wasn't what was ever seen. That wasn't what was ever reported. So, who's misleading who here?

So, that's the basics to start from – the human experience and work from that. We take our lead, I guess, from archeologists because if archeologists are looking for old structures, they start with what they know and work towards the unknown. Paranormal investigators seem to start with the unknown. Somebody sees a ghost in the middle of the afternoon while working in an office.

Q. You have some amazingly big groups in the U.K. that have 40 or 50 people in them for an investigation. It's not an investigation. It's a mockery and a money event.

A. It's a circus. It's not just here in the U.K. When I was in New England, there was an investigation with eighty people in a very small building. I don't think the situation is very different on either side of the Atlantic.

The vast majority of paranormal investigations, things that are actually public, are marketing events. Tickets are sold, the events are promoted on Facebook and social media, and a large number of people who are not part of the group are turning up. They are taken, or dragged, from room to room. In the session, we are going to do table tipping, and then we will have one or two of you look through the full spectrum camera. Then our group resident sensitive will sense something in the corner of the room, and then we will have a tea break. That's what happens. Then, of course, they'll say, "We're not for profit." I know how much a lot of these locations are.

Q. I can see that, but the only way to come up with £1,000 to pay for the location is to bring people along.

A. I've got to make a clear distinction between going there for the purposes of conducting an investigation which is completely different than going, for example, to one of the courses – groups like what was described earlier here. Despite what I just said about these groups, within every group, there are people who are dedicated and interested in the paranormal.

What I have a problem with are groups who do this under the guise of an investigation. They will advertise that people are going on a real investigation, and with thirty, forty, fifty people, and more, you just are not going to have a real investigation.

The problem is what happens is people are just dragged from room to room or location to location, and it's divided up into a very set pattern. We will do calling out, we will do EVP, and even some of the more bizarre ones, we'll do the human pendulum. Which when I first heard of this, I had visions of them swinging the medium on a rope from the rafters. But that didn't take place.

Q. You're not saying that regular people can't investigate ghosts, are you?

A. Ghostology is about putting a little thought into what you are doing. All of the great breakthroughs in amateur science in astronomy, archeology, chemistry, and physics have been made by amateurs. The academics came along later and claimed the glory and mopped up the Nobel prizes. It's the same in the paranormal.

There are huge advances. There are huge areas where we have no understanding. The academics aren't really interested in going there, so there is an opportunity for investigators. Really good, dedicated investigators. But they need to up their game. They need to produce results that they can then take to the scientists and challenge them with them.

There's no use saying, "We got this really cool video last Friday night," then discover the clock on your camera or your sound recorder was set for the first of January 2000 because nobody bothered to set the date properly. It's those little basic things.

They're the sort of things that make what you're doing credible and meaningful, that you can show the skeptics that you have considered the flaws, considered that you are, in fact, not in a controlled environment, and you've taken steps to mitigate some of the problems, and giving your evidence a degree of more credibility. If you are going to measure something, people often measure temperature.

Q. Yes.

A. It's very commonly measured and one of the few things that I honestly believe investigators should spend a great deal of time on focusing measurement. But none the less, people will measure temperature but in a way that the results are meaningless. You cannot just wander around a room armed with a laser thermometer or an air probe thermometer, blindly taking the temperature and putting it down in a book.

Any environmental research, any environmental scientist, any HVAC engineer would look at you and laugh and say that your measurements are meaningless. But, if you measure in a different way, if you measure temperature to a given set of standards, and those standards have existed for tens of years. They're internationally agreed and laid down within legislation, the ISO standards, and if you measure your temperature to that standard using the right thermometer, then your data is meaningful. Then you can challenge the skeptics. There is evidence made with a calibrated thermometer and obtained to the relative ISO standards. Then watch the skeptics squirm.

Q. That level of knowledge you have, that common sense approach to an investigation, is this how the ParaScience group was set up?

A. That was why ParaScience was set up the way it was. It was set up twenty-two years ago. There are five simple steps:

1. Observe a phenomenon,

2. Hypothesize about what you think might be taking place,

3. Test your hypothesis. Were your tests supportive of the hypothesis or negative,

4. Re-hypothesize & retest,

5. Reach a conclusion.

We all did this in high school. You would write down the name of the experiment, the aim of the experiment, the equipment you were using, the method, the results, and the conclusions. Everyone did it, yet when they become ghost investigators, all of this stuff, walking around in a building saying, "Can you hear me?" or "If you can hear me, say my name," or "Can you tell me how many people are in this room? Oh my God, it said five!" That's not evidential.

Q. Do you believe in ghosts?

A. My new book coming out is sub-headed *Ghosts Exist* because every day, people experience ghosts. They see ghosts, they hear ghosts, and they interact with ghosts. Our problem is, "What are ghosts?" Because one person's experience and description of a ghost might be completely different from another's in terms of the mechanism.

A few days ago, I was sitting downstairs in the living room, and Elizabeth Taylor appeared in the corner of my room. She was talking, and she was a vision of loveliness, in full color, and at no point did she seem like a ghost. It was clearly the television.

The point I'm making is that ghosts don't always necessarily equate to the survival of death. It might be some form of replay. It might be some form of hallucination. It might be some sort of walking dream. It might be dead people coming back. We just don't know. If anybody tells you that they know what a ghost is, then they're making it up because we still don't know what ghosts are.

Let's look at some of the definitions according to the Oxford Dictionary. "The ghost is an apparition of a dead person which is believed to appear or become manifest in the living typically as a nebulous image." That's what the Oxford

Dictionary says. Yet, we've got lots of examples of which apparitions of living people have appeared. There are as many definitions of ghosts as there are people. In Parapsychology, they consider the study of ghosts to be related to aspects of survival beyond death. But there's actually very little to indicate that ghosts are entirely visions of the dead. They could be hallucinations. We just don't know. There's no doubt that ghosts exist.

Q. Tell us about your investigation into orbs?

A. It started back in the late 1990s. ParaScience invested in a digital camera, and back then, it was .8 megapixels, so state of the art. It took five pictures on a floppy disk, and we paid over one thousand pounds for it. We started to get these little glowing circles in some of the pictures.

Naturally, we were intrigued. This was something we hadn't seen photographically. They only seemed to appear in haunted houses, which is probably because we were only taking pictures with the camera in haunted houses. We were left with some questions. Was this new technology able to show us something that was unusual? Were we getting an insight into the paranormal?

But what happened was, wherever we took the damn thing, we got these little circles of light. It didn't matter if we took them at home or in haunted places. You get to the point that if you get them that often, then it's not going to be paranormal. Not unless the air is saturated with ghosts who all come back as a soap bubble. I don't want to come back as a soap bubble.

So, we sent off a batch of pictures that we had taken to Sony, the camera manufacturer, to see what they make of it. They went, "We haven't seen this before. We don't think it's a fault or defect with the camera." Of course, that made it more intriguing, but we were still not too happy about it.

What we did notice quite quickly was that when we were in an environment that was misty or raining or indeed occasionally an insect that was there, then the light started to go on. We started to realize that what we might be dealing with is a simple optical reflective phenomenon.

So, we started to do some rudimentary experiments. We started blowing talcum powder in front of the camera. We started to just see what would happen if this were what would take place. We then very quickly realized that was the case. So, we set out a series of experiments in order to test it properly.

We got the results of this in about 2003 and produced a paper. The results are available on the ParaScience website and have been published elsewhere also. We were absolutely convinced that the vast majority of these phenomena are entirely natural in their production – that they were moisture, they were pollen, they're dust, they're all this sort of rubbish that floats around in the air and an occasional thing with wings, and I don't mean angels.

We couldn't definitively prove that there wasn't a very small percentage that was unusual in some way, even potentially paranormal. But we eliminated in our own mind a big chunk of them. We tried several times to design, back in the early two thousand, using stereo photography, we had stereo film cameras with the team, but we didn't have stereo digital cameras. What we needed was to replicate a stereo digital camera, and it couldn't be done using two digital cameras side by side for technical reasons. The results would not be one hundred percent identical. Therefore, there was a flaw in the experiment.

In 2007 or 2008, we got wind of a 3D stereo camera that was being produced by Fuji Film in Japan, so we got in touch with them, and we started begging them. And eventually, we got one of the very first ones in the U.K.

We had to go to London to collect it, and coming back on the train from London, I put the batteries into the camera, and playing around with it, I took a picture. On the screen of the camera, I could see an orb. I knew, at that point in time, we had already demonstrated the camera was going to work.

In order to prove that these phenomena are airborne and close to the camera reflecting the flash, not at the opposite end of the room flying over Auntie Florence's head, or flying out of the dog's bottom, or wherever else they appear, and therefore paranormal.

But they are very, very close to the lens of the camera and reflect the lights of the camera. We took 1,800 stereo pictures, which is three thousand odds, close to four thousand stereo individual images to demonstrate this. Then to date, we've actually taken over 10,000 pictures, and we still use the camera regularly. We might find a paranormal one, one day.

It's always surprised me that nobody else has used stereo photography as an investigative tool. There are lots and lots of ghost photographs that are offered up. The photographs are two-dimensional, and they give you almost no information at all.

Ghost hunter Harry Price back in the 1930s, the great investigator, one of the cameras he used, although primarily in the séance room, photographing mediums, was a stereo camera. Can you imagine how much useful information we would get from a shadow person that was taken from a 3D camera as opposed to a two-dimensional photograph? But we still use the camera.

What I'm saying is that we have taken over 10,000 pictures, and we have a zero percent rate of paranormal hit rate. Investigators will often console themselves by often saying that 99 percent of orbs are dust and moisture and insects and other known phenomena, but one percent are paranormal. What they're really saying is everybody else's is rubbish, and theirs is the one percent. The ones they have on their website or Facebook page are paranormal when, in actual fact, that's just not the case.

Q. What else were you able to pick up from a 3D camera?

A. We were able to see other phenomena that appeared as paranormal. For example, on one occasion, the strap from the camera had fallen across the lens and produced one of these spirally white vortexes that used to be quite common in paranormal photography. We were one hundred percent sure it was the strap as it wasn't on the other stereo image.

Likewise, there was a human hair that got in front of the image and also breath because it wasn't the same on both the left and right images. Although we have never pursued those other lines of experimentation, after we demonstrated equivalently that the orb was, despite what people write down, because if you are looking at the bookshelf here, we have orbs. There's a whole raft of ludicrous books written about them where they represent angelic beings, or you can tell the sex of the orb by the color of the orb, people see faces in them, and that they are otherworldly beings.

The reason we did it was not to ridicule these people and their beliefs, but it was about doing meaningful research, collecting meaningful information and evidence. How many thousands of hours have been wasted by people sitting in front of the computer, blowing up pictures and fiddling with them in photoshop, determined to see a photograph of a demon in an orb? Stop wasting time with the known, and go and look for things that we genuinely don't know anything about.

Q. What are your thoughts on EVP?

A. There are two types of EVP. There is the Electronic Voice Phenomena. This idea that the dead are using electronic means to communicate with the living is far from a new phenomenon. It goes back to the very early days of the twentieth century. They were studying these phenomena and trying to use electronic devices to try and talk to the dead back in the nineteen-twenties.

Now that's completely different from this relatively new phenomenon that you're talking about, which has swept the paranormal world in recent years. It's always been there. People have always had sound recorders. It's developed from the EMF meter because you go back ten years, and the EMF meters, the ghost detectors, were the big thing. Every group had to have their EMF meter.

People discovered that these things weren't working as ghost detectors. They spent thirty-five or fifty dollars on this, and it actually wasn't detecting anything.

Q. You mean the ghost radar apps don't work on my phone either?

A. No. Not really, but what they did notice was these things had flashing lights, so they thought they had a communication device. Maybe they can't detect the ghost, but the ghost can flash the lights, which gradually develops into electronic speech because it crosses into EVP.

We've done experiments with people where we could pretty much control what they think they are hearing. The best EVPs are the ones you tell people in advance what they are going to hear. Otherwise, people tend to hear different things. People hear what they want to hear, and it's very easy to do experiments where you play the same sound clip for people, and they all hear completely different things if you don't tell them what you want them to hear.

When you go into an investigation, the question is front-loaded to prime the people listening. If you say, "Can you tell us how many people are in this room," people are listening for a number response. And it doesn't matter what the number is, whether it's one, four, five, if there are eight living people and somebody hears fourteen, they'll say, "Well, there's eight of us, there must be six of them." The easiest one to get them to respond to, the simplest form of EVP experiments is you get everyone to introduce themselves, so everybody knows everybody's names. Then you say, "Can you say my name?" or "Can you say one of our names?"

Everybody is listening for the names, and it doesn't matter whatever is said. It'll sound like the syllables of somebody's name. One person will say, "It's said, Steve." Then everyone will say, "Yeah, it did. Didn't it." Even though they were thinking it said, "Leave, I believe." It doesn't matter. You are front-loading the question, and you are priming the hearing of the people.

An example of that is YouTube has misheard song lyrics. Everybody who knows the ABBA song, once they heard "Chicken Itza," they can never ever hear "Chiquitita" any other way. It's proof of this fallibility of the human mind. We think, "I know what I saw. I know what I heard." Well, you just don't actually because you're living in a constructive world.

Your brain constructs the world from the sensory information it is supplied at a very simplistic level. The only reason you know the color red is red is that you were taught that that's red, and that's blue, and that's white. You have no inherent understanding of that. Likewise, your brain constructs an environment for you to live in.

You have to trust it. You have to rely on it. Your life depends on you, relying on what your brain tells you is there. If you're driving along in your car and you come to an intersection, and you see another car, you've got no time to say, "Oh, I'm hallucinating." You have to rely on the fact that your senses know it's there.

Occasionally, your brain makes a bad guess. It will hear a sound and try and make sense of it in a way that is not accurate. But you have to believe what you are hearing. You have to believe what you're seeing. That's why we see faces in clouds. That's why we see shapes in fires where none exist.

Q. You were Ciaran O'Keefe's replacement for the one season that he was moving from the U.K. to France. What can you tell us about that?

A. *Most Haunted*. The standard line is, it's a good thing because it makes people more aware of the paranormal, and it's a really bad thing because it makes the locations more expensive. That's the standard answer when, in actual fact, that answer is completely erroneous.

Television ghost hunting programs like *Most Haunted* exist purely as entertainment. They are as close to reality as a soap opera.

They are all staged reality like *Lizard Lick Towing*. All the scenarios are created.

It has never been an investigative program. If anyone believes that to be the case, then they are mistaken and misguided. What you are seeing is a program designed to sell advertising space, and therefore, in order for advertisers to buy revenue slots on the program, then the program has to attract viewers.

Initially, it was, "we're going to spend the night creeping around a dark building with night vision." Where it's been real harm to investigating is that a lot of people cannot see that. A lot of people believe that the methods portrayed on the paranormal shows, be that in the U.K. or the U.S., and the equipment and the methods that are being used are an inaccurate gauge of what's out there.

Ten years ago, back in 2002, the year *Most Haunted* arrived, the following year with *Ghost Hunters in America*, people were happy to look for floating phantoms. Floating phantoms became fashionable. Then they had to fight demons. Do battle with these things.

These guys are like S.W.A.T. troops going in these days, armed to the teeth with crazy bits of equipment. If you can get your equipment onto one of these programs, then you can charge the Earth for it. There are some wacky bits of equipment, some wacky ideas.

It doesn't portray paranormal investigations. It betrays paranormal investigation. It has misled a lot of people into believing that the methods portrayed on television are in any way adequate or useful in determining or forwarding increasing knowledge of death and what constitutes the paranormal. It's just wrong.

But as an entertainment genre, as a format for entertainment, it can be brilliant. Because some of the episodes have been shot in locations where people report experiences, it can be fascinating. I had an experience while I was with *Most Haunted*. The experience, of course, didn't make it on television because it wasn't exciting enough. There are lots of times where I know the camera crew was in the right place at the right time but have chosen not to have the unusual, interesting thing that took place because it wasn't big enough or spectacular enough for television. They are too busy burying each other, or hanging each other, electrocuting each other, and throwing things, and screaming and rushing about. It has been a bad thing, as you said before. Look at the cost of locations.

Listen to the full interviews with Steve Parsons on my website:

www.alanrwarren.com/hom-podcast-episodes/episode/b4071e7b/steve-parsons-parapsychologist-part-one

www.alanrwarren.com/hom-
podcast-episodes/episode/
b3afe569/steve-parson-
parapsycholgist-part-two

www.alanrwarren.com/hom-
podcast-episodes/episode/
b4124c0e/steve-parsons-
paracoustics

Professor Paranormal

INTERVIEW WITH LLOYD AUERBACH

Along with being a parapsychologist, Lloyd Auerbach was a mentalist performing under the name of "Professor Paranormal." Mentalists demonstrate great intuitive abilities, which might include hypnosis, telepathy, clairvoyance, divination, precognition, psychokinesis, mediumship, mind control, memory feats, and rapid mathematics.

It is also considered by some to be a form of magic; only mentalists don't perform stage magic, but mental magic. Most skeptics will say that mentalists perform their abilities from reading people's body language and a good knowledge of behavioral sciences.

Auerbach was also the editor of *Fate* magazine from 1991 to 2004, which is a magazine covering paranormal phenomena that started in 1948, and by 1955 had well over 100,000 subscribers. It primarily focused on UFOs and alien abductions, but by the 1960s, it started to include haunted houses and ghosts.

Auerbach has a master's degree in parapsychology, has authored ten books covering topics of ESP, hauntings, poltergeist, reincarnation, and possessions. He now sits on the Rhine Research Center and teaches a course on parapsychology.

This interview took place on December 15, 2015.

Q. You are the president of the Forever Family Foundation. What exactly is that?

A. The foundation was started a little over ten years ago by a couple who had lost their daughter in an accident, and they had been grieving quite a bit. It turned out that a medium that was being seen by one of their friends got a message from their daughter. After verifying evidence that came in from the medium, they were convinced that the messages were real, and it made them feel good and helped them out significantly.

They found other people who had also been helped with their grieving from mediums as well, and so they decided to start a foundation to support the work of mediums in the family grieving process and also to support the research work in a variety of areas of looking at experiences of life after death, survival of bodily death. So, everything from controlled research in the laboratory of mediums to apparition research, reincarnation, and so on.

Q. Is there a goal for this foundation? What exactly are you trying to accomplish?

A. Well, there's two goals. The primary goal is actually education and helping the public understand what mediumship is and what the evidence is for life after death in general. The secondary goal is to support mediums by actually vetting good mediums. They actually have a certification program which they do every so often, even at a distance, to see how evidential the mediums are to make sure the mediums are real. The mediums that go through the certification process have to volunteer, not a lot, every year, some hours to the foundation.

Q. As president, how do you see your role there?

A. Well, I have been president for a couple of years now. I oversee the conferences that we have for the general public, and those conferences brought together scientists who were doing research both in the field and the laboratory as well as mediums who are part of the foundation. Now I'm overseeing some projects we have. We are working on a project to reach out to other organizations in the parapsychology and the consciousness world to see if we can help spur on some cross-pollination and support for each other. The whole idea here is this is about the "family of man" here.

Q. Now, you are a parapsychologist, and the ones that I have met so far, tend to stay away from the mediums and ghost hunters and things like that. Is there a particular reason for that?

A. Well, a lot of my colleagues, are laboratory-based, and they have to deal within the structures of laboratory research. Actually, some of them are connected to academia or academic situations where they have to be extremely careful because there's so much prejudice against any of these topics in and from academia.

Others don't believe in life after death. They look at experiences with mediums, for example, as extraordinary psychic ability, but not necessarily communicating with the dead. Part of it is also who funding sources are. There are so few funders that they have to be careful and stick with what they can sell to the funding organization.

Q. I think the role or even what a parapsychologist does is confusing for the general public. So, what is a parapsychologist?

A. A parapsychologist is someone to studies psychic phenomena and psychic experiences. That runs the gamut from Extra Sensory Perception, which includes things like telepathy, precognition, and remote viewing. Clairvoyance to psychokinesis, which is the concept of mind over matter. We have different types of research that we do there. Mostly the lab research is done with computers as it can be very difficult to control from fraud when you are talking about something that is happening in somebody's hand. I've seen a lot of fraud over the decades.

Then, of course, parapsychology also covers looking into the survival of bodily death. Many parapsychologists are actually interested in things like "Near-Death Experiences." The University of Virginia has a whole division, the Department of Perceptual Studies Medical School, which looks at things like evidence of reincarnation. Evidence of children who remember past lives. Near-Death Experiences and Out-of-Body Experiences.

So, we cover the gamut. But some people are more dedicated to laboratory, and other people really reach out and look at experiences in the real world. Even the laboratory researchers are aware of and look at the experiences in the real world because that informs what they're doing in the lab. People who are doing the other, those of us who do field research, have to keep up on what's going on in the laboratory because that's where things get tested.

Like psychology, there's the laboratory and out of the laboratory, experimental and non-experimental. While we may not be counselors, we are educators, talking about and providing information about this.

Q. Where do you draw the line on evidence. When you are a parapsychologist, you are trying to gather evidence scientifically. I think the problem lies in what people see on T.V. The ghost hunters in the different shows often get excited about the loudest noise on the piece of equipment that they are holding at the time, with no explanation of what it means.

A. The ghost hunting shows have no concept of science, and they have no concept of parapsychology. The shows have been very carefully avoiding the field that's been studying this subject for well over one hundred years because they don't want researchers, whether they are field researchers like myself or laboratory researchers, to take away from the so-called talent, as they call them, the teams that are focused on, in the show.

They are not meant to be science shows, and unfortunately, what's happened because of these shows, that even if the people on the T.V. shows, which I suspect only some of them do, knew what the equipment does and cannot do. The producers have crafted or edited the episodes so that you're not getting the whole story. If they get a big beep, they get excited, then the next moment they figure out that there is some other cause, a non-paranormal cause for that pretty evident, you're not seeing that non-paranormal cause on that show because they've edited it out.

The sad thing is, I think, and it speaks to, unfortunately, a segment of the American public believing reality T.V. is what you see on T.V., without asking questions about what's missing or what's really going on. It is a deficit in our education system.

Q. Right, we've become crystallized in thought. We are no longer trying to figure out things or question them.

A. Right. Even the news media has been responsible for undercutting this.

Q. Is there anything that you find worth watching as far as paranormal shows on T.V.?

A. Well, personally I don't watch them, I find them boring. I'd rather watch a scripted show that actually has some thought behind it. The shows I have seen that look interesting are there's a show from Canada called *Ghostly Encounters* where people actually told their own ghost stories.

They found people that could actually tell a good story, positive, negative, or neutral. That is kind of what we do. It's shows like that that I find interesting.

Q. It's kind of like interviewing a witness to something.

A. Yes. Even the celebrity paranormal shows, when they're telling their stories, they found actors and actresses that had experiences. Those are more interesting than the ghost hunting shows. When I see these shows, I think we do not investigate in the dark, and the only reason people are is because of television. It has nothing to do with science. It has nothing to do with our history in parapsychology. It has nothing to do with people's experiences. They have created this mythology around how and why ghosts appear, and oddly, a lot of it comes from beliefs of psychics, or things psychics have said over the last one hundred years. Even phony psychics would say, "Ghosts only appear in the dark."

So, these shows are using that mythology, that folklore, and at the same time, they'll say, "We're not going to work with psychics because psychics are useless." But they are using the information from psychics that they don't even believe.

Q. Where did ghost hunting in the dark come from? Was it just scarier in the dark?

A. Exactly. Back in the eighties, when I started doing television, the number of times that we went out on location to a haunted place, the directors would always say, "Can we lower the lights," or "Make sure we record at night," even though people were experiencing things in the daytime. Fortunately, the camera guys would say that we can't turn off the lights because we can't see anything. Then all of a sudden, we had Sony night-shot cameras and the infrared cameras showing in the dark.

Even more than just being in the dark, people's eyes shined and looked spooky. So, they had their own inexpensive, atmospheric technology that allowed them to make things even spookier. It looks good on T.V. The T.V. is a very visual imagery medium, and you're always trying to come up with something visual, and rather than having people wandering around a place with the lights on, you can at least create some suspense in the dark. The odds are that you're going to have something happen in the dark. This is scientifically documented. There have been studies showing people are terrible observers in the dark.

Q. But I think it's the whole atmospheric conditions that help to create or suggest something scary or haunted going on. So, how can you prove something like this? You can bring pieces of evidence into the investigation, but...

A. Right. The word proof is overrated in science because there's been very little that has actually been proven. We experience gravity. But what gravity, if it's not been proven? There are many things that have significant evidence, and you have a theory. You do want theory, and you want to be able to explain these things. That leads to what we would consider proof or evidence.

Q. So, what is a ghost hunt then?

A. What we're starting with here is a human experience. A person experiences a ghost. A person witnesses something happening. You don't have psychical evidence, except maybe the aftermath. So, if it's a poltergeist case with things moving around, you might have some broken stuff. You might be able to, if you're lucky, catch it on camera moving. But even then, you still have to watch the video, and you have to question whether the video was legitimate or whether it was fake.

Parapsychology is a social science. We are dealing with human experiences. Living or dead, we are still dealing with human experiences. Like all social sciences, the evidence is based on people's subjective experiences and attempts at objectively understanding what those experiences relate to.

We can apply the scientific method but not so well in the field because we're not in total control like we would be in a laboratory. We can still apply some of it. So, you might say that the investigation part of the file is an applied science. We're applying what we learn in a laboratory, what we've learned in history, to the investigations in the field.

Q. Have you had any paranormal experiences in your earlier life before you became a parapsychologist that might have had an influence on you today?

A. No. It's just because I was a bit of a science fiction and comic book nerd. Probably in the sixties, it was a combination of hearing about ESP and a couple of T.V. shows. I certainly had experiences much later when I got into the field. But personally, I was undecided. In the literature that I read, I was certainly leaning towards the concept that survival of bodily death was happening. One of my earlier cases left me with no other alternative that made sense.

Q. Consciousness. Does our mind survive after our body dies?

A. Right now, we have no consensus in science. There's consensus in small parts or segments of science. We don't know what consciousness is, not even a good definition. The question for people looking for the survival of bodily death is, "What is it that survives?" That's the question. There's a secondary question is, "How is it that the thing that survives can communicate or connect and interact?" For us, if consciousness survives, the way ghosts or apparitions actually interact is through psychic ability. They don't even have eyes, so how in the world do they see the world except maybe with their direct consciousness, which is the definition of ESP.

But we're kind of stuck here because we don't know about consciousness in the body. To say that there is something or not something there, or is there something that could survive? I think that we're just not there in science.

Q. Another thing that has been brought into the world of the paranormal is religion.

One particular area is reincarnation. How does that affect you in your research?

A. Well, you're programmed just like any education program. Reincarnation is believed by more than a billion people on the planet. It's not a small belief. There are many variations or flavors in the reincarnation belief. We, in our field, stick with young children who spontaneously recall past lives. While it seems like that's what's going on, there are some other folks that are trying to work on some other possibilities, including genetic memory or even accessing information or accessing memory. We don't even know where memory is stored in the brain. There's that issue too.

A different interpretation of "reincarnation" is actually "possession." Some people even suggest that it might be a spirit that is actually temporarily possessing the kid and working through them. So, you have different interpretations where reincarnation, the idea at least, some part of former person's personality has survived. Whether it is memory alone, or consciousness intact, it's hard to say. But you're right. Most major religions have talked about reincarnation as a possibility, even if it's only been a minor possibility. But religions change over time, and certain things get omitted.

Q. In Near-Death Experiences (NDEs), it seems that people who have a certain belief or religion quite often see the God that they believe in. So a Christian will see Jesus. Do you find that in your research as well?

A. There is definitely a cultural-religious context. So you can see relevance if there are going to see anything at all. It can simply be some light which they may interpret as an angel. In some cross-cultural studies of Hindus and Hindu Gods, Christians that seen Christ or an Apostle, other people have seen specific interpretations of what they considered as a voice of God. There have been experiences by atheists, and they don't believe in God. They typically run into their relatives or some sense of coming back or being sent back. So, there is an interpretation here, but the core experience seems to be the same for the NDEs.

There's no question that religion does inform us to some extent. I grew up in a very reformed Judaic family, and I don't believe in demons. I was taught that you don't take the bible literally. It's just something to discuss. So, the stories are allegorical or parables from which you learn, but they're not all strict history to take literally. We really haven't seen any evidence of demonic presences in our field at all. Even the angel thing is interpretation.

Q. Also, how does one know that it is a demon and not just an asshole coming across or some residual from a bad person?

A. Exactly. This is a good example of those T.V. shows. It's just crazy to me that I'll get people telling me that we just went into a house and there was a demonic presence. Well, how do you know there was a demonic presence? Well, because we got an EVP of a voice saying, "Get Out!" I would ask, "Really, did you challenge the ghost, or were you friendly when you walked in, or something like that?" Personally, if I was a ghost and you came in and yelled at me, which a lot of ghost hunting groups like to do, I would be saying things stronger than "Get Out." To me, they're acting rude and more like demons.

Q. When do you draw the line when someone is talking about demons and possessions, and you know that it's not?

A. Frankly, we always have conversations with people upfront about their cases, and if somebody thinks it's a demon, demonic, or evil on the pre-interview, I give them some background and let them know that we typically find that things are not as evil as you think they are. They may be harmful, and we can see what we can do about that, but jumping to that conclusion can be difficult.

The whole idea is to reduce the fear, and you definitely don't want to tell people that it's demonic or evil. Certainly not before you do an investigation on-site and you figure things out. All too often, people are, for some reason, sometimes because of the T.V. shows or a horror film, imagining sounds and things that they've heard that are actually explainable as something that could indicate a demon being present. You rarely ever have people being attacked, at least in their reports.

So, we have to kind of educate them, and if I run into somebody who is just absolutely positive and will not even consider that it's anything but a demon, my question is, "Why do they want a scientist to come in?" We don't deal with demons. We can go in, but are they going to listen to me? If not, we're not going to do any good. So they need to be referred to a religious perspective.

Q. I have heard about a show where they are going to do an exorcism on the house.

A. An exorcism is of a person, not a place. You can call it a house clearing or cleansing. But it's certainly not an exorcism, and you don't need a religious figure to do it.

Q. I have noticed a huge amount of ghost-hunting shows in the last few years, and since then, it seems that there are tons of ghost-hunting groups popping up everywhere? Why do you think that is?

A. I think it's a new kind of fandom. It's not like *Star Trek* or *Dr. Who*, and you can't be on the Enterprise. You can buy some extensive equipment, and you can go out and emulate them. I think if people could actually get away with going out and fighting crime after they were watching the T.V. show *Cops*, it would probably generate the same thing to some extent. They don't want to put themselves in danger from criminals. So, it's just the nature of television and movies have fans. These are a group of fans that emulate what they see on T.V. without question. I mean, there's a small percentage of them that either immediately or after working with the groups realize, "This can't be right," and they do seek out educational opportunities, of which there are many now, to understand how one should really do this, and what the phenomena might really be.

If they recognize that a couple of guys working for Roto-Rooter, who admits to never having read anything or having done any research or any education, how can they possibly do any more than stumble around in the dark. They may encounter some stuff, but their conclusions are based on stumbling around in the dark. They're not based on anything that has gone on before or any actual research.

I think most of the ghost hunters are thrill-seekers. The ones I have a problem with are the ones who become experts and usually because they buy a lot of equipment. Or claim to be scientific because they have a lot of equipment. They think that science and technology are equivalent, but they are not. They do more harm than good when they go out there. Even the conferences are based on the fans of the show.

Listen to the full interview with Lloyd Auerbach on my website:

https://www.alanrwarren.com/
hom-podcast-episodes/
episode/a9831f7f/lloyd-
aberauch-parapsychology

MEDIUMS AND
PSYCHICS

Qabalah

INTERVIEW WITH DAVID WELLS

David Wells was thrown into the paranormal spotlight when he took over for medium Derek Acorah on the popular U.K.-based television series *Most Haunted*. Wells was the popular astrologer for the national U.K. newspaper *Daily Mirror* and had appeared on other supernatural television series such as *Jane Goldman Presents* and was a popular local medium before that.

Since leaving *Most Haunted*, Wells has written several best-selling books covering past life regression, Qabalah, astrology, and Tarot. As Qabalah has become one of the most popular new-age religions by so many famous people, including Demi Moore and Madonna, it was time to find out what Qabalah was and how a medium uses it.

David Wells' website is https://www.davidwells.co.uk/

This interview took place winter of 2018.

Q. Do you have siblings? Were you brought up in a spiritual family?

A. Yes. I have one sister, and no, not particularly. If it came through any line, it would be from my paternal grandmother. She is the one that would see things or give you these little nuggets of spiritual information. In Scotland, she was in the Brethren, and then she was in the Salvation Army. Not strong or strict in any form. But she is the one who kind of nurtured in me. She was there in my first spiritual experience around my grandmother's house. I would speak to my grandfather, and he would sing to me, and talk to me, and he had been dead for years when he was doing that. The thing is, she would believe me. She wouldn't disbelieve me. So,

I didn't feel that it was something weird or something truly odd.

Q. I know there was a time when you were very unwell and everything sort of switched on. Did you just automatically know and accept that you had those abilities and that was mediumship or spirituality, or did it take some getting used to?

A. Certainly, I didn't accept it. I would always defend things like astrology or mediumship, even while I was in the Royal Navy. You're right. So many people come to it through that moment of suddenly everything is different. It can be an accident or a lot of different things. People can be just walking across the road, and suddenly, wham, it happens.

But for me, I couldn't come to grips with it. The biggest thing was energy loss. The biggest thing was not sleeping or resting at all because the minute you go to sleep, you go straight into the other world. You're drained of your energy, or they're zapping your energy. You are constantly on. You are effectively an uncontrolled medium, and that's just not a good place to be.

Q. Did you not want it?

A. For me, I just didn't want it. At that time, to me, it seemed too difficult. It was certainly psychically draining for me. Also, for me, I wasn't picking up on other people's stuff, I felt like I was being attacked all the time, and spirits were just draining me. At that time, I couldn't see anything of value in it. I wasn't hearing anything that was particularly positive. It was all very exhausting, really.

Q. You talk about a term that some people will be familiar with, "Qabalah." You talk about that as keeping you grounded, a way of life, or a way of being. Tell us a little bit about that because I know you're very passionate about it?

A. It really truly is because, without it, I really don't know where I would be. I tell people it saved my life, and the truth is, it really did. I did start with Astrology, which in it is quite grounding itself. There's lots of different Qabalahs. That's because there are lots of different Qabalah. But the one I studied, the western mystic tradition. Essentially, it's like a map that when you are kind of stuck, you can find out where you are and find your way back.

I always say to people it's about symbolism. I can look at the tree and see different symbolism every single time I look at it because I'm focusing on a different part of it. Same with Tarot Cards. I can show you a Tarot Card, and you can say this means this, and I can see something completely different in it. But there is also within that a universal structure. So, for me, it's like a huge oracle, and it never stops giving. I've been with it now for nearly 25, 30-years now, and I still go, "Of course, that means this."

Q. So, how does it influence your life?

A. Well, I use it in my work. So, I use it to bring a deeper understanding to perhaps my Astrology or to the Tarot. I use the Faulk deck in Tarot, and there's very strong

Qabalistic references there. So, I can use it in my work.

But on a daily basis, in practical daily life, if I'm going through a particularly difficult time, then what it does to me is I know the pathway I'm being held on. Actually, what it does is it kind of takes the pressure off in a little way because it helps me understand the process of what's happening. So, I'm not going blindly through it.

But that's really a double edge because part of me sometimes wishes I didn't have this information because I would maybe crack on and get on with it. Just crash through it. Then another part of me thinks, thank goodness I've got this information because I know what's happening.

It can be everything from physical well-being, when I know that I'm in the process of shedding, or the process of transforming in some way, shape, or form. If I do know that I am ill, I look and think, "Well, where am I in this? Why am I not feeling so great? What do I need to do to change this?"

Q. So, this diagram, tree of life, how do you physically use that? How do you understand it?

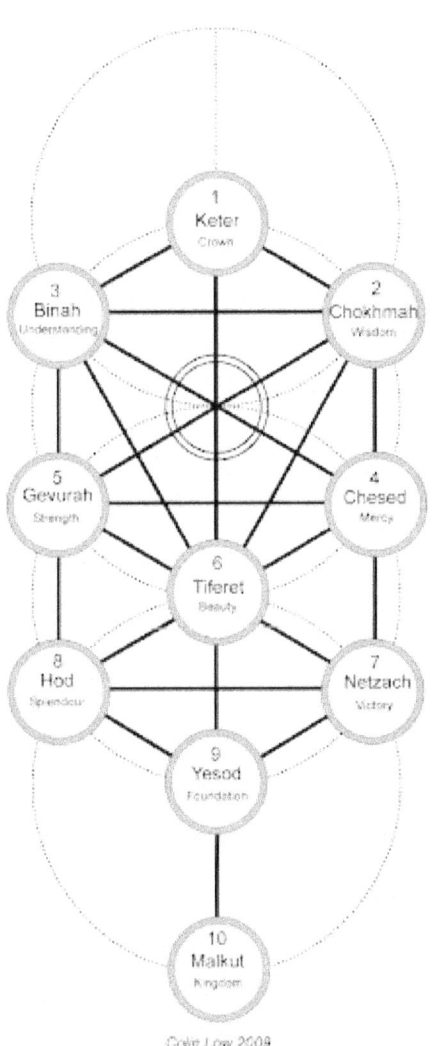

Colin Low 2009

A. You understand it through many, many years of studying. I think the best way to put it is, when you look at a Buddha, if you have a room with an altar and a Buddha in it, and you'd looked at it, immediately you yourself feel peaceful. You feel calm.

That's because the image of Buddha has been instilled within everybody's energy, thinking calm peace, calm peace. The truth of it is that it's a piece of marble, or it's a chunk of concrete. That's what it is. But because people have invested in the symbolism of it, it automatically changes it. It transforms it into something else.

With Qabalah, that drawing that you see, and if you've never seen it before, you'll see it's a geometric shape. It's very interesting. People are naturally drawn to it. But once you understand it more, it does that Buddha thing. I look at it, and it can bring me great peace. It can bring me energy, or sometimes it can make me melancholy, and sometimes it has me screaming at the wall. But it always has an answer.

You know, if you are passionate about your country and you are traveling, and you see your flag, and everything about your nation comes up inside of you. You're proud of your nation, and you feel those moments, you feel high school, you feel apple pie, you feel bangers and mash, or whatever. It's all within a symbol. You can attach all of that to a symbol. That's what Qabalah does.

Q. So, if I was to look at it tomorrow, I'm attracted, and there's something pulling me into this symbol, but I don't know what it is. Where do I start?

A. You start at the beginning. So, you start by, first of all, getting yourself a copy of that symbol. But also do a little bit of research because there are various types. We all know there's Qabalah with a "K" or a "C," and it's all spelled differently. You will find that there's some very negative about the one that Madonna follows, unnecessarily, for they are all just different forms. You find which one suits you. I suggest that if you love your Astrology or love your Tarot, then probably the one with a "Q "is probably more for you.

Q. What are people looking for when they come to you for Qabalah?

A. They are looking to understand this symbol. They feel actually drawn towards it in some form. Some are ready, and some actually can move rather quickly, and some really not so much. It's a rather big commitment, but wherever you leave the Qabalah, it stays with you. The information never leaves you. The point I'm trying to make is it's a bit of a long journey. I always tell people that if you're going to call in the Gods, whether it's Qabalah or no matter how you do it, you better be sure of yourself, and you better be ready. But they will come, and you better be ready to walk alongside them.

Q. How does it all fit together?

A. It fits together personally. That's the key. Whether you are consciously doing the tree of life or not, you are doing the tree of life. I hear people talking about it that have never done it, and I know where they are and what would help or where to go with it.

I heard a quote that was from someone famous. I don't know whether it's true or not, so I won't mention the name. But I thought it was very sad. She said the difference between her and her friend was that she was on a spiritual path, and they weren't. Now that's shocking to me because we're all on a spiritual path. Regardless of whether you know or don't know what that symbol means or what that Angel is, you are on a spiritual path.

I think the beauty of learning a system like Qabalah for a lot of people now is that it makes more sense of their Astrology, or it makes more sense of their Tarot, or more sense of their Past Life work, or Crystals, because they're held in some way, shape, or form in the structure. The one thing I see a lot with people is they do a workshop in Crystals, and they'll have a weekend away on Angels, and then they'll just do a little bit on this and a little bit of that, and they won't bring it together. They won't see the correlation between all of this is that it's just more of the same thing. They won't be able to match it up together, and it slows them down. No matter how you do it, it slows them down not to have some kind of structure.

Q. So, is it Spirit Guides or angels that are coming through, wherever you are on that diagram to guide you?

A. Yes, they are definitely there. Your own guides will definitely walk with you, and your masters, etc. They also have all the Gods and Goddesses from every faith and every religion you'll find on there. The same in Crystals and incense, you'll find a number, you'll find a letter or words, you'll find lots of things. If you break it down to its simplest form, the circles are the planets, and the pathways between them that you see are the Major Arcana of the Tarot. That, in itself, tells you how magic works within it. You have all the planets and all the Tarot Cards.

Q. So, Qabalah is a representation of our energy frequencies. In order to connect with our guides, we have to raise our energy up to that level through our studies, learning, and karma?

A. Yes, exactly. People will say to me, "I can't contact my spirit guide. They never make themselves known. Why won't they come to me?" I always tell them that's because you go to them. There are guides that are around us all the time, but seeing them, you need to raise your vibrations a bit. The more you work with it, the more your vibration changes. The higher up that you can contact, and you're are getting longer-term information rather than just short term stuff.

Q. So, the longer you stay up in that vibration, the longer you want to stay? It's almost addictive.

A. Yes, it kind of is. You move up a level, and it's kind of like most things in life. If you get a gold badge from the teacher, then you want a platinum one. But the karma thing is really what's important because, karmically, we're all trying to refine ourselves through the challenges we've chosen. Again, there's an astrological thing. Your astrological chart fits on the tree, highlighting your karma.

Q. Are some people more prone to Qabalah than others due to where they are astrologically?

A. I've yet to see anyone who sees the tree and doesn't think that's interesting. I think it's within all of us. Yes, you're right. It's equally as sound astrologically to say that some people don't want anything to do with any of it because it's not where they're at. They don't care about astrology. It doesn't make them wrong. It doesn't make them any less spiritual. It just means that in this life, it's not for you.

Q. Are there particular astrological signs that find it harder to understand?

A. I think that's a good question. I think harder or approach differently. For example, Gemini and Aquarians are really good at astrology because they have a mind that can have six conversations at a time. Therefore, they can make connections. Whereas a Virgo, for instance, needs to write it down and be more practical, and make a list about it, and make sure they check and double-check those facts and figures and things.

Q. When you receive a message from the tree, is it the same as when you receive a message from Spirit?

A. I think it is the same. It kind of activates something within you. What will happen is I will look at the tree, look at the cards, look at their chart, and never look at them again for about 40 minutes because it all just fires within you. The very hardest part of this work is getting out of your own way, stepping aside so that you're not putting your standpoint in, and you're letting that channel be as absolutely clear as you can make it.

Q. When we hear about past life regression, why is it that it's always famous people only that seem to have a past life?

A. Myth. It's an absolute myth. That's not true. I've done hundreds of past life regressions, and I think I can count on one hand how many famous people. It's an absolute myth. I think what that is, is people who have had a famous life are likely to shout about them. They want everyone to know they've had one. Here's the thing you know, so what if you've had a famous life. It usually means that it was extraordinarily difficult, I suspect, and also that you created because you affected so many people's lives. You've created huge amounts of karmic conditioning because nobody's going to get those ones perfectly.

Equally, so what if you were Cleopatra? Probably thousands of other people have had that life, too, because, in the multi-universe, we could all have a go at being Cleopatra because we need to maybe understand that for our souls to grow.

When I get someone who is having a life of notoriety, I love it because the history either matches up perfectly, which is interesting. Or it's completely off, and I love that. I did a past life regression who it doesn't matter who she was, but she died in a particular way in this past life, and I said to her, "That's not what history tells us." She said something that was really important, and I've never forgotten it. She said, "History is written by men and by winners." So, in other words, don't believe history because it's not always true.

Q. What was the most interesting past life regression you've had?

A. I've done past life work where someone was an alien. So he went to life as an alien being. Interesting in many respects—not just only because of what they saw and how they were—but also in my consulting room, they were shaking. Their body was physically vibrating, and I actually panicked a little bit because I had never seen this before. But I persevered because his voice was still calm, and he was still describing what he was saying. Afterward, when I mentioned this, he had no idea that he was moving in any shape or form.

I did another past life regression for someone, and I just thought, why are you wandering around into other people's houses and just living there, and there's no care for anyone. I got him to look in a mirror in a house that he just walked in and taken over, and he looked in the mirror, and his face was half hanging off. It was like a skeleton with flesh hanging off. He actually regressed to a life where he was a ghost.

He was haunting in his life, and we had to regress to find out why he was stuck here on Earth. Then we did some timeline therapy, so you release the pain of that. And you release that fact that he was, in fact, haunting in that life. We worked forward so he could release the feeling of isolation that he always had. He felt like he had never fit in and that people didn't see him in this life. That was his big thing— that people don't see him.

Q. In past life regression, do you automatically go back to a poignant experience, or could it be quite random? So, if somebody was taken back a few times, would it be to different places each time?

A. Absolutely. I say to people that if it's your first time, let your soul decide. Let your soul decide what's relative right here, right now. If you have a calling to something, let's say, Egypt, you can ask and try to go back and find out if there's something you need to know. But there's no guarantee that you'll be able to get there.

Q. Can you go back as an animal?

A. Interesting question. I have never experienced a past life regression where someone stays as an animal. But I have seen them where they have returned to being an animal. But it's been part of a journey where they have been going backward, and they go, "Oh my goodness! I'm a horse!" But then they are in another life. So, I've heard them say it. From what I understand, when I've been talking to my guide, you can remember the life, but you don't go back into the animal's life.

Listen to the full interview with David Wells on my website:

www.alanrwarren.com/hom-
podcast-episodes/episode/
b42297a0/david-wells-past-
life-regression

Spiritualist Medium

INTERVIEW WITH DEREK ACORAH

Derek Acorah was a popular U.K.-based medium for over thirty years who started out by making appearances on the television shows *Psychic Livetime* and *Predictions*, where he would tell people their future. Acorah joined *Most Haunted* as their house medium in July 2001, which followed a crew of ghost hunters and paranormal investigators in reportedly haunted locations throughout the U.K. The show prided itself on being 100-percent real, and there was nothing seen on the show that was faked or exaggerated.

Eventually, Acorah was let go from the show after he was accused of not being a real medium.

During an episode of the show that was being filmed in 2005, the team skeptic, Dr. Ciaran O' Keefe, left a fake name on a piece of paper for Acorah to find before they started the investigation. After they started filming the show, Derek claimed to be possessed by a person who had the same name that O' Keefe had left for him to find. After the event was leaked to the media, a major scandal erupted, not only the show but the paranormal field. The show replaced Acorah with medium David Wells and continued successfully for several more years.

Acorah continued with a few other television series. *Derek Acorah's Ghost Town* was the most popular, running for three years. Acorah made the spotlight again in 2012 when he claimed to have received a message from missing U.K. girl Madeline McCann, saying that she had indeed died and was about to be reincarnated into a new body.

Acorah considered himself a spiritualist-medium and published several books about the paranormal. So, what better person to talk to about it. This interview took place in 2018.

Acorah died on January 4, 2020, at age sixty-nine, following a short illness. His wife later confirmed that Acorah had been hospitalized with pneumonia and later developed sepsis.

Derek Acorah's website – https://www.derekacorah.com/

Q. You're such a personable person, and I think that obviously comes with lots of experience with knowing who you are, knowing what it is your purpose is in terms of your spirituality. But it wasn't always like that, was it?

A. From a young boy, it seemed that I had a certain talent within sports. I played all sports, and my love was football and still is until this day in sports. I was getting watched by what we call the scouts from professional football clubs at the age of eleven. Come the age of thirteen, I was so shocked and surprised that one of the major football clubs, Liverpool Football Club, was interested in signing me. The year I signed for them was in '65 and '66.

I ended up playing with them for years before going to Australia, and there, I continued to play until I got an injury and was out for a while. I tried playing again for a couple of games and got the final diagnosis that the injury was permanent and that I could no longer play soccer and had to find another career.

Then my wife said to me that I had a grandmother who was a lovely medium, and she had the gift. And you also have the gift. I said, "Well, yes, but I don't want to do that sort of thing." I guess I was a little dubious or a little scared. So, we came back to England after about a month or so, and we settled, and I had to figure out what I was going to do as a breadwinner and look after my family.

This is where my journey began. I had only been home about a month, and no matter where I would go, into a large store like Tesco or Morrisons, a woman or a man would come up to me, and I would be with my wife and small son Carl, and start talking to me in this strange way, saying,

"You now know what you've got to do. You now know you've got to follow your grandmother's life with your gifts." Total strangers would say this, tell me things about my future and what I should be doing. It was mind-boggling at first.

A. Yes, I'm sure.

Q. So, my wife found in the paper this Spiritualist Church, where she said, "Spiritual people like your grandmother would meet and actually do demonstrations. So let's go along and have a look at this place." So, we went, and there were about 60, 70, or 80 people in this small room. And, of course, the medium walked in and introduced herself. She just gobsmacked me. She astounded me. I was at the very back of the room so that I could just fade into the background. I didn't want to be noticed.

She then came at me and said, "I need to speak to Derek." Of course, my wife gets a hold of my hand. The medium continued, "I need to speak to Derek because there's a lovely lady that's here that's come to say a big hi to him. A big hello, and she loves him dearly." I, of course, couldn't speak out. I didn't know if I should speak out. It was my first time.

Then she said, "Look, there's only one Derek in this church, and he's in the back, according to his grandmother." Everyone in the back row, men and women, all were looking at each other. My wife told me to put my hand up. So I said, "This could be for me."

She said that it was for me, so I questioned her. Because it's my grandmother, I questioned her. "If you are telling me you're talking to my grandmother, tell me how she died." She said, "She suffered from a cancer that spread in different parts of her body." Then she said, "Just say fifty-six to him." And I said to my wife, "Oh my God, that was the year of her death, when she was 56 years old, a relatively young woman." She brought along two of my grandfathers and one of my uncles – even my baby sister.

Q. You were certainly getting a message.

A. They were really giving it to me strongly, weren't they? My little sister was a baby child. She was only a matter of weeks old, and she was found and had passed away. There she was coming through as a young woman to say hello to her brother. That afternoon, I stayed behind and spoke to the lovely woman medium who was from Scotland. She said to me that I was going to be doing this kind of work (mediumship) like me, and more because it was meant for me. She brought the football up, "You were allowed to play the football for a period of time." The many years to come, you'll hear about the great diaries your grandmother wrote, which I've got them presently in my company. She wrote these three diaries recording from the age of nine right up throughout my life. Things are still happening that I've written in the diary to finish them off. The diaries finish off in fourteen years' time.

Q. That's mind-boggling.

A. It is just bonkers. I've got them here, and all of my family has scrutinized them, read them. When the diary was written in those years, the television had not become what it is. Everyone had radios. But in the diaries, grandmother had drawn a rough drawing of a box, and she put "T E L E," and underneath it, she put "G R A N D" and an "A." I went onto television on Granada T.V. that year to do my work. I did so many shows with Granada.

Out and About with Derek Acorah – a program that they wanted me to do even before *Most Haunted* was even in existence. *Out and About with Derek Acorah* was with a production crew going to haunted locations, going to old homes, going to places where there could have been a case history of the paranormal nature. That's where the idea came for *Most Haunted*.

Q. Did it scare you? You haven't mentioned at what age you knew this gift also, but did it scare you knowing how powerful that gift could be? I mean, your grandmother writing those futuristic diaries, predictions about your life?

A. It scared me in my younger years because I had my first encounter, hearing encounter, with someone that was like a disembodied voice to me. I was sitting in my mom's lounge. Dad was a seafarer but happened to be home, thankfully, at that time. We were all sitting in the lounge. At the time, there were four kids in our family. And a Saturday afternoon – I'll never forget it – I was reading a football magazine, and I heard this voice. Now, I knew it was in the room, but I had never heard this voice before, saying "Derek" three times and then something else. I looked around the room and asked myself if I was going mad.

So, I left the room and went up the stairs quietly and went into the toilet, because I was a bit shocked. I closed the door, locked the door, and sat there, numb. I went out of the bathroom and went into my bedroom, and sat on the end of the bed. Then it happened again. "Derek," three times, but then he told me that he was my spiritual guide. "I know you can't see me at this time, but you can hear me, just popping in to say that you will get to know me over the next months, over the next years. You will know everything about me, and to work with you spiritually, we've been designated together."

Now when all this happened, I must have lost the color in my face because I went downstairs and thought, "I can't speak to my dad. I can't speak to my mom. I can't speak to my brother and sister about this." That evening I was asleep. I heard this sound like someone shuffling sand on the floor, and then someone sitting on the bed, and then I was totally awake. I quickly switched the light on and there I saw Sam.

Q. How old were you at that time?

A. I was seven.

Q. What about your parents? Were they psychic at all?

A. No. It skipped them. In actual fact, mom was very sympathetic because she knew her mom experienced all of these things and realized it was true. Dad came from a very strong religious Catholic background. He did not like the idea of his wife being the daughter of a medium. However, he loved my mom, and I suppose for that, he put up with it. But it was a little bit too much for dad, realizing later that there was another one in the family that was going to follow in the shoes of Gran, and it cracked my dad up. I was fine when I was a footballer for my uncles and dad. I was the bee's-knees, so to speak, in the family.

However, when the football stopped and later on, it was apparent that I was going to follow in my grandma's footsteps, Dad couldn't cope with it. Dad didn't want to cope with it. Dad, on a number of occasions, made the statement, "I do not want a son of mine dealing with something he doesn't understand, doesn't know the power of, doesn't know the depth of it, and the evil." Then he would start to say things through scriptures. God saying that you leave the contacting of spiritual souls, leave them in the heavenly state in eternal sleep.

But my mom would always say, "This is your vocation. It's what you were meant to do. He (dad) will realize this later." So, many years later, when I was doing things everywhere with my work and touring, my mom was so proud. I'm going to tell you a story, I was in Boston doing a demonstration, and a medium approached me after the show. She told me that she had a man named Frederick with her, so I asked what he was saying, and she told me he was saying to tell you, son, that he was awfully proud of you and that he was sorry he didn't realize or understand it until he was there.

Q. So, how does your mediumship work for you? Because we obviously all get information from different ways?

A. Mine started off with "clairaudience," where I could hear. I demonstrated with the clairaudience for a couple of years, then I found in a natural way by coming into the company with a number of other mediums that were more experienced and being around a lot longer. They said that my abilities in "clairvoyance" are going to develop so to get ready for it. So, of course, that came. Whereas at one time, I could only hear spirit, and then I could see spirit, and then "clairsentience" was always there with me. I could always sense when I walked into a room whether there was a spirit energy there, whether it be negative or positive. But what happened, which I wasn't always happy about was, when I was doing my demonstration, something else, a little added extra would be thrown in there using my psychic abilities.

The psychic abilities are a poles apart too, you know, directly the world of spirit. I thought, what are they going to say to me then? They are going to say their observances to prove to their loved ones they do visit them whilst they're in their own homes and listen to conversations when they are visiting and if some kind of guidance from a mother or father if the children were having problems when they were here, they would give them guidance.

Now, at first, I wasn't sure about this. But now I think it's a wonderful thing, an absolutely wonderful thing because if that's mom and dad, and I'm being used as a conduit, as an instrument for spirit, and I'm telling them something responsibly. If I can tell them something that their mom or dad says, this is the way you should go with this because we've got stronger foresight than you back there in the physical world.

Oh my gosh, did I see it work! People making contact with me a week later, two weeks later, "Oh my God, you told me mom said to go to a solicitor because of my situation, so I went, and it's over and went well." I've got these letter correspondence, sack loads. My home is quite a big home here, up in the loft area, I can promise you, and I'll keep every single letter. I've got big black bin bags of letters that have been sent in from all over the world for years. There's millions up there, not thousands, but millions. I've been moved to a realization of where's all this coming from. If it's not come from loved ones that have moved on.

Death is not death. It's a transition to a higher consciousness or understanding of who we are. We're eternal. We can never perish.

Q. Tell us a little bit about that. People will hear mediums talk about things like levels, plains, angels. What are they?

A. In the world of spirit, there are so many levels, dimensions. Each dimension is where the soul is coming over, who has progressed. In other words, a mom might go over after her mother many years later, and suddenly they are not really together at first because the lens of the grandmother far outrides or outreach what the mother had to do in their physical life. So, she's had more hardships, and she's gone to reap the rewards and gone to a higher plain in life. But the eventuality is they do join up.

If we can put that into perspective, in the sense that the only way you can achieve this is what in certain religions say, or the belief systems of reincarnation and having so many lives and going back over to the world of spirit for a period of time, resting, and enjoying the fruits of your hard labor, and then coming back again. If you asked the question, "Does Derek believe in reincarnation?" Absolutely.

However, one of the biggest questions, the hardest question, whether it be a non-believer or believer, has to cope with this. Look, Mom's gone over, Dad's gone over, and I feel really lonely without them, and I'd have reassurance if you could tell me that I will meet them eventually. I always give that reassurance. And yes, as sure as night follows day, that will happen. That's the system.

The world of spirit comprises of my knowledge okay – of the dimensions, which is the lowest dimension to our planet Earth and is very close to us actually. It's intermingling with us. It's unseen by the naked eye. It's unheard by the ear, but in your state of awareness, as an instrument of spirit, you can interlock with that very quickly. When doing so, you can get so much information. I call it getting information from the great pool of knowledge.

So, that very first interaction with that great pool of knowledge is quite close to us. This is why when we get visitations from our loved ones. They come into that lower level in order for them to come into this atmosphere, this ether, one of the most difficult things. In wintertime in any country, you'll always get to a point where there's a deep fog, icy cold temperatures. We call it in England, the pea soup of fogs, where it's that bad if you walk in it and breathe, you cough. It's like that coming into this atmosphere, to our loved ones. They have to adjust their acceptance into this atmosphere in order for them to get through, and then it does relent. It does relax, and then they can see you. They can hear you in your atmosphere. If I was to do the opposite and take you into their atmosphere, what you would experience is just the opposite. What it is is the brightness would be that stunningly sharp, it would blind your eyes.

Q. Does this come into line with the people that have had a Near-Death Experience and described a bright light?

A. That's exactly it. That's what they bring with them around their aura. They bring that bright blinding light of where they come from. That's why people even talk about the sighting of angels because they see them in this glow.

Q. I can't let you go, Derek, without clearly talking about the one program that probably has for a lot of listeners really opened up people's thoughts in terms of capturing an investigation, that being *Most Haunted.*

A. Yes.

Q. I know there's been a lot of critique of *Most Haunted,* but the one thing that came out of *Most Haunted* was that it opened up people's understanding of the links between spirit and our world.

A. Yes.

Q. I think that's a good thing.

A. I do.

Q. What was the most interesting or the most rewarding time for you in the eight years that you did *Most Haunted*?

A. I think really at the beginning. I thought not only was it one of the most refreshing I've ever entered into because up to that time, I only had ever linked with, in my demonstrations on television, on radio, and personal readings, the goodness, and the brightness – the higher side of the spirit world. Suddenly, I'm launched into a challenge, not realizing it was a challenge. Not realizing that some of the stuff that I'd experience, or all of us would experience, was seeing the darker side.

That darker side comprises only one thing. On a lot of levels in the world of spirit, God, in his wonderful way, has provided a place in that dimension, in that realm, where all the not-so-goodies go when they leave the physical life. They are there in a constant vigil of the higher beings in the angelic field, waiting and listening for these souls, who are in what we call a "Struggling Meyer," and all wanting to hate each other like they hated people when they were here – still ongoing, constantly still wanting to hate, not knowing any better. Until suddenly, and it does happen, it dawns on them that they were doing wrong and they need to call out, "I am sorry that I did what I did, to whom I did it to, and if I could pay back or have my time again I would like to repent." This is where the life cycle of reincarnation comes in.

I had to encounter, on my years with *Most Haunted*, things, to speak honestly, I didn't quite think or believe existed. I had to experience it physically and mentally. And at times, a horrible experience, however, a great experience of God's kingdom and the doings of things, and I accepted that. I had to correlate with Sam and his protectiveness, constantly reassuring me.

I remember saying to Yvette, I think towards the end of the third series, "You know, Yvette, now I've experienced this over a period of how many shows." It was a lot because we did *Most Haunted* live as well. "I don't think that I want to continue in my capacity as the medium for this program because I've seen now. I understand it, and I don't want to. Who I want to link with are the loved ones where there's only going to be happiness and joy?"

Of course, there were arguments about that, and she said, "Do you realize the show wouldn't be this without you, and you'd be letting all the public and the viewers down?" I was even called to the network and had a conversation, and they said, "Please don't even consider trying to leave because everyone would turn off." And I said why or how? And they fit it was because of the mediumship, not the presentation. So, we continued on with it.

Q. The question I'm going to ask you, I'm going to leave it pretty open because I think in our line of work, you're going to get critique. You're going to get people trying to trip you up. You've been through that, and some of that was with *Most Haunted*, and I think for many listeners who follow you, Derek, and certainly, in my networks, people were mortified that things had been done in that way and thought it was quite underhanded and unnecessary. And a little bit immature, really.

A. Can I just...

Q. Yes.

A. I don't use the words "sour grapes." It's just not in my forte.

Q. Yes.

A. But the simple truth to all of this is, I did a three-hour interview a number of years ago with an American radio station when things were happening then. I was threatened by the program, not the network, but by the program people—the producers, Karl Beatie and Yvette Fielding —that I was on the confidentiality clause and that if I said anything negative about *Most Haunted*, they would sue me. They would take any properties, money and would just drain me of everything.

I would still be criticized by Yvette coming out and saying that I was phony, saying this, that, and the other. The simple answer to all of this is, and I've said it before, when Yvette Fielding and Karl Beattie found out whilst I was still conducting my mediumship on *Most Haunted*, that Living T.V., not I, quietly got me to London and asked me if I would like to do a new program for Living T.V. They would develop the program because the viewers loved me. I, with my agent, sat for hours in London. This is exactly what happened.

They said they knew that I was on a confidentiality contract, but you can speak to us. We can do this secretly. You carry on with *Most Haunted*, go forward, do the sixth series, three more months of *Haunted Lives*. We'll get someone else in, and then we will announce that you are starting your own new program called *Derek Acorah's Ghost Towns*. That's exactly what happened.

Why I don't see people on social media reading and looking it up, I don't know. That was the reason that it came from one certain party that I had been sacked for cheating. People need to take the time out, journalists, reporters, and get in touch with Living T.V., and see that I wasn't sacked from Living T.V. I did *Ghost Towns*. I was with Living T.V. five years after leaving *Most Haunted*. I was never sacked.

Q. There's been many mediums after you on *Most Haunted*, and the program has moved on. And you have rightly moved on, and you've done amazingly since that. You've said that you had some good times and that you enjoyed the experience and...

A. I did. I don't have any bitterness there. Honestly, in my heart, I think I've been a very fortunate man. The only thing that stopped was it hurt my family. It hurts my family more than it hurts me: my wife, my son, and my daughter. My grandchildren are always saying, "Granddad, you're not like that. You've not done that." Especially my mom, when all this stuff started to come out, mom took ill and came to live with us the last few years. She said. "Son, these evil people who have done this – they will get their comic rewards, believe me."

Like I've said before, and I want the listeners to know that it's not stopped me from working with spirit. If anything, it's strengthened me up.

Q. I think you're right because the very popular T.V. programs have promoted the fear factor in investigating and spirit work, and I think that has done wonders for raising the profile of mediumship with some very well-known mediums appearing on the programs. But I think it also has minimized the risk associated with it. So, it's made it quite normal for people to go out and shout out and call out for spirits and for things to happen.

A. The only thing that bothers me about investigating well-known locations with the different paranormal groups is, I've been to some locations where the energy has been really high, and you go onto those locations, and the energy is really flat. There's nothing there. You have to accept that you know that in this location, we're not feeling anything. That's being completely honest. If you are honest about what you are receiving, then that's got to be a good thing too. The energy can sometimes be flat because, you know, maybe the spirits are going, "I'm so fed up with this, I don't want to perform again tonight." You have to be very careful about how many times you investigate one place.

Q. I absolutely agree with you. I think it's a shame because there are groups of twenty, thirty, forty. I have seen groups of up to seventy people. It's advertised as a paranormal investigation that just could never be one. People go along because it's on the tele. It's the fear factor. It's something that spookies do, and there's no way in the world that they are experiencing a true investigation in any way, shape, or form. These large events where something has got to happen because you've got to keep these people coming back. There's pressure on the company to perform. Likewise, that's very hard in our world because you know that you can go into someplace, and there's nothing. I recently did an investigation for a group, and there was absolutely nothing. The whole evening was very flat. They did everything they could to try and conjure up something that wasn't there, and they couldn't understand why I was saying, "No, nothing there." I found myself in that position where I was thinking actually, "I don't need to justify this." I had to keep reminding myself and reminding them, and that's hard. You've seen that on television as well. We've seen television mediums not perform, like a performing monkey, and not make things up, and therefore be cast aside by television companies.

A. That's reality. I think if you stay honest and true to who you are and what you are receiving, then that's got to be a good thing. But you are right, especially with T.V., which is very visual. It's got to be very visual, and it's all about the ratings with T.V. as well. You have to perform. You have to do this, and you have to do that. You know, many years ago, before we started to work on *Rescue Mediums*, Christine and I did some work for a German T.V. company called ProSeven, and they took us to a few places to investigate. Just the two of us with a film crew. On one of the places that we went to, it was a little bit flat. There were things going on there. When we said to the producer, "What do you want from us? What do you expect from us?" because we were giving him clairvoyantly what we were receiving, but he was quite disinterested. He said, "What I wanted is for something to come from the sky, for something to happen right there and then, and my camera to be focused right at that moment in time so that I get the fireball that comes from the sky. And I can hear the chains clinking up and down those stairs as you're telling me about this story. That's what I want." I said to him, "If that's what you want, then you go out and find a couple of actors because we don't act." We walked off because we wouldn't perform. We weren't going to make something there that wasn't there.

Q. We saw that with Chris Conway when he said, "I am here to work spirit. I'm going to work spirit. I'm going to stay true to spirit, and I'm not going to just make stuff up just because I've got five minutes to come up with something. I can't not talk about your artistry, your psychic art. I've never tried psychic art, but I'm impressed with yours. That leads me on to asking how many drawings you've done if spirit guides?

A. I don't know. I've lost count.

Listen to the full interview with Derek Acorah on my website:

www.alanrwarren.com/hom-
podcast-episodes/episode/
b3e56631/derek-acorah-
interviewed-by-julie-saville

Survival Medium

INTERVIEW WITH JAMES VAN PRAAGH

So far, I have had a medium the does past live regressions, uses qabalah, and is a spiritualist medium. Next up is a survival evidence medium named James Van Praagh. As I understand, he is not using any tool or new age religion to help him communicate with the dead. Instead, he just does it.

Van Praagh says that he gives the people he reads for evidential proof that he has communicated with the dead by providing detailed messages from their loved ones and has done so for over thirty years now. Over these years, he has developed quite a large following which led to his own cable television show called *Beyond with James*

Van Praagh, where he brings messages to people from their loved ones live on television. He has also produced some television series that portrayed either himself or other real-life mediums and the lives that they led.

Van Praagh has also had a successful career writing books about life after death and the paranormal world. With such an extensive background Van Praagh would be the perfect guest to have one to answer our questions on what a survival medium is and does in their work. This interview took place in the fall of 2016.

James Van Praagh website – https://www. vanpraagh.com/

Q. You call yourself a "Survival Evidence Medium." What does that mean?

A. I was born with the ability to see a spirit and hear them speaking to me in my mind. I feel that personality, so I'm called "clairsentient." So, I can sense their personalities. I hear their thoughts, so that's called "clairaudience." Also, they'll show   me   themselves,   and   that's "clairvoyant."

Q. Meditation is really quite important in order to connect with spirit, isn't it?

A. Exactly right. Our soul has to connect with their soul, and we really have to have a relationship with our soul. And the best way to do that is to really sit in the quiet and start listening to your inner voice. That's really the best way to do that – sit in the quiet. I know past mediums and well-known mediums used to sit in the dark and meditate for a long time and let the spirit world work with their sensitivity of their energetic body and also work with their own human sensitivity.

I was the same way. I sat for seven years every Tuesday night for at least two hours with a British medium and learned to open up my sensitivities. Nowadays, we live in a society where mediums don't feel the need to sit and develop that, and I think that's a big error because I think the best way that you can develop as a medium is to have a relationship with your soul first and foremost.

Q. In your videos, you also mention for somebody to sit quietly and to imagine that space above you because that's inherently where spirits reside. Can you tell us a little bit more about that?

A. I believe that the soul is the mind, and the mind is the soul. I think in physical death, the brain dies with the body, but the mind continues on. I believe the physical body that we have right now, it's just about twenty percent of the soul – where eighty percent of our soul is outside the body. I believe that the spirit world is all around us and vibrating, if you will, at a different frequency of energy. But they are always around.

It's not that they're living here in our physical world, and they go somewhere and then come back. They are connected to us in some way, whether it's through bonds of love or a certain commonality that we share. But they are always with us.

So, the space around us, if we start paying attention and place our minds to the space around us, that's when we can open up the door to the spirit world and really start to begin to hear them and become one with them. Again, done through meditation, mind journey, focus work, just to open up to that space above us and around us is where they are.

Q. You talk about mediumship as in you opt-in and out of it. So, is mediumship for you something that you're able to switch on and then you do, or is it something that is always with you, and if a spirit needs to get through to you, they do?

A. Yes, the way I developed as a medium, and I think the correct way, is to learn how to open up the chakras of the body. It's almost as if you turn on the radio and tune in to a station. Before I work, I will open up the center. I will use the rainbow colors and open up each energetic center. Then I'll put myself through a mindset where I'll ask a prayer often, an intention to my guide that I'm ready to work and I'm receptive. That's not to say that when I'm walking down the street, sometimes a spirit comes to me. Yes, that does happen. But your focus isn't there. Your focus is not as clear.

So, I always say to mediums who are just starting that you can't always be "on" constantly because your adrenal system will burn out. It's very much like a ceiling fan being turned on and leaving it on all the time. That motor keeps on going, on and on and on. Eventually, it'll burn out if you leave it on. So, really the adrenal system of the medium needs to be respected and only used when you go to work.

Now that's very different than a psychic. Where a psychic—we are all psychic, every one of us has psychic energy—which is intuition, which is the soul's voice. So, you can feel energy, sense energy all the time. That's very different than mediumship which is communication with the higher forces.

Q. You are quite willing to help others develop their mediumship, and you give a lot for free demonstrations on your

YouTube channel. A lot of mediums aren't so willing to give that away.

A. Why wouldn't they give that away because it's certainly not their information. It's the spirit world's, and it's theirs to share. I was given this information when I was first starting, and I think it's ours to share. Spirit gave this to me in my head very recently and said, "You human beings have what's called time, and you borrow time, and just like you might borrow an item from your neighbor, like a cup or some dinnerware, you want to make sure that you return that item even better than you got it."

The same thing with time, I think we have to return time when you leave this world in a better way, same as on the Earth. So, we borrow this time on the Earth. We need to leave the Earth in a better way than we found it. If sharing this information does that, which I think it does, then we need to do that.

Q. One of the most frequent questions that mediums get is what happens to us when we die? But so many of these mediums all answer that question differently. Why do you think that is?

A. I don't know. I don't know what their background is, and I don't know what their experience with it is. I know that for me, my experience is that there is no death. We very much leave the body painless. There is no pain in death. It's a change in consciousness, if you will. I think our spirit leaves the body every night we go to sleep. I know that we are met there. We don't die alone. There's really a reunion of loved ones who come to get us – that really helps us cross over. I think that's our homecoming, if you will.

I think that when we all first pass over, there's what's called a life review. I think you look back at your life, and you see all the lessons that you passed and those you didn't pass. How much love you left on the Earth and how much you didn't. The opportunities that you had that you didn't fulfill. They'll be around their loved ones for sure, letting them know or trying to let them know that they are alive.

Q. I see quite often the idea that your loved ones are trying to come across with signs like a bird or butterfly. Do you believe that is the case?

A. People often ask me, "Are the birds, or robins, and butterflies, are those my dead mother?" My response is yes and no. To me, what it could probably be is that the spirit of the mother is standing right next to the loved one and projecting herself into the mid of the loved one. At the exact time, they see the butterfly and therefore associate their mother with the butterfly. I think that's more of what happens.

Q. I think that's too bad about the misinformation.

A. That's one thing I found out with mediums and this work. The responsibility is a big one, and some people who work in this field don't seem to get that. To me, it's like working as a medical doctor or a lawyer. You have someone's life in your hands. Work as a medium should enable people, not disable.

Q. Mediums can say anything you want them to say, but unless it's evidenced, it's not believable. I see some mediums that just react to the belief system of the person they're reading. Someone has a picture of themselves, and in that picture, there seem to be orbs floating around, and they believe it to be their lost loved one – things like that.

A. When somebody sends me a picture with an orb in it, I always ask them, "What did you ask the orb when you saw that? What was the thought that you received?" I have a little more discovery and not just accept it for what they say. It could be some phenomenon, but I don't know necessarily that it's a loved one. So, I like a little more investigation to be done.

Q. Is there a challenge to give a reading for somebody who has just passed?

A. I think people have to realize that just because someone has left the physical Earth and they're in the spirit form, it doesn't necessarily mean that they know how to communicate. They might not know the process of communication. Even I found spirits who have been over a year or two years, and they still don't sometimes know the exact process of how to concentrate on thought and really transmit feeling or a memory. It takes a lot to do that, from my understanding. They don't know immediately how to do that. Just like on the Earth realm, there are good recipients, and there are bad recipients. There are good communicators, and there are bad communicators – the same thing in the spirit world.

I find that for me, personally, when it's a very strong and emotional link, and I'm able to bring them through much easier with the emotion. For me personally, and many of my friends who are mediums, it's not easy for them to bring some family members up on their own. It's not easy to bring your own personal moms or dads up because there's also a part of them that gets in the way, and we can't really be objective. We would like them to say this or that.

Q. How do you think spirit helps best for people to move on?

A. Thoughts are things, and they can see our thoughts. They see the color of the thoughts, the texture of the thought. Thoughts are things. So, when you think of your loved ones, they see that. We have to realize that they hear our thoughts. They know our thoughts, and they're alive. They're not a figment of our imagination. They are very much alive, and it's kind of a little disrespectful to think that they are dead.

Of course, being in the human world, it's hard for us because, being in the physical world, we want to see it. We want to see it with our eyes. But we can't. It's really a test of faith. But the most important messages have been the ones like, "I'm not dead, I hear your thoughts, I hear your prayers," or "I don't want you to hold back your own progression of life."

Sometimes I hear, "I'm here to help you on your journey. I'm destined now to be on this side of life to help you progress on your journey on the Earth. That's why I had to leave." So, it's all these different kinds of messages about, "Life is not over, and your life has just begun, and it's only a temporary time that we cannot see each other, but I still influence you every day. I'm around you every day. You don't need to put a picture of me out and say a prayer. I hear you. I am there. You don't need to go to the graveyard."

Q. How can people tell when the medium they are going to is the right person?

A. If you go and see a medium for a reading or session, you should try and be as open-minded as you can. The more you think about connecting with your loved one and thinking, come to me, come to me, they're actually blocking the space for the spirit to come through. It's like a garden hose, and you are watering your garden, and if you have a kink in the hose, the water can't flow. It's the same thing with the space around the medium. The more you try to force that energy, it'll block and make it harder for them to come through.

You should really be referred to them, and if their price is rather extravagant, I would say no. Pay attention to what comes through, there should be at least five pieces of information that no one would know about, and I'm talking about whether it's a name or a birthmark or a t-shirt you have with a name on it, but something specific. They should really have some evidence.

Q. You say that you've heard from some quite prolific and popular people who have come through to you after they've passed.

A. Yes.

Q. Quite often, when those moments are publicized, they are open to public criticism, like when we saw Derek Acorah here (England) with Michael Jackson, and he was completely vilified really. There seems to be a higher amount of criticism when that person has been in the public eye.

A. Yes.

Q. Have you experienced that?

A. A lot of the celebrities that have come through for me have not been done in public. One was Heath Ledger, who came through. He came to me after he passed away when I was shaving, and he said, "I screwed up." Lucile Ball came through once. A lot of people have come through to me. Princess Diana came through to me. Again, none of this was made public. Edward Casey has come through to me a couple of times, and he called me Doctor Van Praagh. When I asked him why he called me a doctor, he said it was because I've healed a lot of hearts. The other night we were working in Phoenix, and Pope John Paul came through. Abraham Lincoln has come through. Winston Churchill once.

Listen to the full interview with James Van Praagh on my website:

www.alanrwarren.com/hom-podcast-episodes/episode/b3afb567/james-van-praagh-medium

Rescue Medium

INTERVIEW WITH JACKIE DENNISON

If you have watched any ghost hunting shows over the last ten years, during an episode, you would have seen the team medium try to get whatever spirit that was haunting the location to cross over or go into the light. It was often explained that this spirit or ghost was trapped somehow or didn't know how to cross to the other side.

One of the nicest mediums I have ever met was Jackie Dennison – one of those mediums that would try to help these spirits cross over to the other side and help resolve the haunting in a location. The show that I saw her one was called *Rescue Mediums*.

So, why does a spirit get stuck here on Earth? How could a ghost not know how to find its way to the other side? Are these spirits here because they are possibly being punished, or maybe they have something to resolve in their now past life?

Besides being on her *Rescue Medium* television show, Dennison owns a paranormal school in the U.K. called the Feathers Academy, located in Northwich. The academy offers both the teaching and healing process using spiritual methods. She has also written books and articles in several magazines on the subject.

Rescue Medium Website – https://m.facebook.com/Rescue-Mediums-166163363400917

The interview took place in 2015.

Q. Besides your *Rescue Mediums* Television program, you have the Feathers Academy. Inherently, this is about offering your skills and expertise and supporting others to learn, correct?

A. Absolutely. Feathers has been open since 2002 now. It's just a little shop in the town where we live, Northwich in

Cheshire. A little shop that we sell spiritual gifts and things. But mainly to offer a place where people can come and get help and advice. So, the shop area is like a sitting room. So it's like walking into somebody's sitting room. We've got a fireplace there with little tables and chairs. So, people can just come around and get some help and advice.

If they've got a problem, like a dream they can't understand, they'll come in, and there's always somebody there that can chat to them and maybe try and explain to them what's been going on. Or somebody who's maybe experiencing a feeling of being watched, or there's just somebody in the house, and they're not quite sure. So, there's somebody there to talk to them in a number of different ways to find out whether it is a spirit that's causing that or whether it's something else.

But we teach there. We teach clairvoyant development there. We do Reiki treatment there. We've got a lovely lady there called Ann Jones, who's our Reiki Master. She teaches Reiki as well as the Reiki treatments. So, there's lots of things offered there.

We do readings there too. We have different mediums in every day. I'm there virtually every day. It's no wonder my bed's not there. But everyone that works there has been trained there, which is what makes it so unique. We are a family. It's like the Feather family.

We also travel around the world. We travel to Canada and to Spain, taking workshops. We take them outside so that other people can enjoy the same sort of workshops. That's in a nutshell what Feathers does.

Q. I think you've touched on something that's very important there. When people talk about going to mediums, they always ask if you're a member of this, or have you done that, or have you done this? You have to go with somebody you trust. You have to go to somebody that you make that connection with. Do not just go with someone because they are local or their availability. You have to find someone that best suits you. It's the same thing on stage.

I would never work with someone unless I trusted that person. So, Feathers Academy and having that family there is critical, isn't it?

A. Yes, exactly. What we do with the students when they've completed the awareness and development course, we don't just leave them high and dry and say that's the end of everything now. We have other things set in place.

We have a meditation evening where it's just meditation. We have a closed circle evening for the group that has developed together so they can further on that development and trust with each other within a very safe environment.

We also provide a platform within Feathers for them to practice doing readings. So, if they're stuck and they're not quite sure how to deliver a message to somebody, then there's always an experienced medium there that can say. "Maybe you should look at it like this? Maybe we should just open this up a little bit." So, it's a continuing thing, nurturing while they're still developing for as long as they want to be there.

Q. When someone comes into Feathers, and they have a problem in their home, a door bangs, noises, or whatever that may be, and for you guys to help them to understand whether that's spirit or whether it's another cause. Is that not something that you would go out and investigate the property in a two-pronged approach both scientifically and psychically, or do you feel that's doable by Feathers?

A. It works differently than how I work on *Rescue Mediums* because on *Rescue Mediums*, we have no idea in advance where we are going. So, we work in a completely different way. So, say somebody was to come into Feathers and present those problems, what we would do once we got all the information from the person either in person or over the phone, we would then ask them to keep a diary for two weeks.

Within that two weeks, we would ask them to write all the things that were happening. Just for example, maybe a clock would have stopped, so what time did the clock stop? Who was in the house at the time? What was the conversation maybe an hour before the clock stopped? All of those sort of things.

Or maybe the lights went out. Well, who was in the house at the time the lights went out? Was anybody having a conversation at the time? It could be that they see a shadow on the stairs or just have a feeling that someone's there. Maybe it's a certain smell or a sound. So, we ask them to write down absolutely everything, even if it seems silly, write it down. The time it happened and who was there at the time because this can be very helpful when we are paying a visit to the house because then we would go out to the house, but only after a two-week time. It could be that we can help remotely, and we have done that on a number of occasions if we didn't feel that it was necessary to go to the property. But nine times out of ten, if it was within driving distance, we would go. If not, we would pass the information onto someone we trust in the country who is very capable of dealing with something like that.

We will take equipment with us, but we always say, and I'm sure you agree with this as well, we've got all of this equipment that can sort of add to what we've got, it can confirm things that we are picking up. The best sort of tool that you can use is yourself.

Q. Where do you think mediumship and paranormal investigation is heading currently, especially here in the U.K. and I'm bringing that question in now because there are various groups around the U.K. that will scientifically look at the nature of orbs, investigations, how people investigate, the use of EMF, and rule them out as being useful. So what's your feeling?

A. I think they go side by side, to be honest. It depends on what the mediumship is being used for. Obviously, a medium will give proof that life is continuous and, therefore, messages can be passed onto loved ones on the Earth plane. If you're doing a paranormal investigation, you are using your mediumship ability in order to make that connection, and if science can confirm what mediums are already picking up on, that's got to be a good thing, surely.

Q. I absolutely agree. There are people out there that we've interviewed, like Steve Parsons of ParaScience. He's done papers on Orbs. He's looked at the use of EMF and largely would say the one thing that is stable in terms of investigating is our own senses. We go in and investigate somebody else's experience, so to go in at different times and try to replicate the same thing happening again is very short-sighted in many ways.

Of course, paranormal groups out there in the U.K. charge a lot of money to go in and investigate. They go into big places, and they can only get in at night, so you're losing that sense of "We're investigating somebody else's experiences and being able to try and replicate that." In that time or moment, with whoever else was there, who was talking, to see if we could have the same scenario happen again. It's making it much more entertainment and money-making as opposed to an investigation.

A. It depends on what purpose it is for going there. At Feather's Paranormal Investigation Group, we do charge. But we don't charge for rescue work in any way, shape, or form. But for a paranormal investigation, where we take members of the public with us to an investigation, of course, we have to as a paranormal group, we have to pay for the venue, and therefore, in order to recoup your own charges, you've got to charge the individuals for that experience.

A lot of paranormal groups go in for the fear factor straight away, and that's what they are there for. Because the people who are on their paranormal group, that's what they want. To me, that's not what Feather's Paranormal Group offers. We always have at least three or four mediums working on the same night, and we split those into groups. Every group does a different activity.

One group may do a séance, another a vigil, another may do pendulum work, or dowsing rods, and maybe table tipping. We have different experiments that we do. But we show those who are attending how to do it and how to do it properly by grounding yourself first, by putting protection around yourself first, and how to open up your chakra so that you can fine-tune.

We teach them how to do it just so that they can get the whole experience themselves, rather than a medium that goes in and says, "I'm feeling this, and I've got Great Aunt Sally here, who's come to say hello to everybody" I wouldn't particularly like to go to an investigation like that where the medium is doing all of the work.

We like the individuals to experience things for themselves. We will try things. If somebody wants to bring something in— except for a Ouija board, we won't ever use one of those—we will get them to try things. But we will do it in a safe way. People don't realize that they can open doorways this way. If they don't know how to close the doorways that they are opening as they're going into properties, they can cause all sorts of problems for the individuals who were attending, also for the property itself. You've got to treat it with respect. That's the way I look at it.

Q. You have done things that you call "Guide Portraits." So tell me, Jackie, how do you do it, how does it work?

A. The spirit guide ones I've done in a slightly different way. The guide portraits I've done for people, so it's either a commission piece or I've felt compelled to do it. What I would do in that case is I would have a photograph of you in front of me, and I would link into your aura. I would have to see somebody's eyes when I am working this way. So, I would link into your aura or energy field by focusing on your eyes.

Then I would ask my spirit guide to connect with your spirit guide to ask them to come forward, or whatever spirit guide happened to come forward. Then I would get a different guide that I have. This is a psychic artist guide to work through me. So, I have three different artists that work with me in this way, and one of them works in color – quite detailed color. Another one works with color but very quickly. Then I have another one that works with a pencil.

Mainly, it's the one that works with color when I'm doing guide portraits, and I feel as though I am complete with that energy at that moment in time. So I get to feel the characteristics of that guide. As you can imagine, there's a lot of love that comes with the spirit guides. So it can even affect the way I sit. If I'm working with a spirit guide who is quite strict, I have to sit up straight. If I work with a spirit guide who was an artist themselves when they were on the Earth plane, there's quite a sort of lots of flair in the picture. So, I can be standing, sitting, or moving around. So I tend to work with the spirit guide's energy in that way.

When I'm working with psychic art like for *Rescue Mediums*, it's done by meditating a couple of days before I go to the location. I would sit and ask my spirit guide to give me a list of things, a bit like premonitions if you like, of what to expect when we got to the property – where we were going, what sort of things were going to be happening.

I would ask the psychic art guide to come forward to work through me to show me either someone who connects to the property or somebody who connects to who is there. What spirit is there if there is a spirit that is haunting the property, and who they are and what they look like. What is their personality?

I tend to do a lot of different types of artwork like that. So, I could actually draw someone who is living in the property and actually still there. It could be the homeowner. It could be that I'm drawing someone from 1920, and it's a male, and he's wearing a hat. So, the hat becomes quite a prominent feature.

Q. How easy do you find it to touch base with people's guides and to be able to have some insight with them?

A. To link into somebody else's spirit guide is not very easy to do, but when I'm working in a psychic art way, I link in through someone's eyes, and that gives me a soul connection with somebody. When I'm working that way, and I try and link into the aura or energy, it's my spirit guide who brings the guides who are connecting with the person's photograph that I'm linking into.

It works in a similar way if I'm sitting with someone and doing a spirit guide portrait for someone who sat in front of me. It works in exactly the same way. It's probably a little bit stronger because I'm working with that person's energy as well as the guide's energy at the same time.

Q. How people present is quite different normally to who they are to help you make sense of something.

A. Absolutely.

Q. So, if I asked you for a picture of my guide, would you see the image they were giving me, or would you see something completely different?

A. Well, everyone sees things in their own way. It's very personal, isn't it? Of course, what I'm linking into is the energy of that person, and the spirit, and the personality of the guide. The thing with guides, and I found this out a few times as well, is that since they've reached a guide level, they have been on the Earth plane many times. So, therefore, they have many incarnations. It depends which incarnation they show themselves to me in.

For example, my main guide that I work with every single day is a little Egyptian fellow. He's very small, very bony, and I have drawn a picture of him. He did a past life regression with me, and I've been working with him for about 20 years before he did this. He said, "You know we've known each other in a previous lifetime." I thought, "I have never known you before." But he took me back to when we were slaves together in Egypt, and we were slaves to a Turkish merchant. As soon as he said that to me and showed me an image, I was straight away back to where I knew him from. We were best friends. His image then was totally different from the image that I see him now.

Listen to the full interview with Jackie Dennison on my website:

www.alanrwarren.com/hom-
podcast-
episodes/episode/b404b85c/rescue-
mediums-T.V.-show-host-jackie-
dennison

Channeling

INTERVIEW WITH MARK ALLAN FROST

Channeling was a popular thing when I was growing up in the 60s, where it was used on several scary movies and television shows. They would show people sitting around a table, holding hands, in a darkly lit room to have a séance. During these seances, the medium would channel the spirit or let the spirit take over their bodies and use their voices to communicate with the living people sitting at the table.

One of the most popular real-life channellers back in the 1960s was Jane Roberts. She claimed to have had a spirit named "Seth" channel her to give her information that was important to the world. Roberts would write several books with this entity called "Seth" so that as many people in the world as possible could get his important information and use it to make the world a better place to live.

After Roberts died, everything on the Seth front went silent until a man named Mark Allan Frost would pick up where Roberts left off by channeling Seth and continuing to write the information in books for the world to have. Only this time, Seth had a different demeanor and a more critical message.

These interviews took place in 2014 and 2015.

Mark Allen Frost Website – https://www.sethreturns.com/

―――――――――――――――――――

Q. How did you come to meet Seth? How did it all start for you?

A. Let me talk about who Seth is and how he entered our system of reality originally. A woman named Jane Roberts—she was a writer and poet, her husband was an artist, and they were living in Elmira, New York, in the early sixties—Jane Roberts began what she called psychic disturbances. She would hear voices. She would see apparitions in her home. She would see figures. She decided to get a Ouija board of all things to explore what might be happening to her.

She and her husband decided to use the Ouija board to decipher some of these messages they were receiving. Specifically, this guy named Seth came through over the course of a few days of exploration. He made it known that he wanted to give messages to Jane and her husband, that they were to put in books, and distribute to humanity. And that began the Seth material.

Jane and her husband wrote a number of books dictated by Seth to Jane, and her husband would take down the dictation in his own shorthand, and they made books out of that. They became very well-known. She's probably the most well known medium of that era.

In 1984, she became very ill and made her transition, as Seth calls it. She passed away in 1984, and Seth was dictating his messages through her up until the very end. Everyone presumed that since she was no longer in a physical body that Seth would stop transmitting his messages, and that was true for the most part.

Then in 2002, I was a hypnotherapist with a practice in California, where I helped people who were trying to stop smoking, lose weight, or conquer their fears. One day, a woman phoned me. Her name was Kat Smith, and she said that she'd like a past life regression. I brought the woman into my office and gave her a few suggestions, and within minutes she was accessing apparently what was a past life in which she was being devoured by lions in the Roman Coliseum.

It startled me to see that. I asked her to project her consciousness out of her body so that she wouldn't have to feel that pain and tell me what was going on. She did that, and I documented that. I video-taped all of these early sessions.

Later, she phoned me and said that some spirit named Seth was interrupting her transmission meditation. This is where this group of people from different parts of the world all meditate at the same time. She was having trouble with these meditations because this spirit named Seth was coming through and saying that he wanted to write books again.

Kat did not have any idea who this Seth was, but when she mentioned the name Seth, well, I had some experience with him, and I had read all of his books. So, we brought Kat into my office, where I had some of Seth's old books that he wrote with Jane Roberts there so that he would feel comfortable.

Just after a few suggestions, I heard this gruff voice coming from Kat say, "Mark, I'm here. You asked for me, and I'm here." I asked if he was Seth, and he said, "Indeed I am." Then I said, "Are you Jane Roberts, Seth?" and he replied, "Of course." In that hour that I talked to him, I asked him a few validating questions to make sure that it was *the* Jane Roberts. Seth answered them to my satisfaction.

Because we thought that this was a one-shot deal where he would come through and not come back, we asked him some personal questions about our lives, and another question I asked was about breast cancer in Marin County, because at that time they had a much higher amount of breast cancer as compared to other counties around it and we wondered why. He gave us a very detailed reason.

Q. What happened next?

A. The very next meeting, Seth started dictating *911 the Unknown Reality of the World*, his first book of new material since Jane passed away, almost twenty years. In six weeks, we got all the material for the book. He does this thing where he puts it in our consciousness. It's like a download. It came to us intact. We had to punctuate, but all the material you see in the book was literally from those early dictations.

It's been that way ever since. Kat left the program after the first book. She didn't know who Seth was in the beginning, but she learned about Jane Roberts and some of the difficulties that she and her husband had, like people looking for Seth's wisdom and camping out on their front porch and that kind of thing. She realized that she would no longer have privacy if she continued this project.

So, Seth taught me how to pick up his communication stream, and I have been his collaborator over the last ten books. That's twelve years.

Q. Well, who was Seth? I'm taking it that he was once alive just like we are.

A. Yes. Well, he describes himself as a non-physical being and an energy-personality. What he does is kind of difficult to describe. He is energy. He is a representation of the reincarnation of the theory of reality. He calls it the simultaneous lives. He maintains that here in this life, we're living separate lives. I'm a separate person talking to you, but in fact, also beyond what he calls linear time, there's this spacious moment where we are experiencing many lives. From the distant path, we might say and lives from the distant future also.

These many lives of his, he used them to assemble personality aspects that are likable. He chooses many aspects of his many lives in which he was a kindly grandfather, for example, because people are comfortable around that kind of energy.

He no longer has need for a human body, and that's why he has contacted people like me. Folks who are in his soul family, he calls it now. He used to call it the "Seth-entity." I'm a Seth-entity human counterpart. He needs us to take his messages and create books in physical reality because he doesn't have the wherewithal to do that because he doesn't have a body.

Q. Do you have any actual input into the books that you dictate from Seth?

A. That's a touchy subject. I think there's always my input, just as it's my belief that when he spoke with Jane, there's always her input also. You can't help it. You're basically translating the inevitable – something that can't be put into words. He calls it "The Ancient Wisdom." I try to keep out of it as much as possible, but after the fact and I read the books, I can see, oh well, here's where my knowledge of psychology comes in so that I can express the inevitable. An idea that Seth was trying to manifest in his books, and I can do that because of my schooling in psychology.

That speaks to a difference in my books to Jane's books. Jane was a female. She was a poet. She was sort of a priestess. I see her in that way. So, her books with Seth have this lyrical, poetic sensibility, I think. She was also a very good writer and profoundly interesting.

Now, my books, because Seth is speaking through me, create a simplification of his teaching to appeal to a broader audience. My books have a different sensibility to them. They are more simplified. They don't have a poetic aspect, but they do have a psychological underpinning to them, you might say.

So, do I put myself into the mix? Yes, because it can't be helped. But Jane tried to keep herself out of it as much as possible, and so do I. I don't think it's my place to put my values or my thoughts and ideas into the Seth books, and I think that I have been pretty good from preventing that from happening.

Q. Is there something different that Seth is doing and saying to you than what he was doing and saying to Jane?

A. I think so, yes. On the first three books he wrote with me, he called it the books on the awakening of humanity. He maintains and still suggests that humanity is awakening. We're all coming up in frequency. We're learning about our other lives and so on. Each of us is at a particular stage. He calls it "Soul Evolution." According to the stage we're at, we are identifying our issues and learning our lessons. In his books with us, all of the material is centered around that dynamic – that we are in really interesting times.

Now, with Jane's books, I don't think there was as much alarm as the books we did with Seth. Back then, it was a matter of Seth attempting to convince people that he was real, and he sort of courted the reader. In a sense, he put on this aspect that "I'm the gentle, friendly grandfather, and here is the truth of your reality. That you create your reality, and you are experiencing your thoughts, your imagery, lifting your consciousness. Your feelings and the emotions that you're having may manifest in front of you like feedback from your consciousness. You see the world in front of you or your personal reality."

He was updating people on the truth of their realities, and a lot of people were calling him the "Father of a New Age" for that. This predates quantum theory also.

But the books he's written with us have a sense of alarm. In the interim, after the last twenty years after Jane Roberts passed away, he says that our world has regressed to a point where these non-physical beings such as Seth and others are worried about the state of the world, and there's a danger that we will destroy it with nuclear weapons and other weapons to the degree that all life will be destroyed. Seth, as an extra-dimensional being, has a stake in it. He exists in the dimensions of Earth. The fourth, fifth, and sixth dimension. He says that if the Earth goes down the tubes, he and the other non-physical beings also go down the tubes.

Q. Is there a reason why the world has regressed, according to Seth?

A. Yes. There are a few reasons that I've noted. The primary one is no leadership. He says that our world is being run by negative leaders primarily. These men and women are driven by not the positive Gods but the negative Gods. They get their energy from lusting after power, not doing the people's will. Now, this is a broad generalization. I think the listeners know what I'm getting at.

These negative leaders don't have our best interest at heart and are extracting the resources of the Earth for themselves, their friends, politicians, business leaders, corporate leaders, and so on. They're taking the essence of our planet for their own benefit and could care less about the common citizen.

Q. Now, you also do personal readings for people with Seth, don't you?

A. Yes. That's how we support ourselves. The books we use as business cards and price them cheaply. Seth says to put the books out cheaply so that people can read them and connect with what he's saying and realize that it's the truth. Then, they often phone up for phone sessions, and in these sessions, Seth acts like a sort of ghost coach or spirit coach, helping people with their everyday issues in regards to relationships and finances. He speaks from this perspective of the reincarnation trajectory.

Q. So we carry over our unresolved issues from life to life?

A. Yes. All of our lives are happening now. It just looks like they're passed because we are in this linear time construct with one moment that seems to occur after another. That's not the way reality works. Everything happens at once. Seth tells us if we can get a grasp of that, we can easily peek into those other lives in times of meditation or when you're walking in nature, and we see the benefits of those communications.

In new age circles, people talk about connecting with their source, the guides, angels, and so on. Seth talks about the possibility of connecting with your other simultaneous lives and achieving guidance, particularly future lives. Because all of our lives are occurring at once, we can access future lives right where we are now at this moment. We can see the results of our behavior today and see if it's worthwhile to continue what we are doing now.

Q. Do you think that Seth will choose others to channel?

A. Yes. He is in communication with a multitude of other souls. He says that he's always in communication with other people. He appears in their mental environment, and some people know him as their intuitive voice or guide, or this message is from my angel beings, and there are some people that identify him as Seth. They have read some of his books and made the connection.

So, he has made himself known over the millennia. So, it's not a manifestation with Jane and her husband or me and Seth only. It's something that has been done since time began. So, the idea of others channeling him, there are a few, but according to Seth, I am the only one that he writes books with and is spreading the word of his return.

Q. Was there a particular reason you think that he chose you to write his books?

A. Yes, there was, and I know that from everything that has transpired since we met. First off, I was a semi-expert in the Seth material because I read most of his books, mainly back in the eighties. So, I was familiar with his teachings, and I was very interested in desktop publishing back in the old days. With desktop publishing, I didn't have to get an agent or worry about publishers turning me down.

So, I had that in place. Plus, I was in graduate school studying psychology with an emphasis on alternative practices, especially hypnotherapy – hypnotizing other people and myself to achieve the trans-state. The trans-state is what Seth used with Jane to make that connection and to make it possible for them to write those books.

Kat and I, she was the client that came to me in my office, both agreed in a past life that once we both turned fifty and all of the drama that comes with reaching fifty, all that comes before that like raising families and settling down, and all that comes with that. For me, I quit drinking ten years ago.

We both signed what Seth calls a "soul contract" and agreed to meet coincidentally and began to work with Seth. It was coincidental when Kat was looking for a hypnotherapist and looked through the phone book and found me. Of all the hypnotherapists in Marin County—there are about one hundred—she chose me.

I later found out that Seth directed her attention to my name and inspired her to keep the appointment. In that sense, he brought her to me. In that same way, he knew that she was going to act as an intermediary here and not stick around. At that time, if I knew that she wasn't going to stick around and put all of the responsibilities for the books on my shoulders, I don't know that I would have done this.

Some people have asked me how I feel about being deceived by Seth because he didn't warn me that there was a bumpy road ahead, but I have to be forgiving with him because the end result is we're here twelve or thirteen years later, and we have all of these great books. We have a network of loving souls all around the world. It was all worth it.

Q. Did you ever have any negative things come from working with Seth?

A. Yes. I encountered a bad case of blindness. I went completely blind for about three months, and everyone was telling me to stop with the project. That it was, somehow I was being invaded, and my sight was being taken by Seth. But I pursued the project further, and in the third book, we wrote about self-healing and a healing regiment. I used that information and his practices to pull myself out of that – to heal myself and prevent a downward slide into death.

Q. Can you tell me what actually happens in a phone reading?

A. Well, we have a 20 minute, 30 minute, or 60-minute session, and for the most part, our people are long-term. We've been having Seth talk to his students for about ten years. Typically, someone would have read one of his books, the book on healing, let's say. They are usually triggered by an example Seth talks about in that book. He gives a lot of examples to pull the reader in, and then he sort of delivers this subtext of ancient wisdom. The main one being that you create your own reality, so take responsibility for your creations. Because it does require a certain knowledge of who Seth is, his practice, his theories, you have to have a little bit of that knowledge, whether it's reading from Jane's books or our books.

It begins simply with people asking questions. It takes about thirty seconds for me to bring Seth in, and people begin asking questions. Seth answers their questions in a context of an individual human with particular issues learning particular lessons. He helps you to identify those issues and see where you may be avoiding issues, or you may be intellectualized.

So, they get to the root cause of the issues. If someone has a health issue, for example, Seth often says, "Well, you created it, you created it for the learning experience." The person might say that was unbelievable. Why would I create cancer to learn? What am I learning from dying of cancer? So, Seth works with people to identify and be responsible for their input into the creation of the malady. Then he helps them revere that by changing how they see it. When you can think of a chronic illness as a lesson, you begin to see where you are helping to create the illness.

Listen to the full interview with Mark Allan Frost on my website:

www.alanrwarren.com/hom-
podcast-episodes/episode/
f5ce1651/mark-allan-frost-
channeling-seth

Seances & Psychic Surgery

INTERVIEW WITH GARY MANNION

Can a person really conduct surgery on another? In the 1990s and early 2000s, there were videos of people who claimed to be healing others who had physical illnesses. But this was not the case where a minister stands at his pulpit, has people unable to walk brought forward to them, and lays their hands on them while calling out for God to heal them. And then, low and behold, they get up out of the wheelchair and walk. This is not what we are referring to here.

These were psychics or mediums that were often not religious, who claimed that they could heal people by conducting a psychic surgery on them.

During their "surgery," they laid the patient on a bed and placed their hands on them. They were not holding any tools but acted as though they were conducting a physical surgery on them. Afterward, the patient got up from the bed and claimed they were cured.

Some of the videos even showed what appeared to be blood on the patients while the psychic surgeon was working on these clients. After considerable searching for one of these psychic surgeons with a good reputation in that subject, I found one that would sit down and tell us what psychic surgery was all about.

Gary Mannion lives in Australia, and we interviewed him in 2014.

Q. Gary, let's tell our listeners what you do?

A. My name is Gary Mannion, and I work as a psychic surgeon and medium.

Q. We have had mediums on the show before but never a psychic surgeon. What do you mean by "psychic surgeon?"

A. When I work or when spirit team works through me, I see two hands going into the body. I see what would appear to be an operation going on, and in most of the world, we don't cut skin. In places like Brazil and the Philippines, we are allowed to cut skin. I get some quite good results, to put it in a nutshell.

Q. How did you know that you could do this, and when did it start?

A. So, for me, I apparently used to see and talk to spirit from a very young age. I have no memory of anything before the age of thirteen, and my very first memory was my dad taking me to the local spiritualist church, and I was sitting down in front and saw the medium tune in. All of a sudden, I hear this voice in me saying, "You can do that."

So, of course, being thirteen and hearing voices in my head, I gave it a go. That started off my psychic mediumship pathway. Then, when I was eighteen, I was invited to Manchester in the U.K. to teach in psychic development. The group that I was working with did some spiritual healing and asked if I wanted to take part. At the time, I thought, put your hands on someone, let the energy come through – how hard can it be. So, I said, yes, I'll give it a go.

When I went to start, all of a sudden, I felt this very strong presence behind me, and I saw these hands going into this woman's stomach, pulling this mold out, which made sense to her afterward. Then I started being scientifically documented by the Scottish Society of Psychic Research and another organization called Prism. They researched me for five and a half years, and through them, we got a 90 percent success rate.

Q. How has this changed your own philosophy or religion?

A. From my personal experience, I can say that when it comes to life after death, I have no doubt. As far as religion goes, I come across it every now and then. Somebody who, say, has been brainwashed by their religion to think what we do is evil.

Generally, I won't cast myself as religious. I believe in life after death, but I don't want to abide by any doctrine. I'm very happy with people who have their own beliefs. As far as I'm concerned, I'm not there to try and convince or change anyone's mind. I'm there to work for spirit for those who want it.

Q. Yes, when I grew up, things like this were considered quite evil.

A. Yes, we see psychics and stuff all over T.V. now, and on the positive side, it's raised awareness that it is around. It's been around for a very long time. The only downside is that it's become very sensationalized, and everyone wants to do it without putting the work in for it, so it's also watered down the whole movement quite a lot.

Q. When you do your psychic surgery, do you do it in a private office, or do you do it on a stage with people watching?

A. We do demonstrations. So, in the U.K., I got about 26 clinics at the moment, and I also work around the world all the time. Every other month I'm in a different country. I also do demonstrations in front of audiences and big crowds.

Q. Can you walk us through the process a little bit?

A. Sure. In the demonstration, I do the introduction of what I'm going to do and who I am. Then, I would ask my guide Abraham—who's the main surgeon—who he wants to call up. Then, I'll get a condition. So, for example, a lower back problem with a compressed disk or trapped nerve, things like that. From that, we'll get all the people to put their hands up who can take the information, which will then help me narrow down who it is I need to work with.

Once I know that, I'll get the person up on the couch. Then, I'll hand things over to Abraham, and he'll take control over my hands and get to work. While that's happening, I'll be explaining what he's doing inside the body, what's going on.

We'll be asking the client on the couch what they are feeling, if anything, as well.

The benefit you get with a demonstration is since psychic surgery is a form of physical mediumship, it takes the energy that we all give off all the time, which means in a demonstration setting, a lot of people in the audience can also receive healing while they are sitting there.

Q. How and when did you get connected with your spirit guide Abraham?

A. Well, I first knew of Abraham when I was eighteen. That day, I went to do healing, and I just started seeing his hands going, and initially, that link would come and go. So, whenever I would do a healing, I would feel his presence. I didn't know anything about the presence. I just started working. Then, as it developed, I got to know the personality of Abraham. And nowadays, he's pretty much with me 24 hours a day.

Q. Do you know what led you to Abraham or Abraham to you?

A. He says it's nothing special. He has something he wants to achieve, which there's a few things he wants to achieve. He found me to be his medium because he knew my energy, and we had a set desire to achieve the same thing. So, that's why he picked me. But again, it doesn't mean that I'm special or anything else. It just means he can resonate with my energy.

Q. Was Abraham previously alive and living on Earth as a human?

A. Abraham says that he has lived on Earth many times. His last life was probably about three and a half thousand years ago.

Q. You obviously believe in reincarnation?

A. Yes. Again, from what I've seen, Abraham gives me a lot of advice, and I have no reason to doubt his advice. So, from what I've seen, yeah.

Q. Do you know how that works? Is there any time length between lives? How many times do we live? Do we get to choose when we come back?

A. Going from Abraham's opinion, Earth, material worlds are all about learning. It's also a world of duality. So, we've got the opposites here. So, in order to progress in spirit, we need to have enough experience and knowledge to do so, which means that we may need to come back in many lifetimes to experience many different things. Whether that's this world or another world in the dimension, or maybe in another form, not just as humans, so, it's his opinion that we have many lifetimes until we've learned all that we need to in order to progress.

Q. You are also a medium, correct?

A. Yes, I'm a physical medium.

Q. What is it you mean by a physical medium?

A. A lot of people will experience it as a traditional séance. So, everyone sits and holds hands, and you can get a range of phenomena – from things flying out of the room to materialization to direct voice from loved ones. That's just a few things.

Q. Can you explain what's different about a séance as compared to a medium giving you a reading?

A. So, a mental medium is if spirit came to you, the energy, and you work with it, you interpret it, that's mental. It's coming through our minds, and we've got to interpret it. A physical mediumship – they use us as the medium or the vessel, but they do the work.

So, traditionally with physical mediumship, they'll work with a substance called Ectoplasm Photo-plasm, and from this, you can get phenomena like things flying out of the room, or things like direct voice, where say your mother or father can actually come through and talk to you, or materialization, where they can actually be a physical mass in the room. You can feel them. You can touch them and talk with them. It's kind of a big step on from mental mediumship.

Q. When I speak to a lot of mental mediums, they tell me that everybody has the ability to do this. It's just whether or not they are in tune with it. Would this be the same for physical mediumship?

A. So, everyone is spirit. So, in theory, we all have the ability to connect with spirit and work with spirit. With physical mediumship, if you work with ectoplasm, every living being has ectoplasm. It's a substance within our body. However, a physical medium has an abundance of it. So, they do say that you have to be born with the ability to produce an abundance of ectoplasm. However, a lot of groups are now working with a substance called photo plasm, which is purely energy-based, and anyone can channel that.

Q. What is the Spiritualist Church?

A. In the U.K., we have the Spiritualist religion, which is kind of run and overlooked by the Spiritual National Union (S.N.U.). So, they have various churches. Some are completely Spiritualists. Some are Christian-based Spiritualist Churches, but they still come up under the S.N.U. What we've got a lot of now in the U.K. are mainly just centers who don't want anything to do with religion. They just want to deal with the mediumship, or maybe the philosophy as well. But they don't want to come under the umbrella of any religion. But Spiritualism in the U.K. is a recognized religion.

Q. Most people listening today probably have an idea of what a Christian Church is and what they believe. What is the foundation of a Spiritualist church? Is there a God involved?

A. The Spiritualist religion is based on seven principles. Basically, it's meant to be open to everyone. We are all spirit. And God, or whatever you want to call him, is the same God accepting that life does go on after death and that we can still communicate with those, and that's the kind of base of it. The problem I find is that adults get caught up very much in Christian religions. So, they have their hymns, they have their prayers, and it can be a little bit political like any other religion can be, sadly. Initially, it was just meant to be a philosophy, but it became a religion for tax reasons, and that's also why I try and stay away from that. And a lot of people in the U.K. now are breaking away from that because of the politics, sadly.

Q. When you are actually performing a psychic surgery, how are you affected?

A. With psychic surgery nowadays, I can take up to about 19 or 20 people a day as long as I don't go over that. I might feel tired by the end of that, but I'll bounce back very quickly. I'll be fine within 10 or 20 minutes of finishing. If I go over that 19 or 20, I can feel very tired for sometimes two or three days afterward.

With the seances, that does put quite a bit more pressure on your body. So, depending on how the séance went, if people weren't following the rules, they were moving around and things like that, then that can leave me quite ill for a couple of days afterward. But the more I do it, the more I can sustain and put up with it.

Q. Are you ever left with the effects of the people you are healing?

A. Thankfully, no. I also don't walk down the streets and start picking up on people's conditions. I can become aware of it if I wanted to. If I wanted to focus on that person's energy, but it's very much when I want it to happen. Abraham is with me 24 hours a day, and he's there when I need him, and I want to work with him. When I don't want to, and I just want to be me, I've got that space.

Q. So, you have pretty good control over this?

A. Yes. I can control what I do and don't want to do. Some mediums burn themselves out, and they like to blame spirit for that. But it's them that's saying, yes, I want to keep working, and spirit is going to take that opportunity.

Q. I was born in the sixties, and back when I was growing up, a séance was always represented as something evil or bad.

A. Yes, sadly, because of things like religion and Hollywood, it's always been given a bad name, but it's not. Not when you're doing it genuinely. It's also an industry where there are a lot of fakes out there. I suppose it's like any industry. So, people have seemed to focus on the negative in the past, and it's not at all. It's a bit like ghost hunting. People think they are going to spend the night scared, whereas, in reality, you spend most of the night being bored because there's very little if any phenomenon, and that's spread out over 8 hours, and it's not scary when you get that phenomenon. It's just the idea that's portrayed to us by movies and media.

Q. What do you want someone to get out of a séance with you?

A. The aim of the séance is to try and allow people in the audience loved ones to come through and communicate. Whether that's through direct voice, through materialization, where they can actually touch and interact with their loved one. But yes, that's the ultimate aim.

Q. I am picturing a séance to be just like a mental medium. Only the spirit is using your body, correct?

A. Yes. Rather than the medium going, "I've got your mother here, and she tells me her name is Jean," Jean's going to come through and actually talk for herself, and she's going to prove to you that she is who she says she is.

Q. So they are using your actual voice and body?

A. Yes, except when they come through with direct voice. It's their voice. So, it would be your mother's voice if she was to come through.

Q. Do you remember this after it's happening to you during a seance?

A. No, I have no idea before the séance or afterward.

Q. Does this leave any sort of memory or feelings for you afterward?

A. If something goes wrong in a séance and the rules aren't followed, it can be very dangerous for the medium and mediums have died in the past while doing it. If everything goes well, I'll just feel tired for a day or two.

Q. That sounds kind of scary that a medium could die from a séance. What rules do people break that can cause this?

A. When a phenomenon is happening, you have to try and sit very still because it's the energy of the sitters that are allowing the phenomenon to happen. If somebody is moving around, they are really upsetting that energy. If your loved one comes through and touches you, until they are ready to be touched back, you need to just sit there and let them work with you.

If you grab them when and they are not ready, the ectoplasm will recoil back into the medium's body very quickly, and that can create burns on the body. Same as if light comes in before they're ready for it, that will cause the energy to disperse and recoil, which again can harm the medium. If you are working with photo-plasm, it is very safe for the medium.

Q. Have you ever had any of these things happen to you while giving a séance?

A. Yes, we've had accidents happen during seances, and they've left me burned. They've left me ill. But we've had no major problems during a séance.

Q. Do you actually get a physical burn, sort of like what you'd get from a fire?

A. Yes, if you look at the history, it's often described as electrical burns. A great example would be Helen Duncan, a physical medium, who got raided by the police during a séance and died three days later from what appeared to be electrical burns all throughout her body.

Q. Do you ever have a séance in front of a live audience, or is it only in a private setting like a residence?

A. We can do it for an audience, but because of the risk involved with a séance to the medium, we are more selective. So, if you were very new to spiritualism, we may not start you off with a séance. We might start you off with mediumship or maybe table-tipping to make sure that you're going to be okay to sit. But it's generally open to the public.

Q. Some mental mediums claim that you don't have to be in person with them in order for them to do a reading for you, such as by phone. Can you do a séance remotely as well?

A. No, not a séance. But I can do distance psychic surgery.

Q. So, you mean distant healing?

A. Yes. Actually, with seances, I guess there have been cases of a medium being in one country sitting for a circle and in another country that medium's home circle has been sitting, and phenomena have happened between circles, even though the medium wasn't there. But they still need to be sitting at that time to build the energy.

Q. When we go back to the psychic surgery, someone can phone you, and you can heal them?

A. Yes, we can connect energy and see what's going on and establish a connection for healing to take place.

Q. Are there ever times when you come across a person who needs some sort of healing that you cannot do?

A. I'd say that Abraham will always help in any way that he can. That said, like two people with the exact same condition, one may make a full recovery for whatever reason, and one might not even respond. So, it really depends on the person. When we're working, we're not just working on the physical problem. We're working on what's triggering that, whether it's an emotion or an experience in their life and what the root of the problem is. We're going to try and work with all of those levels because if we don't, the condition is not going to go, or it's going to come back in some other way.

Q. There is no guarantee?

A. No, sadly we can't make any guarantee with it. We have some very good reported results, but everyone's different. So, I can't make any guarantees.

Q. If a non-believer comes to see you, someone who has been talked into it by someone, will the healing still work? Does the person being healed have to believe in what you're doing?

A. Yes, some of my best cases have been skeptics. The only requirement we ask from somebody, you don't have to be religious, you don't have to believe in why it works, you just have to want to get better. As long as you have that one thing, we can work with you.

A great example was when I did the BBC documentary quite a few years ago, I had a friend who knew what I did, and he was a complete skeptic of anything spiritual. He was developing this breast tissue because of his hormones. So, I said to him one day, "Why don't you let me work on them." He said, "Okay, you can have a go." After the psychic surgery, his breast issue disappeared within a number of days.

So, when the BBC interviewed him, he said, "I am still a skeptic." When they asked him what he put down to his healing, he said, "Its placebo. I allowed him to work on me, and that triggered something in my brain to get better." So, in his case, he still doesn't want to believe. He doesn't want to say that the spiritual stuff worked, but he just wanted to get better.

Q. How do you feel about the medical community? They are probably not very supportive of psychic surgery.

A. You'd be surprised. There are a lot more doctors who are taking an interest. Some will take the stance that if it's working for you, keep doing it. Some will say this has worked. Let's not address why. Let's just accept it worked. Some will 'pooh pooh' it, and that can't possibly work. It's a real mixed bag. But there is a lot of interest in it now from the medical community.

Listen to the full interview with Gary Mannion on my website:

www.alanrwarren.com/hom-podcast-episodes/episode/1a46953f/psychic-surgeon-gary-mannion-2014

Pets in the Afterlife

INTERVIEW WITH ROB GUTRO

Many of us have had pets throughout our life from childhood to retirement. They often become an essential part of our family, and we love them as such. The unfortunate thing about having a pet is that they don't live nearly as long as we will, so we will all face the times when they pass on.

Like any loved one who passes, we feel great sorrow and loss. But one thing that is different about our pets is that they never once speak to us. I always find it fascinating that I can love my dog so much, and he has never spoken two words to me.

This tells me a few things about how our pets communicate with us. If you ever watch two dogs together, they often communicate with each other purely by closely observing and sensing what they are doing, and they know exactly what they're thinking. With every dog that I have had, they begin to do the same thing with us.

Now comes the question of our pets in the afterlife. Do they continue to live on after they have left their physical body? If their consciousness does live on, how do they communicate with us? They are great at reading us and what we think and feel, but we're not always so good at reading them. We need words and expressions to understand what another is trying to tell us. So, if the animal doesn't speak, which in my experience they don't talk even when they are alive, how do they speak to us from the other side?

I searched for the answers to these questions and found all sorts of explanations, but nothing that was very believable. Some mediums claim that they don't need to know how to speak or know our language, just as spirits of people don't. After death, there is no need to understand each other's languages to communicate. I'm a pretty logical guy, and that doesn't ring true for me.

So, now it's time to speak with some of the best animal after-death communicators around. I found and got several animal spirit communicators and interviewed them all. After much thought and reviewing these interviews, I chose to be what I consider the best. I say that not only because of the information that he gave but also the feeling that he was being absolutely sincere.

I have to say that with most of the animal spirit communicators, they would often, over the phone during the interview, try to impress me by connecting with an animal of mine that had passed away. All of these attempts were embarrassingly wrong. I was still very polite in my early radio days and never called them on it. But that's not something that I would let pass by today.

The animal spirit communicator I chose to use in this book is Rob Gutro. I interviewed him three times and produced a paranormal show that also interviewed him on this subject. He has written several books on the subject as well. His website is www.robgutro.com

Like the other interviews used in the *House of Mystery* radio show interviews, I have taken the highlights of all three interviews. The interviews are posted for you to listen to anytime in their entirety. The interviews took place in 2015, 2016, and 2018.

Q. How did you become a medium?

A. Well, I have been able to get messages from people who have passed since I was a teenager. In 2010, I joined a paranormal investigation group, and we have done lots of paranormal investigations since then, mostly in private homes.

Q. How did you get turned onto communicating with pets after they passed?

A. It was about 2005, and it was all triggered by the loss of a puppy that I had. His name was Buzz, and he passed suddenly when I was walking him, and his leash opened, and he ran out in front of a car, and he was killed in front of me. He became the world's best canine communicator from the night he died and over the last ten years.

He gave me so many signs that he actually inspired me to write a book about how he was communicating with me. Before that, I never got messages from dogs or cats. He kind of opened the door to that.

Q. The next question would be, how did you know that it was Buzz who was communicating with you? Mediums, in general, will talk about getting images, pictures, feelings, and even words from a human spirit. How is it different from an animal?

A. Well, animals communicate pretty much the same as they do in life. But the additional thing that they could do is that they can actually give you words. They recognize a lot of words that we teach them. They know their names. They know where certain things are in the house by identifying them. They also show pictures. They give mediums pictures that we can decipher. They'll identify a favorite toy. So, if someone lost their cat or their dog, and their cat or dog comes through to me, they will give me a specific image of something that was very personal to them. Something that they liked. Or they'll tell me about a companion animal or something like that.

Q. Do you get something different from animal communication than from human communication?

A. Both really come through with a lot of messages of love. I don't think pets know anything different than unconditional love. People, on the other hand, are a different story.

Q. But a person will try to get a message through to you besides their love. Do animals do that too?

A. Animals do the same thing. They have reasons to communicate with us. Many of the reasons they have to communicate with us are to let us know that they are still around us even after they pass. Oftentimes, we find that we grieve just as much, if not more, for the loss of a pet than we do for the loss of a human. I think because we feel responsible for them.

Q. Is there something different that you have to do in order to connect with animals rather than people?

A. The messages just came when they came. I'm not actually able to ask somebody to come through. The next thing to trigger an animal was the passing of my other dog, a Dachshund, who, at 16 and a half, provided clear messages. Then after that, all these animals started communicating with me. In 2005, I also met my partner and fell in love, and that actually enhanced my ability, if you will, to receive signals. The more emotional somebody is, the more likely they are to receive signals.

Q. Do the signals from these loved ones go away after a certain amount of time?

A. They do give you a lot of messages when they first pass, but the problem with that is grief acts as a block for messages from spirit. Most people are so grief-stricken they don't even realize anything that a spirit is trying to get through to them. Spirits come back and forth whenever they're needed.

Four years after the passing of Buzz, I was on vacation in Puerto Rico, and I felt the urge to walk down one particular street. We were at a five-corner street, and I felt the urge. I was being nudged to walk down one street. So, I did.

We got to the end of the street, and there was a dog walker, and he had a dog with him that looked like Buzz. It was right then that I heard Buzz say to me telepathically, "Dad, do you know what day it is?" Then, I remembered that it was the fourth anniversary of his passing. So, it doesn't matter how long they've been gone. When they have something to tell us, they are going to be around us. Birthdays, anniversaries, and holidays particularly are the times when they notify us that they are around.

Q. What about those who say that animals don't have a soul?

A. Every living thing has a soul. There are some conservative religions that claim that animals don't have a soul, which is bologna. Our pets are going to be waiting for us on the other side. Animals would have never been able to survive long before man even showed up on Earth if they didn't have a soul, which is basically intelligence, emotion, and instinct.

Q. Now, your third book is called *Pets in the Afterlife*. What inspired you to write that book?

A. It was actually the passing of our second dog, a Dachshund named Sprite. He was a 16 and a half-year-old dog when he passed. My partner and I do dog rescue and have for about eight years now. Sprite came to us as a foster dog, and he was turning fourteen years old. He was abandoned because both of his parents passed away. He ended up living for about two and a half years. He had a heart murmur.

The next day after he passed, we were in the backyard with our dogs, and a yellow butterfly came into the yard and lingered around for ten minutes and around our other three dogs. If you have a dog, you know that they'll chase a butterfly, but our dogs didn't do that. In fact, they just let the butterfly sit on the grass, and I got close enough to the butterfly to take a couple of close-up shots with my camera.

I realized that it was sent for Sprite. Sprite actually influenced the butterfly, and that all comes back to spirit. The spirits of humans and pets can influence things in nature: birds, butterflies, feathers, any small thing. Actually, also pennies are a common sign of spirits after they've passed. People should look at the year to figure out who it is.

So, Sprite sent us a yellow and black butterfly, and I wrote about this butterfly on my blog. Two friends of mine later that week were reading the blog – one in Maryland and one in New Mexico – and they were reading about it on the iPad outside, and a yellow and black butterfly landed on each one of them when they were reading it. One thing that I have learned about spirit is there is no such thing as coincidence. Sprite was letting them know that they were reading about his passing.

Now, this past July 8th—he passed on July 8, 2013—I was driving to work, and a yellow and black butterfly flew right in front of my windshield on my way to the office. Then I realized that it was July 8th, the anniversary of the day he passed. These are the kinds of things that pets can actually provide.

Q. When you go to a pet shelter, do you find that you can pick up things from the living dogs that are there?

A. You can, actually. Being a medium, you actually tune into their energy, which is different than a reading. I can pick up on their emotions. Each of the dogs and cats has emotions just like people do. You can also tell if they are an old soul, someone that's come back. They have come back in a certain body for a reason, even if it's for a very short time. I think my dog Buzz, the one that was killed as a puppy by a car, was an old soul. I thought that right from the moment I adopted him.

Q. Earlier this year, we had the comedian and television star Brett Butler on our show, and now she claims to have become a medium that can connect with animals. Only she claims that it's horses and other more wild animals that she communicates with.

A. Yes. I find that besides dogs and cats, some birds and horses also have the ability to communicate. It's basically any animal that's been around people. Any animal that's been domesticated in some way has the ability to communicate with us.

Somebody asked me if I could get messages from a lion. Not really because lions haven't been domesticated unless they were in a zoo and they know words, and they study human behavior like dogs, cats, or horses.

Q. Do you do readings for people from their pets?

A. I actually do. I don't charge anything. I don't make my living out of being a medium. Since I published *Pets in the Afterlife* about a year ago, I receive about ten emails a week from people all over Canada, the U.K., Italy, the U.S., and I've, fortunately, been able to tune into a lot of their pets. So, if I get a message, I'm happy to pass it on. I've actually received so many confirmations from people I am going to publish a *Pets in the Afterlife 2*.

Q. Were there any that surprised you?

A. Well, they all surprise me. It's surprising that a dog can give so many details. Where sometimes I am on a ghost investigation, you'll be lucky if I get a few things from a human. But there was one particular dog that I wrote about in *Pets in the Afterlife 2* that told me about his favorite place in Germany. He described the trees, he described the pathways, and he gave me the name of the woman he had stayed with whenever they visited. His pet parents were able to confirm everything and give me pictures of the whole environment where their dog loved the most and stayed whenever he went there.

Listen to the full interview with Rob Gutro on my website:

www.alanrwarren.com/hom-
podcast-episodes/episode/
51e0e6b5/rob-gutro-pets-in-
the-afterlife-3

www.alanrwarren.com/hom-
podcast-episodes/episode/
c0706c1e/rob-gutro-kindred-
spirit

www.alanrwarren.com/hom-
podcast-episodes/episode/
b4311604/animal-
communication-after-death-
rob-gutro

MIND OVER MATTER

Near-Death Experiences
INTERVIEW WITH DIANE CORCORAN

Since I can remember, people who have died for whatever reason and then been revived have told stories of what they experienced during that time they were dead. Over the years, I have seen documentaries or movies where the people who died and then were revived quite often explained an experience of floating over their dead bodies and seeing others who were around them. Eventually, they would float up and go towards a bright light and then suddenly be brought back into their bodies.

During their time dead, some would claim to have met Jesus or some other religious figure, while others say they don't remember anything.

Science has quite often explained this phenomenon because the brain was actually still alive and functioning and that this was some sort of dream state. I've even read where this experience was just something the human body did when it knew it was about to expire.

Instead of just using the interviews that we have had with people who lived through such experiences, I found someone who was not only keeping track of these events but also reporting them to the government.

Diane Corcoran is a retired Colonel for the U.S. military and has her doctorate in Nursing from the University of Texas. She is now the president of the International Association for Near-Death Studies in North Carolina. Corcoran started this organization from her years serving as a nurse during the Vietnam War, where she would hear many Near-Death Experiences from her patients who were wounded during a battle. Originally, the group was there to help support these patients to work through these experiences and get back to normal life in society but quickly ended up being a great resource in the field.

This interview took place in 2014.

Diane Corcoran Website – https://www.corcoranconsulting-nde.com/

Q. What is it that you do now?

A. I'm the president of the International Association for Near-Death Studies, and essentially, I'm a retired military officer. I have been working in this field for a very long time since I first saw a patient in Vietnam who talked to me about one of these experiences.

Q. What was it about that experience that made you go into this subject further?

A. I had the distinct feeling that this was something all doctors and nurses needed to know about because it was an intense experience, and somebody had to be there to support these patients. So, I kind of went on a crusade for the last forty years to teach nurses, doctors, psychologists, social workers, and clergy – because you can't assume, for example, that if they're clergy, they should know this. One would think so, but not really.

Now, of course, the experience is everywhere on television – every movie star has had a Near-Death Experience. So, it's a much more known entity now. When I started out, there really wasn't one book, and now there are thousands of people's experiences and lots of other books talking about the Near-Death Experience.

It took that experience of the young man to initially say, "I think there's something there." Of course, in 1969, there wasn't anything. So, by the mid-seventies, I started to hear about it, and I was in graduate school at the University of Texas. So, I started to do some investigation. My work was really in decision-making behavior, but the thought of studying Near-Death Experiences also was very intriguing, so I used some time to do that.

In the early days, it wasn't that easy. I look back, and I know some of my supervisors thought I was crazy. Nobody was talking about it then.

Q. Why do you think that was? What was so bad about talking about these things in the sixties?

A. Well, nobody knew what it was. The word wasn't out there. The phrase "Near-Death Experience" wasn't coined until the mid-seventies. It wasn't that it was a bad thing, just nobody knew about it. It takes a long time for a brand new phenomenon. Although it's been written about it by Plato and other philosophers, nobody was really aware of that.

Q. How do you define what a Near-Death Experience is?

A. A Near-Death Experience is a set of criteria that are universal—there are about fifteen of them, and they're all the same all over the world—that happens during a crisis. It could be a medical crisis. It could be physical trauma. It could be an accident. It could be surgery. It could be an illness, It could be anything like that. They go on to have one, two, five, or fifteen of these characteristics.

It was coined the Near-Death Experience because Raymond (Moody) did his research with heart patients that had a cardiac arrest. So, he was working with a population that almost died all the time. We found that's not true anymore. There are many circumstances where people are not near death so much as they might be very ill or have some kind of crisis.

Q. What would count as a Near-Death Experience?

A. Let me give you a couple of examples. Let's say someone has a heart attack, and they are taken to the hospital, and they are resuscitated, and they feel like they are separating from their physical body. They are watching and hearing everything that's happening. There's the immediate loss of pain. Then they might go further.

Some would talk about a tunnel or seeing a bright light, and going to the other side of the veil was the description. Or I went to heaven and saw these beautiful flowers. Then, I was greeted by departed loved ones who I knew and were friends of mine or relatives that had already died. And I might be addressed by some kind of a superior being and told that I couldn't stay there, and I went back.

Those are some of the characteristics of the Near-Death Experience. Just being near dead is just being near death. You might hear, think, or feel anything. So, they are distinctly different. One is a physiological component. It might accompany a Near-Death Experience, but the other is an exceptional spiritual experience that changes people's lives forever.

Q. Now, for me, I have had a heart attack and been in the hospital, but I have had none of this happen to me.

A. Okay, we don't know why. It's a question that I get all the time. We do not know why some people have this experience and others don't. We don't think it has anything to do with necessarily good people or bad people. We just have no idea why some people will have this experience and others don't.

Q. So, when we have these Near-Death Experiences, and you describe some of the things that people have claimed to experience, do you find it usually to be the same type of experience for different kinds of people?

A. Well, they have similar characteristics, but everybody has a little different experience. A child might say, "I died. I went to heaven. I met God, and I saw the angels." That's their experience. Somebody else might say, "As I was going through this tunnel, I saw different color bricks, and I saw the light in front of me." People have different experiences of the characteristics. So, the tunnel doesn't always look the same. The other side doesn't look the same, but basically, they have the tunnel experience, or they have an experience with music or flowers or smells, but they aren't necessarily exactly the same thing.

Q. Would I be correct in saying that it would be a different experience because of what brought you there? So, for instance, if I were a soldier and I was in combat of some sort and got wounded enough to be near death, would it be a different experience because of that?

A. Not really. In many of these circumstances, in combat, a whole bunch of people is injured at the same time, like with a mine or bombs. They will talk about seeing the other souls or spirits, whatever they call it, at the same time that they are raising out of their bodies. But they have typically pretty much the same ones. They might fly out of their bodies and fly up. One soldier just talked about he felt like he was catapulting out above the universe. He could see the whole Earth, and he talked about that and very specific things about how he felt when he came back in. Now the aftereffects of having a Near-Death Experience and their availability to have somebody listen to them that's very different for soldiers.

Q. Why is it so hard for soldiers to have the opportunity to have somebody listen to them about their Near-Death Experience?

A. The issue, I think, is twofold. Part of it is that this is a very intense personal experience, and without somebody to validate that this was real, some of them they've already got major physical illnesses and PTSD, so they're beginning to think that they are going crazy. The other part of that is there's very limited resources on the other side if they try to tell somebody. I know that I had a soldier tell me he went to the VA and tried to tell them about this experience, and they told him that he was bipolar and filled him full of drugs.

All experiencers usually need is some support, and they need somebody to listen to them and own their experience. And they need some resources. They need some things to read. They need to be able to talk about aftereffects. They might have special effects after. With some of the aftereffects, it might be very difficult to go back into the military and into a combat zone.

Q. Is there a higher percentage of soldiers that have Near-Death Experiences?

A. We don't know, but I would assume so because of the huge number of TBIs and amputations that happened in Iraq and Afghanistan. I think it is probably true that they have large numbers of soldiers out there with having Near-Death Experiences, but they are afraid to talk about it because they think people will think they are crazy. They're afraid that some of their benefits would be taken away from them, which probably isn't true.

Q. A lot of healthcare professionals don't really understand much about Near-Death Experiences to help these soldiers out?

A. There is no scientific proof. They are working on it. Right now, we understand there is a lot of work in consciousness where they understand that it's not in the brain. It's not associated with the brain. Consciousness does not have to exist in the physical brain. So, there's a lot of work going on in that area.

But we have researched how they (Near-Death Experiences) exist in other countries and how they exist in other countries that don't believe in an afterlife and don't have it as part of their religious dogma. But people are having them all the time.

Q. There's no religion attached to Near-Death Experiences?

A. No, we take a very non-religious approach. It doesn't matter. We've had people who are atheist, agnostic, all kinds of people from all kinds of different religions who have these experiences. We really go to great lengths not to attach any religion to it.

Q. Do people ever say that they have real distressing Near-Death Experiences?

A. There are some reports of them, but we hear very little about them? Nancy Bush has written a book about distressing Near-Death Experiences because she had one. But we don't hear about it very often. In all my forty years, I have maybe heard of three people who have talked about them.

Q. What are the most commonly reported experiences that people report?

A. People feeling the sensation of an out-of-body experience is the most frequent, and the next most common is people claiming to see or go through a tunnel. Another common thing is seeing loved ones on the other side.

For me, having children tell you about seeing loved ones on the other side was one of the things that made this very real for me because kids don't have a frame of reference. They just tell you what happened to them. They are not at the library reading about it. You know, when a four-year-old who's never been off the block tells you about going to heaven and meeting his great grandfather who died in a fire in England, and he had all these details that even his family didn't know. But once they were told about it went and researched to find out it was true. For me, that's really a strong indication that these kids aren't making this up. They're just telling their experience.

Q. Have you heard of people ever having more than one Near-Death Experience?

A. We do have some people. PMH Atwater, who's the most prolific writer. She's written eight books now. I think she was on her ninth when she had her first Near-Death Experience. She was told that she would write seven books. She was directed to do that, and she did it. She did consequently have three Near-Death Experiences in one week from the same illness. So, she really had a lot of aftereffects and discussions. She's been around for a long time and has some great books on the subject.

Listen to the full interview with Diane Corcoran on my website:

www.alanrwarren.com/hom-podcast-episodes/episode/cbce4bbd/near-death-experiences-diane-corcoran-2015

Lucid Dreaming

INTERVIEW WITH ROBERT WAGGONER

We have all had dreams and even some nightmares throughout our life. Have you ever thought about why we dream? In the last ten years, I have interviewed some great dream interpreters and even doctors who have scientifically studied these dreams. But because this is a book focusing on the paranormal or supernatural, I only used those interviews which looked at dreams from that perspective.

The main two areas of dreams and the paranormal have been either remote viewing or lucid dreaming. This chapter focuses on lucid dreams, what they are, and how do they happen.

Probably the most popular person covering this phenomenon is Robert Waggoner. He has not only had lucid dreams himself, but he has studied them for over forty years and written several books on the subject.

Lucid dreaming is where the person dreaming is consciously aware that they are in the dream and are able to interact with other people that are in the dream. Is this really possible? If we can talk with people in our dreams, can we control our dreams? When we dream of lost loved ones who have passed, does this mean we can talk with them too? When we have these lucid dreams, can they affect our future? There are a lot of questions to ask.

Robert Waggoner's lucid dreaming website – www.dreaminglucid.com

This interview took place in 2015.

Q. Where did it start for you?

A. I am a person who taught myself how to lucid dream or become consciously aware of dreaming while in the dream state. I taught myself how to do that back in 1975 when I was a junior in high school, so I've been doing it for basically forty years. I graduated with a degree in psychology and always had a deep interest in dreaming. I joined a wonderful organization called the International Association for the Study of Dreams, and there I held the position of president a few years ago. But all of my comments today are just my personal opinion and don't reflect the IASD people.

Q. So, you say that you've taught yourself how to lucid dream. How did you do that?

A. There wasn't a whole lot of information on how to do this, so I just created my own rules. So, this is what I did. Each night before bed and before I went to sleep, I would just look at the palm of my hands while telling myself, "Tonight in my dreams, I'll see my hands and realize that I am dreaming." I would just stare at my hands, repeating this over and over for about five minutes. Then I would fall asleep. When I'd wake up in the night, I would try to remember if I had seen my hands in the dream.

After three nights of doing this, on the third night, I was walking through my high school hallway, and all of a sudden, my hands popped right in front of my face. I couldn't believe it. I saw my hands and thought, oh my God, this is a dream. These guys over here I saw that looked like football players; they're dream figures. This wall over here that I touched that felt so cool; it's made of dream stuff. I went on to have a wonderful lucid dream for a number of minutes. After that, I was totally hooked.

Q. Some people are not going to know what the difference is between a lucid dream and a regular dream. Can you explain that?

A. That's a good point. So, if you can remember a dream from last night, like you found yourself in China and you had to get on an airplane, but you couldn't find your ticket, and they were holding the plane for you. In a regular dream, we just go along with whatever happens. We never ask ourselves, "What am I doing in China or where am I flying to." We just accept what the story is and go along with it and react to it.

But in a lucid dream, we have this moment when suddenly it occurred to you, "Wait a second, what am I doing in China? I don't live in China. This must be a dream." In a lucid dream, you get that moment of awareness where you suddenly realize that this can't be. It's too impossible. It's too strange. I'm dreaming. This is a dream.

Once you become lucidly aware, then you can begin to direct the dream to some degree or direct your awareness within the dream. So, if you want to go flying, you can go flying. If you want to talk to dream figures and ask questions, you can do that. That's how you can differentiate between a regular dream and a lucid dream.

Q. What do you do to prep yourself before you go to sleep in order to control your dream?

A. There's incredible stuff that you can do when you become lucidly aware, so I taught myself how to do this in 1975, and the scientific proof didn't come out until 1980. So, in the first five years, I just used it as a playground of the mind. I would just fly around and go through walls. I would have fun with dream figures and that kind of thing.

But later on, I went deeper and deeper into it and realized that in lucid dreams, you could, for example, access inner creativity. You are consciously aware there in the subconscious mind of dreaming. Later, I realized that you could communicate with a larger awareness. You could even use it for emotional and physical healing if you knew how.

When you become consciously aware in lucid dreams, sometimes your thinking isn't as clear necessarily as when you're awake. So sometimes, you would make up experiments in the lucid dream state that weren't really valid ones. So it's much better to make it up when you are consciously aware in the waking state. Then, you can remember what the experiment was and conduct it in a lucid dream. Sometimes I would have a plan to achieve when I would become lucid, and other times, I would just wing it and see what came.

Q. You mentioned scientific proof. So, have lucid dreams been scientifically proven?

A. Back in 1980 or 81, I think that it was in January that year, I was at Drake University library, and I saw the *Psychology Today* story by this guy Steven Laberge, who got his doctorate at Stanford. He had provided the first really solid evidence for lucid dreaming, and this is how he did it.

He realized that when you're consciously aware in the dream state that the only part of your body that's basically movable at that time is your eyes because when we're dreaming, we have rapid eye movement. So, he thought that if you decided to set up an experiment where you brought a lucid dreamer into the lab and put the rapid eye movement polygraph pads on his eyes. He told the person that when they become consciously aware in their dream, move their eyes left to right eight times. That would be so unusual on the normal random pattern of rapid eye movement that it'll clearly show that you were consciously aware in the dream.

Using himself as a subject back in February of 1978, he went to the Stanford sleep lab and became consciously aware. He signaled with his eyes, and he did it in twenty other subsequent trips to the sleep lab. At first, people could barely believe this because lucid dreaming has been talked about for thousands of years. There are Buddhist traditions, shamanic traditions, Hindi traditions – they all talked about lucid dreaming, becoming consciously aware in the dream state. But no one had ever been able to prove it. When he had this irrefutable rapid eye movement polygraph pad print out that showed consciously being aware and moving his eyes, signaling, it was truly an epic achievement.

Q. Is lucid dreaming being used today for any practical reasons?

A. Yes. They do some experiments to try and understand the nature of the dream state. So after you get into the lucid dream state and start to do math problems, they are measuring which part of your brain hemisphere is activated. As it turns out, while doing math problems, the left hemisphere of your brain becomes more active. If you do music and you're in a lucid dream state, the right hemisphere of your brain becomes more active, just like it does in waking reality.

You can also use it for something I think is really important, and that's emotionally healing. For example, some therapists have used lucid dreaming as a way to help people who have post-traumatic stress disorder. One of the common symptoms is recurring nightmares. Somebody's been to war, or an event happened in their personal life, and it's almost every night the person has the same dream over and over of the horrific event or some symbolic version of the event.

When you learn to become consciously aware, the therapist teaches people that this incident only occurs in your dream state now. So the next time you see it getting ready to happen, and all the conditions are right, stop for a second and think, "This is a dream. I'm dreaming this." Normally, when the person becomes consciously aware in that recurring nightmare, just once, normally, the nightmares cease.

Q. When you change what's happening in your dreams, does that change what is happening in your waking life too?

A. Exactly, you can definitely influence your emotional life. Lucid dreamers are taking this idea even further than just recurring nightmares. You have lucid dreamers now talking about how they overcome phobias. If you think about if you had, let's say, fear of heights, or a fear of snakes, or fear of flying, or whatever, if you use that lucid dream as a form of virtual reality, you can begin to resolve that phobia in that lucid dream state.

Stephen LaBerge, whose kind of the pioneer of lucid dreaming on the scientific level, did some other experiments as well, looking at how the body would respond to lucid dream actions. So, for example, he would have people during sleep become lucidly aware and signal with their eyes. Then he would have them signal that they were ready to begin the experiment. Then they would do the experiment.

One experiment might be to flex your right arm in the lucid dream. Then flex your left arm and back and forth ten times. Then signal with your eyes that you are ending the experiment.

So, what they found was that on a very small level, there were actually muscles being activated in your physical body in a right-left pattern. You begin to see that an action performed in a lucid dream affects your dream and causes your body to respond in kind.

He did experiments on breathing, respiration, singing, and counting, all that kind of thing while measuring brain and body activity.

In a lucid dream, if you decided to focus on your physical body and tried to heal it in the lucid dream, would that be possible? Here's an example: There's a woman named Amy. She had these horrible planters warts in her feet for months and couldn't get rid of them. She decided to try and use lucid dreams to make them go away. So, she became lucidly aware in a dream and remembered that she wanted to heal her planters warts. In the lucid dream, she created this ball of healing light between her hands and put it over each of her dream feet, intending for them to be healed by this healing light, and then she woke up.

When she woke up in the morning, she looked at her feet, and overnight all of the plantar warts had turned black. Within ten days, they had all fallen off and never returned. You can see that by focusing your intent, you could affect your body.

Q. Have you followed up with these people who had actually healed themselves?

A. I think the mind is involved in all healing of the body. It's part of the equation. Obviously, if the planters warts turned black overnight, there's been some sort of physical response. The medical establishment could easily do lucid dreaming research.

Q. So, why isn't modern medicine taking this on?

A. It's getting out there, but it's a conceptual barrier. Most people, when they become lucid in a dream, they just play around. They go flying. They have fun or talk to dream figures. They go through walls. They just do whatever they want. It never occurs to a lot of them that they could heal a physical illness.

LaBerge even had people in a lucid dream have lucid dream sex, and he had them all done up in nineteen channels of physiological data on respiration and heart rate and all sorts of other channels – seventeen of nineteen of the physiological responses. It was just like the real thing, even though it occurred in the virtual reality of the lucid dream.

You also have to look at examples of failure in order to understand the examples of successes. So, when people started sending me their examples of when there was no physical improvement, it quickly became obvious what the difference was.

When you succeed normally, you act on your intent directly. So, when you want to heal your foot of planters warts, you create the ball of healing light and put it over your feet, or you do something similar to act directly.

The people who failed didn't act directly. They would become lucidly aware, and they would go to find the lucid dream doctor, and they would ask that lucid dream doctor to help them. So, instead of acting on themselves, which any lucid dreamer could do, they sought out a doctor. The doctor gave them advice, and they ignored the advice because they didn't care for it. The sense of power is invested in another person or a special pill or potion and never invested in themselves.

Q. The other thing that you talk about is lucid dreaming to interact with the deceased how does that work?

A. What happens is people that have good dream recall and can remember two or three dreams that they had in a night. During the dream state, all of a sudden, you see grandma, and it occurs to you that grandma has been dead for over ten years now. If you are lucidly orientated, you will realize that this is a lucid dream, and at that point, you have a choice. You can direct it as you wish.

Some people just fly away, but other people will have an interest in what grandma is doing in my dream. Then you can go and interact with that dream figure. You have to decide if you are dealing with a dream figure, a symbolic projection of myself or am I dealing with the spiritual essence of somebody.

Q. So, are you actually contacting the person that is dead?

A. Well, I think that there is a way that you could determine whether it's just a symbolic projection or if it's truly the person. For example, if you were having a dream that it was Thanksgiving, and all of a sudden, in the corner, you saw Grandma. Grandma might be there because you're having a dream about Thanksgiving, and she's associated with Thanksgiving because she always cooked up Thanksgiving dinner for everybody. There it might be a projection.

But, when you're lucidly aware, you have the capacity to talk to dream figures and see how intelligent, responsive, and aware they are. Sometimes when you're lucidly aware, you'll go up to a dream figure and ask them a question, and it'll just turn away and walk off. Sometimes it'll respond with gibberish. Other times you'll go up to a figure and say, "Hey, you know I'm dreaming you?" And the dream figure will respond, "How do you know I'm not dreaming you?"

What you see is there's this whole range of dream figures. Some of them seem hollow that I think are truly projections of your mind. Occasionally when you're dealing with deceased dream figures, they'll seem much more consciously aware, and they'll look you in the eye. And if you ask them an intelligent question, they'll give you an intelligent response. But if they don't, then they are probably just an act of your subconscious mind.

Listen to the full interview with Robert Waggoner on my website:

www.alanrwarren.com/hom-
podcast-episodes/episode/
d2a66845/lucid-dreaming-
robert-waggoner-2015

,

Controlled Remote Viewing

INTERVIEW WITH LYN BUCHANAN

During the 1960s, what is known as the "Cold War" emerged out of major distrust between the then two major superpowers in the world, the United States of America and the Soviet Union. At the center of this distrust was primarily each of their political philosophies. Both countries were scared that the other country would get ahead of them scientifically and perhaps even develop a secret weapon that would allow them to become the most powerful nation on Earth. So they developed major spy organizations in order to keep a secret watch on each other.

The Soviet Union was the first to take a group of known psychics and use them to try and see what the Americans were planning. These psychics were situated in hidden locations and spent their time remote viewing America. They were trying to collect as much secret information as possible.

When the Americans learned about this Soviet spy work, they developed their own remote viewing group of psychics as well to do the same thing to the Soviets. Lyn Buchanan was one of these American remote viewers who has since released his story to the public and written books about his life as a spy.

Lyn Buchanan's website is at www.crviewer.com

Our interview took place in 2015.

Q. Tell us about your history and where it started.

A. I was in the military, and I was doing programming over in Germany for the listening post that we had listening to Russia and East Germany and all of that. I was asked to do a special program that was going to tie together computers and the listening posts of twelve different countries. This other Sergeant wanted to do the job, but I got it awarded to me.

Right as I was to present the thing after it was done, all the Generals from twelve different countries came in. This other Sergeant that wanted the job did too, while I was out. When I started to show it, it crashed, and he pointed and said, "Gotcha!"

Since I was around twelve years old, I've had problems with – if I get mad, things happen around me. Things break. I got flaming mad (when the computer crashed), and all of a sudden, the entire field station just went kablooey. One of the officers there knew what a PK event was—Psycho Kinetic event—and knew that all of the electronic equipment, especially the very sensitive stuff that they had, is subject to that, and he reported me.

A couple of months later, the Commander of the U.S. Intelligence and Security installed a new base commander where we were. He called me into his office and said, "Did you kill my computers with your mind?" I thought, what a crazy question. I knew the answer was yes, but I could see myself paying for computers, and so I was going to lie about it. Then I kind of heard myself saying, "Yes sir, I did." He said, "Far f***ing out! Have I got a job for you!"

He took me back to D.C. to start a unit where we would destroy enemy computers with the hopes that we could learn to control the information in them, so we could send their missiles into the ocean and things like that. But Congress wouldn't fund it, and so he took me out to a remote viewing unit that was out at Fort Meade and put me in there. I just took to it like a duck to water. It was the greatest thing I had ever seen in my life. So, that's where I stayed for the rest of my military career.

Q. This was a very secret military operation, correct?

A. Yes, very much so. In fact, it was even kept secret from the military and the government customers who used it. They would ask for intelligence information, and we would turn in information reports as sort of eyewitness reports and things like that – open-source information reports.

When people got to know and associate our name with what we were doing, our project would end. It would be scrapped completely, and the next day we would go back to work under the name of a new project and just continue working. So, yes, we were even kept secret from the government.

Q. So, even the Congress, Senate, or President of the United States didn't know?

A. Oh Yeah, they knew. Those who needed to know knew. Those who didn't need to know, that's why we kept changing names and all of that. But the President was always briefed on us. When the helicopter crashed in Iraq, our information that it crashed got to the President ten minutes before the electronic notice came through and went up the chain of command. So, we turned the information in first, even before they could report it on the radio.

Q. How did that affect you in your day-to-day living with your family and friends? Did they know what you did at the time, or did you keep that secret?

A. I couldn't tell my family or anything, and my Church group would say, "What do you do?" and I would say, "I program computers." Because that was largely a part of my MOS (Method of Service), I was a Russian linguist and computer scientist as my method of service on paper.

Q. So, nobody else knew except those that were involved in it?

A. That's right. Our most dedicated customers who knew what we could do were kept apprised of it, but anytime the word got around, all of a sudden, our project would be scrapped for the reason that nobody was doing that kind of stuff anymore. Like I said, we would go to work the next day with a brand-new cover name.

Q. What happened then? Did you work there and retire?

A. I retired from it about two years before this last time when they scrapped the whole project. People ask me if they still have another project going like that under another name, and I really don't know. I hope so. I think they would be stupid not to. But of course, that raises the question of whether our government ever does anything stupid or not? I'm afraid I already know the answer to that.

Q. But why would they scrap it if it works?

A. No. There was actually a good reason to scrap it. That was at the end of the cold war, funding was just being cut severely right and left, especially on intelligence services and many of the old, more experienced ground spies, ground agents, and all of that just had no funding, no jobs. If the funding question was to dump these crazy psychics out in Fort Meade or keep a good 007 spy, then I'd dump the psychics out at Fort Meade too.

Q. So, how do you go about doing Remote Viewing? I know you can really show us but maybe explain it.

A. Yes, you can't do this in a sound bite. Basically, this whole process is, not in and of itself, psychic. It has nothing to do with being psychic. Everyone does tend to have some psychic ability, but the trouble is it only happens when your daughter was in an accident, and all of a sudden you know it, or someone dies and things. It's only available to some people during a crisis, and for those people that have an easy time with psychic ability, they tend to be in its control rather than controlling it.

There is a guy named Ingo Swann in New York who devised a way to use the body to act as a translator between the conscious and subconscious minds. Well, it's your subconscious level that does anything psychic, not your conscious level. He found that when you can set up a line of communications like in an interview and report, you can interview your subconscious, ask it questions, find out what it knows, and then report the answer.

So, the remote viewing that he invented actually was actually nothing more than an interview and report process using the body —in a martial arts way—as sort of a connecter between the conscious and subconscious. The remote viewing itself is only accessed through your subconscious, which knows things. It's not in and off itself psychic at all.

Q. How is it that the subconsciousness knows things? Are they all connected somehow?

A. Everybody has their own explanation, their own belief system, and all of that. The fact that I found is that nobody knows. They come up with all these fancy explanations that some of them deal with spirit guides, some of them deal with holograms and the universe, and some deal with alien beings from the planet Scooby-Doo, or whatever. Nobody knows. It seems to just be part of our being.

Q. Yes, there are some people that have all the answers, and I don't trust them as much. It's usually someone's own superstition.

A. Or religion.

Q. Yes, you're correct.

A. That's one of the things I liked about the military method was that it was a science. You go get trained in it. You learn it. It's a step-by-step method that you do. You use martial arts methods to train your body to respond to subconscious awareness in different ways. You actually train it, sort of like the "wax on, wax off" type stuff. We train for months and months and months and never quit training.

As a result, we'd go to work. We would do what everybody called miracles for eight hours a day, and then we'd go home and watch T.V.

Q. So, a job like anything else?

A. Yes, I liked that. In fact, two years after I got out of service and they declassified the remote viewing effort, people found out I had been the trainer in the unit, and they started contacting me for training. All these different authors were writing about ETs, and I didn't know what they were talking about. I was a soldier that went to work every day, did a job, and went home. I never looked at any of that stuff.

I was getting about eighty requests for training a day, and some of the people who would call and talk to me on the phone made me start to get paranoid. Some of these people are walking the streets and going to Walmart where I shopped, and it's kind of scary sometimes.

Q. I find that anyways when I walk through Walmart. Now the Russians were doing this same thing as well, weren't they?

A. Yes. In fact, they were doing it first. That's why we started doing it. A man named Oleg Penkovsky, who had evidently been involved in some of this, tried to defect, and he got some of the Russian paperwork and documentation over to the U.S., and of course, everyone had a good laugh about that – the Russians are using psychics. They actually started reading, and they found out that they were getting our secrets. So, they felt that if the Russians were using it and it worked for them, maybe we better at least look into it.

They started looking around for psychics and targeting them with top-secret information and not letting them know what it was. One guy named McMoneagle, not only perfectly described the M1A1 Abrams Tank but actually drew highly accurate pictures of the interior and didn't even know what he was working on.

With Joe's session on that, they thought maybe there's something to this. Maybe we ought to at least start a pilot project and try to find out. So, they did, and it wound up being a military unit in the military.

Q. A lot of people that talk about remote viewing talk about it as if they leave their body and they travel somewhere else, and they watch people. But that's not how it is with you?

A. No. When the information came out that the military was using "Remote

Viewers," of course, it hit the newspapers with "Psychic Spies." But nobody said what it was. The information that was coming out was bogus, and all of a sudden, the message that got through to everyone on the internet was, "This has been scientifically proven. Psychics work." All of a sudden, we had "Crystal Ball Remote Viewers," and "Palm Remote Viewers," and "Tea Leaf Remote Viewers."

People had no idea about the science of controlled remote viewing and just started calling themselves "Remote Viewers." Even at present, I would say that close to 90 percent of everything you find on the internet about remote viewing is just totally bogus and has nothing to do with remote viewing at all.

Q. Most of it is just entertainment.

A. Yes. I think most of the people who are calling themselves "Remote Viewers" are doing so honestly. They're not trying to cheat people. They really think remote viewing is psychic when it's not. It's just really a scientific process.

Q. How do you define yourself differently from that then?

A. The thing that Ingo Swann invented, he called "Coordinate Remote Viewing." When that information came out, everyone started calling themselves "Coordinate Crystal Remote Viewers." So, Ingo thought about what he figured nobody else would want to be called and decided to call it "Controlled Remote Viewing," and that's what we used. The fact is that most people think that remote viewers are controlled by all of these protocols. Actually, what it means is that the remote viewing is controlled by the viewer. So, the people into crystal balls trances don't want to be controlled, so they shy away from that name.

Q. Can this process be used to control other people's minds?

A. As far as it being used to get into other people's minds and all of that, yes, you can do that. With the training, you can do it clearly and accurately. Without training, you can't. It's advanced stuff, and what a lot of people think of remote influencing is sort of where you get into someone else's mind at the subconscious level, and you try to persuade them to be healthier, to cure themselves, or to change policies or to listen to other reasoning, and so forth. It is not at all remote control where you control the person. But yes, it is possible.

Q. Is it in some way connected to hypnosis?

A. Remote persuasion, I think, really is. But the Russians have now developed what they call "Hypnosis at a Distance," where they really go into this, and they've had quite a bit of success at it. In the military unit, we were absolutely forbidden to do any what was called "Active Mental Work." That is the remote persuasion or control. But that was limited to U.S. citizens. If you weren't a U.S. citizen, you were fair game.

I hear people saying, "The Remote Viewer got into my mind and messed my mind up." No, we never did any active mental work. It was all passive. We went, and we got intelligence information, reported it to the chain of command to the intelligence services, and that was it.

Q. How did doing this kind of work change your own personal beliefs.

A. You learn that time isn't what you've been told it is in school. But what makes a greater impact is the fact that you can ask your subconscious what's going on halfway around the world, and it tells you. It can also tell you why you do those things that you don't want to do, but you wind up doing them anyway, and why you don't do the things you wanted to. Also, it tells you why you're really angry about something or why you're really scared about something. It can do in one hour what can take a psychiatrist five years on his couch to do.

Q. A common question when it comes to psychics or remote viewers is why don't you use it to find out the winning lottery ticket numbers?

A. There were about eighteen different forms of "Controlled Remote Viewing" created out at Stanford Research. One of them was called "Associative Remote Viewing," and this works really well. In fact, we did this on a radio program and had 27,000 people participate and correctly predict the stock market for the next day.

Numbers and letters and things like that are human constructs. They are not real. They're not really things. They are constructs. So, they are very hard to view. However, something like your taste, smell, or things like that, you are using your body as the go-between. If you were to say, "View the number on the first ball on the Pick Three Lottery at 7:30 tonight," people would be stuck for it because that's a human construct.

But if I were to say to you, "At ten o'clock tonight, tell me what you taste." If I make a list and say, "If a zero comes up on the ball, I'm going to let you taste vinegar. If a one comes up on the ball, I'm going to let you taste sugar. If two comes up on the ball, I'm going to let you taste coffee," and so on through the numbers.

Then knowing whatever I give you is going to reflect what number was on the ball, I'd tell you to move to ten o'clock tonight and tell me what you taste. Oh, I taste coffee. I know that a two would have been on the ball. By doing it that way, I give you something easy to view that is associated with something that is hard to view. It works very well.

Q. You have had a school for training Remote Viewing. Do you still operate it?

A. Not now. I have trained about 850 people, and five of those people are trained to the point where they are just excellent trainers. I could have started a thing where they worked for me and all of that, but I didn't want to do that. They went into business for themselves, and they're teaching, and they are doing an excellent job. So I figured it was time for me to bow out. But now I am starting some online courses, and I am having troubles keeping up the quality because it's not face-to-face. So I'm mixing face-to-face stuff online with the online videos and all. I really love teaching this. I will be starting that this year.

Q. Are there some bad teachers out there too?

A. There are some people out there training "Remote Viewing," but it's just crap. They are taking people's money and teaching them this stuff that one doesn't work, and two isn't "Remote Viewing" at all. Buyer, be very aware. There are six people: the five that I have taught to teaching level, and Paul Smith in Austin, Texas, who was one of our remote viewers who is also teaching. So, there are six people out there that I would recommend for training, and those are the only six.

Q. Are there any big things that you discovered while working for the military that you can talk about?

A. I discovered myself, actually. You can't do this without dipping into your subconscious, and your subconscious knows you better than anyone else, and you better become friends with it. In fact, you're exposed to it so much that you do become friends with yourself.

But there have been some military things that since then have been declassified: what was called a "Death Ray" over in Russia, the plans and intentions of foreign leaders. We did a lot of work on scientific developments in foreign countries. So yes, there are a lot of things that have been declassified. In fact, it is available throughout the internet by applying to the Freedom of Information Act.

Q. What do you think about the people that don't believe any of this?

A. Well, they have their thing. Everybody has their gimmick. The debunker that they hired to Stargate Project—which is the last name that I knew about for the remote viewing unit—hired a statistician and a debunker to evaluate the project. The statistician found out that it was reliable and that there was actually something going on. The information provided was fairly accurate, even though all they looked at was our practice sessions. They were not allowed to look at anything classified.

The debunker wound up by saying that, "They should at least postpone this—any use of it for intelligence purposes—until the science of statistics could get its act together."

Listen to the full interview with Lyn Buchanan on my website:

www.alanrwarren.com/hom-podcast-episodes/episode/d21fe4ee/remote-viewing-lyn-buchanan

Psychokinesis

INTERVIEW WITH URI GELLER

When I was a kid living in the 1970s, some of the trends in paranormal television shows were centered on subjects that included E.S.P., telepathy, telekinesis, or psychokinesis. Movies likc *Carrie*, where the protagonist was able to make things happen or move only using her mind, were popular.

The act of telekinesis or psychokinesis is a person who has the ability to influence or move a physical item without any physical interaction by them. The term was created back in 1914 by Henry Holt who wrote the book *Cosmic Relations* in reaction to the many live shows traveling the country that included several types of paranormal entertainment.

The scientific community, which has spent over 100 years studying paranormal activity such as psychokinesis, has yet to come up with any solid proof of its existence. Not to mention that if psychokinesis were real, it would violate the laws of physics.

It's been said that quite often, people have this illusion that they have some sort of power that others do not. Their kind of thinking leads them to be susceptible to believing it to be real. Humans also look for and see patterns regularly, which also makes them susceptible.

One of the most interesting parts of our history on psychokinesis is the fact that the governments of several countries, including America and Russia during the cold war times, has taken it seriously enough to have set up tests to study the subject and hopefully be able to use it against any of their enemies.

Magicians were able to simulate psychokinesis as well by bending spoons, levitation, and even teleportation of items. These shows were so powerful that people watching believed that what they were seeing was actually happening.

So, is this phenomenon real? Are there people who can actually move things with their minds or bend spoons? One of the most popular of the illusionists from these times that's still alive is Uri Geller, who became a popular television personality primarily because of his spoon bending on several variety shows. Geller also appeared to be able to stop a watch from running or make it run faster with only his mind. Mainstream America would call it the "Geller Effect."

In the early 1970s, Geller was to appear on the then famous *Johnny Carson Show* to be interviewed. When he arrived, the show's producers surprised him and wanted him to perform in front of their live studio audience. Geller was unable to perform any of his abilities while on the show for over twenty minutes and left. This ended up making him even more popular than he was before, and suddenly, everybody who then had a television show was booking him on.

Being in the spotlight, the American government's Defense Intelligence Agency set up the Stargate Project in order to study Geller and his claims. Both parapsychologists, Harold Puthoff and Russell Tag, isolated Geller in a clinical setting and asked him to reproduce drawings that were made by somebody else in a separate room. Geller was successful enough that both parapsychologists in the published article from 1974 recommended that Geller be studied more seriously.

Shortly after this, the CIA would also perform tests on Geller where they reported that he had demonstrated a paranormal perceptual ability in a convincing and unambiguous manner. Now knowing Geller personally, this is a claim that he mentions in public and on social media regularly.

So, is there such a thing as psychokinesis? Is Uri Geller really as powerful in moving items with his mind as he claims? I'm really not sure what the answer is, but I tend to lean towards science and proof that can be seen.

I decided to have Geller do an interview and ask him all the questions I could to try and get the answers. This interview was done in 2018. Uri was in Old Jaffa, Israel, where he was in the process of opening up his Uri Geller museum, and I was in Seattle.

Uri Geller's website is www.urigeller.com

Q. I have heard that you are going to have the largest bent spoon in the world in your museum?

A. Yes, I wanted to create something that was very unique, and I hope that it gets into the *Guinness Book of World Records*. As you all probably know, I'm the originator of spoon bending. Even today, I cannot believe how I managed to instill spoon bending into world culture. I decided to create this giant spoon. It'll weigh ten pounds. It'll be eighteen meters in length. And it'll be right outside my museum. So there's no doubt that every single tourist that comes to Israel will want to photograph the spoon. I've already had requests from the Russian Space Agency to photograph the spoon from space. If you ever come to Israel, I will definitely be more than happy to show you around.

Q. Did this start out as a normal spoon, and you bent it with your mind?

A. If I could bend an eighteen-meter spoon, I would probably be the most famous man in the world. No, the spoon will be manufactured bent already.

Q. Where did it start for you with this paranormal life?

A. My career started here in Israel when I was five years old, and I was eating soup, and the spoon bent in my hand. Then I became very well known after my army days. I served as a paratrooper for three years. I was wounded in the Six-Day War. Then I worked for the Mossad for a few years, and then came the big jump. The Mossad, for people that don't know it, is kind of the CIA of Israel. They really didn't understand how I was delivering to them the very important information that they asked me to deliver to them.

So, they called the CIA, and the CIA said that they would love to study this Uri Geller character. So, in 1972, I left Israel, and I went straight to California in Palo Alto to be studied by the American Government. I was studied at Stanford Research Institute, which today is Stanford University. There are some very interesting documentaries on my website, Alan, where you actually see CIA agents talk about the experiments. The one documentary is called *The Secret Life of Uri Geller*, which was a BBC production. Because I'm hugely controversial, there are those who try to debunk me or attack me.

Q. Is that what you thought *The Johnny Carson Show* did to you?

A. Yes. I was on *Johnny Carson* for 22 minutes, humiliated by him, but at the end of the day, I learned something very important. One hundred years ago, Oscar Wilde said something very powerful, "There's only one thing worse in life than being talked about, and that's not being talked about." So, you know, the skeptics and the controversy fueled the wheels of publicity around me. I guess maybe that's why my longevity. After 50 years, I am still around.

Q. Now, because of the release of some secret files by the CIA, it appears that you were actually used by them. How did that happen?

A. When they discovered that what I do is real because you know you can't cheat conditioned controlled experiments. You can't be a magician. Once you're locked in a shielded room and a drawing is done in Langley, Virginia – we are talking about the early seventies when there are no mobile phones, there's no Skype, there's no Twitter, there's no Facebook, there is no Instagram. There are the old fashioned black phones. So, when they drew drawings thousands of miles away, and I duplicated them in a shielded room, in a floating room, it's real.

When the CIA realized that it was genuine, I started working for them. I did some amazing things. I was asked to spy on the Russian embassy in Mexico City. I was asked to see if I could see if Lee Harvey

Oswald, who assassinated President Kennedy, visited that place.

Then there were many different missions. I remember when President Carter was interviewed by a student in a University and the student asked him if there were any unusual things that happened throughout his presidency. He said, "Oh yeah, a Russian plane crashed in Zaire, and a psychic found the plane for us."

I've done things that are still top secret. What the CIA released, which was just over a year ago, was just the tip of the iceberg. There was one instance that is not secret which was when Ambassador Max Kampelman, from Washington, and the head of the American Foreign Relations Committee, Senator Claiborne Pell, where they asked me to bombard the Russians to sign the new Nuclear Arms Reduction Treaty.

So, they came to London to brief me. I was living then in England. Then they flew me with Al Gore, Vice President at that time, to Geneva. My task was to get close to the

Russian negotiator and bombard his mind telepathically to sign the Nuclear Arms Reduction Treaty. I know it sounds far out, and it's almost bizarre and strange to hear this, but I got very close to him, and I bombarded him to sign, and he signed. Of course, I cannot take full credit for it. There are others implications and other things like emotion. But those were the types of things I did.

For the FBI, I induced into Russian diplomats the word "defect" successfully. I remember the FBI asked me to locate a serial killer called the "Son of Sam," who was David Berkowitz, and I pointed exactly only at where he lived in Yonkers, New York.

So, there were some very unusual tasks in missions that I had throughout my life, and the show business side of Uri Geller was perfect because it was a cover. I have to thank the skeptics for making all that noise that I'm not real because that was an inbuilt safety device for me, Alan.

Q. To what do you attribute these abilities that you have. Were they natural, or did it come from some sort of outside force?

A. Okay, let me tell you how it started. And again, it'll sound like describing a science fiction film. But when I was around about five or six, I was playing in an Arabic garden across from my apartment building – a small, tiny four-floor apartment that no longer exists. Suddenly in this Arabic garden, I encountered a light, and out of it emanated almost like a laser beam type of light which hit my forehead very strongly with a powerful force, and it pushed me into the grass. I don't know how long I lay in the grass, but I ran home to tell my mother. And of course, she didn't believe me. She thought I was creating it or lying, or I dreamt it.

Many decades later, maybe about ten years ago, an Israeli Air Force Officer actually validated that encounter. He wrote me an email after he saw me on the BBC documentary where I was talking about this. He said, "Uri, I was walking and on my right was this Arabic garden, and I saw this little boy with black curly hair, with a white shirt, and a huge ray of light. Then I saw the little boy running across the street to his doorway, and this thing followed me, and it exploded on the building, leaving a black residue and black residue was there for years." So, to me, this was an amazing validation because I wrote about this experience. Of course, nobody believed it. But I never shied away from it because it happened. I know it happened, so this was an incredible validation coming from a very credible source, an Israeli Air Force Officer.

So, that's how it began. Very soon after that, I ate soup, and the spoon bent in my hand. Well, I showed up in the school with the spoon, and the children were amazed. I blew the mind of the teacher. Then I realized that was what was going to pull me out of the poverty we were in, and I focused on it. I enhanced it. I exercised this ability, and then I could just do it on command. This is how it all developed.

Q. How was this on you and your family?

A. If you didn't know, I am related to Sigmund Freud. My mother was a Freud, and she was from Vienna. My mother always thought that I inherited certain abilities from the great psychologist Sigmund Freud. I don't know if that's true because my kids can't do this. They can't bend spoons, and they cannot read minds.

This happened just after the Six-Day War, and mother's and families lost sons, and they saw me as a kind of connector to the other world. I looked at it as show business. I bent spoons on stage. I read minds, and I became incredibly famous in Israel until the Mossad grabbed me.

When I look at it today, and if I ask myself what it was, I will tell you what the theories are. First of all, I am a great believer in extraterrestrial life. There are no doubts in my mind that aliens exist. I've never seen an alien, but I have seen UFOs. So did millions of people. So, I'm a great believer in beings from outer space.

The most far-out theory could be that this was an extraterrestrial encounter. Now, let's put that aside because this is the most far-out. Second, it could have been a spiritual experience. Third, it could have been a geophysical experience. The fourth one would be that we all have these powers. We all have these abilities, and I have them stronger than others. That's simple because throughout my life when I did interactive television, millions of spoons bent in people's homes. Broken watches started ticking across America, across Japan, across Germany.

I can do an experiment with you right now. Let's do the following. Before a commercial, I am asking everyone at home to go and get spoons, cheese, and broken watches, old watches of your grandfathers, your grandmothers, and bring them to the radio. Because when we come back from the commercial, I will do an amazing thing in your homes, and then you'll be able to let Alan know. So, when we conclude the experiment, let Alan know what happened to you in your home – only if something happens, of course. It doesn't happen all the time for everyone.

You will see, Alan, that you have a very unusual reaction.

For many years I thought that it was my energy that was flying through the television, out from T.V. sets. I thought my energy was coming out of radios. But I was wrong because, at UCLA, there was a scientist called Doctor Thelma Moss, who tested my powers on students. I didn't know that I was filmed secretly by her, and when I went back to New York, she played my video two weeks later to another set of students with broken watches and watched. And low and behold, their watches started working from that video.

When she called me in New York telling me this, I said, "No way. I wasn't even concentrating and didn't even know that you were playing my video." But she said yes, the watches started. That's when it dawned on me that I was only a catalyst. I was only a trigger. I was only an enabler to the powers of the mind of people at home.

Q. Do you compare this to group thoughts or prayer? Is it the same type of power?

A. Maybe. I'm a huge believer in the power of prayer. I believe in God. I get three hundred emails a day, and a lot of people think I'm a healer. But I'm not a healer. So I immediately tell them to go to a doctor and have themselves checked out.

But there are experiments—and you've probably talked about it before on your show—where a group of people was prayed for who was ill, and another group of people who were not prayed for, and the people who were prayed for healed faster. Any doctor will tell you that if you have a patient who is a positive thinker and he has a positive frame of mind, he will heal faster than someone who is negative.

So, maybe you're right. I am a believer that all of humanity is attached to each other with an invisible spiritual thread in which we can send energies all around the world to humans. Look, Alan, if you can go there with your body, you can go there with your mind, because whatever you can visualize, you can materialize. There is nothing that you cannot be, do, or have because, at the end of the day, you are the architect of your life.

Q. What do you think the mechanics are behind what you claim to do, such as starting to make watches run?

A. I don't understand either. I can only theorize that it's some type of energy that leaves my mind. It's nothing to do with my hands or fingers. It penetrates the watch, and it fixes it. By the way, I have thousands of stories from people around the world that have pocket watches that were over 100 years old, and there were parts missing in them. The watchmakers told them that. There were broken parts in it, and they started ticking. Parts materialized.

Edgar Mitchell, an astronaut, was the sixth man on the moon. He tested me, and there was materialization and dematerialization when we did experiments. For those people out there who don't know what scientific testing I have done from Stanford, I went to the Lawrence Livermore Remediation Labs. That's where they build nuclear bombs. People studied me there.

From there, I was taken to the American Naval Surface Weapons Center. From there, I was taken Werner Von Braun, the German rocket scientist, to be tested in NASA. Professor Victor Weisskopf, who studied under Neils Bohr, who worked on the Atom bomb, tested me. I could go on. I've gone through hundreds of tests. In many of them, there were materializations and dematerializations. and that's a fact.

During some of the tests that I went through with MI5 in London, one of the scientists who was leading the tests was David Bohm. David Bohm worked with Albert Einstein. David Bohm experienced something so phenomenal that the National Security Agency decided that if I could materialize or dematerialize and object, then what about ten Uri Gellers, or twenty Uri Gellers, or thirty Uri Gellers working at the same time on one point. They could probably make a city disappear. These words that I am telling you are in the CIA documents that were released and are on my website.

Q. You remote viewed for the government as well?

A. Yes, I started the remote viewing, I believe, for the American government in 1972. The tests were conducted by Harold Puthoff and Russell Tag in Palo Alto, both physicists. A lot of people think the remote viewing project was terminated, but it's not terminated. It's simply goes deep black. In the documentary by the BBC called *The Secret Life of Uri Geller*, you will see these people tell you why it was terminated publicly, but also why they think it is still going on deep black.

Q. If you are making items appear and disappear, where do they go with your understanding?

A. The big question we are asking ourselves today is, "Am I creating you now? Do you exist? Or am I creating you with consciousness?" Consciousness is the state or quality of awareness or of being aware of an external object or something within oneself. It's the ability to experience or feel wakefulness, having a sense of selfhood, and the executive control of the mind. So, it is possible, Alan, that I am creating you now. Or vice versa, that you are creating me.

Q. You wanted to talk about the number "11 11." What did you want to tell us?

A. I wanted to enlighten you about the number "11 11," which I started noticing when I was about 40. I wrote an article on my website, and I received thousands of emails about it from around the world. People telling me, "My God, when I drive my car, I see 11 11. When I'm in my hotel and my back to a digital clock on the wall and something makes me turn around, and it's 11 11. There are endless 11 11 stories.

What is fascinating is that if you come to think of it, John Kennedy is 11 letters, Bill Clinton is 11 letters, Jimmy Carter is 11 letters, Barrack Obama is 11 letters, George W. Bush is 11 letters, Donald Trump is 11 letters, Jesus Christ is 11 letters. I mean, I can go on and on.

What I believe is the phenomenon of 11 11.

Q. Something else you mention on your website is that you dowse. What is that?

A. I discovered I dowsed. You know I found oil and gold for big mining companies. As a matter of fact, I found oil for Pemex, which is the national oil company for Mexico. The Mexican President was so impressed that he made me a Mexican citizen. After I bought the land to place my new museum on, I dowsed in the museum. And I felt that there was something under the ground. So, I got permission from the Israeli Antiquities Department to clear the dirt. And low and behold, I found a soap factory, which is probably hundreds of years old because the Muslims didn't find soap from Europe because it was made from pig oil. This is the first olive oil factory in that region.

Listen to the full interview with Uri Geller on my website:

www.alanrwarren.com/hom-
podcast-episodes/episode/
2da3aa2e/uri-geller

PARANORMAL TOOLS

Ouija Boards

Throughout my many years interviewing folks that have been involved in the world of the paranormal, there has been one item or tool that seems to have everyone divided – the Ouija board. Does it have powers or is it just a toy? I've come across those who are absolutely terrified of the Ouija, believing it to be a tool of evil or even the devil. While others calmly explain that an Ouija board is only a game made of wood and ink that you can buy in any store, and it does nothing.

I tend to lean towards that it is just a board game like so many others that are manufactured and sold to the public, and it has no power at all. The power that it possesses comes from the people that use it. If they believe in any kind of dark magic, then the board is evil. If they believe that it can be used to communicate words from the other side, then it tells them what they need to hear from their dead loved one.

It certainly doesn't hurt that there have been some popular horror films made with the Ouija board being used to commit some sort of evil and death to those who use it. But we are living in times where things of this nature are believed to the point of worship.

Robert Murch is considered the world's foremost collector and Ouija board Historian. He founded and is the chairman of a group called "The Talking Board Historical Society." (Yes, there actually is one!) Murch has gained popularity over the last ten years or so during the paranormal revolution that has taken place since the early 2000s, appearing on shows like *Paranormal State*, Travel Channel's *Ghost Adventures*, and *Mysteries at the Museum*, to name a few.

I found Murch to be a very nice man and believe him to be legitimately into the history of the Ouija board and his motives to be true. (Even though he will go on radio shows like *Coast to Coast*, which has turned into the evangelical right-wing conspiracy central – RIP Art Bell)

Robert Murch website is https://robertmurch.com/

This interview took place in early 2016.

Q. What got you into the Ouija board?

A. My grandmother, who we lived with for a while, loved science fiction and loved horror movies. She would take me to everything that my mother would tell me not to go to. In 1986, she took me to a movie that would change my life, and that was *Witchboard* by Kevin Tenney. For people who don't know or haven't seen *Witchboard*, if you're into talking boards or have any strong feelings, you should see this movie. It's the reason most people feel the way they feel about Ouija boards. He did a brilliant job of taking a lot of these "Ouijastitions" (I know it's not a real word, but probably you have noticed that throughout the paranormal world, there seems to be a lot of new words being used) or urban legends and weaving them into a tale that we believe and pass on today.

I used to go antiquing, flea marketing, yard sales, you name it, with my dad every weekend for my whole life. After a while, I realized that I actually had ten different Ouija boards, not just one, and that struck me as being odd. This was pre-internet, so I had to go to the library to find out about Ouija boards by looking them up in encyclopedias. Every single encyclopedia that I looked in had a different story, and I say "story" because today, we know that not one of them was true. That sent me off on a two-decade-plus journey to track down the Ouija board story: its urban legends, its myths, as well as its real history.

Q. Why is the Ouija board still holding the fascination of people?

A. If we look back, the Ouija board turned 125 this year in April. One hundred twenty-five years ago, the Ouija board got its mysterious name. Its name really set it apart from all the other talking boards. That name was able to be mass-marketed, and it had a story.

How did something so simple, whether it's today and made of cardboard and plastic or it's yesterday and made of wood, how can it be that it's something that's lasted? I think it does something unique that the other gadgets don't, and one of those things is just the experience. Today, we have like K2 meters or electric-magnetic field readers, and we have EVP recorders.

Today, machines make people feel much safer and also push them apart from the experience. You can put the thing down, walk away, ask your question, see if it records, or see if it blinks in response to you. But the Ouija board you are a part of, no matter what anyone says, the Ouija board doesn't work without you. You have to be touching it. You have to see it. So if you believe it's using your subconscious, then you still need your eyes; you still need your hands.

If you believe that you're talking to something other than you, outside of you, the same thing, then this entity or spirit outside of you is guiding your hand. So you still need to see. You're still using your hands. You're touching it. You hear it move and feel it move. You are part of the communication device. This communication device does not work without you. It's very eerie because it's a collaborative thing.

When Ouija came out in 1890, it was definitely sold as an amusement party game, something to be done with multiple people. If you were going to spend $1.50 in 1890, that's a lot of money, so it needed to be something the entire family could enjoy, and that's really what Ouija was. But there was always a segment of the population that did not like the Ouija board. It just wasn't as vocal as it is today. Today with Hollywood using the board to show demonic possession, to show some really scary stuff, that belief plays into why it's still here.

Ouija has its own life now. It has its own stuff now that people talk about: how to get rid of the board, how not to get rid of the board, what happens when you try to get rid of it, or what happens when you burn it. All of these things keep it alive and pass on to the next generation.

Q. There are a lot of people who are scared of the Ouija board, claiming that when you are using the board, you don't know who it is that you are communicating with, and it could be someone evil.

A. When I hear someone say that you don't know what door you are opening when you use an Ouija board, I start laughing. Wait a minute, you just picked up a K2 meter, stuck it on the floor, and walked away. And you ask if there's anyone here, or does anyone have any messages for us, and the thing is blinking to answer. This thing, whatever we're talking to, seems to be making it blink when we ask it to. So, who's to say that it can't pick that up (K2 meter) and hock it at our heads? I don't know what the rules are, but for someone using digital devices, we feel safe. We feel like technology keeps us a step apart from whatever it is that we are communicating with.

I had a conversation a few years ago with Lorraine Warren, who is against Ouija boards and all kinds of spirit communication devices. In our six to eight-hour interview that we had together, we actually agreed a lot more than we disagreed on, which was to say that the Ouija board is no more dangerous than any spirit communication device used even if it's just calling out to something because the danger is made in the act of conjuring.

You are asking something to communicate with you and giving something permission to talk to you, whatever that is. That's where the door is opened. What you use is just a personal choice. But if you believe that Ouija boards are more dangerous, I guarantee you that you're going to have a more dangerous session.

Q. What about those who claim that the Ouija board could be possessed?

A. We say that there are attachments with things that can possess inanimate objects, but that's so rare, and yet with the Ouija, we believe this to be common. Again, by giving it that power, we've done something unique. We have created something, unlike anything that's come before or after.

Q. Where did Ouija get its name from?

A. Talking boards popped up out of the spiritual movement in 1886 in Ohio. We know that in 1848 when the modernist spiritual movement began in New York, they were using lots of, let's say, alphabet pointing devices, including just laying out alphabet cards and asking a spirit to make a knock as we pointed towards the letters and when you hit the right letter it would knock.

Then there were devices that would be used where you would put your hand on them, and the pointer would point out letters – what we call dial point devices that never really caught on because they were expensive. Also, early on, they had planchettes. For your listeners, if they don't know, the planchette is the device that's used as the message indicator on the Ouija board today. But, around 1850 in France, it was its own device. It was an automatic writer. It was much bigger and had two wheels on the bottom and a hole at the top. Not like the viewing hole, but just a hole small enough to fit a pencil. You put your pencil in it, you place your hands on the top over the wheels, and you ask the spirit a question, and it would write out the answer. Your hand would write out the answer guided by the spirits.

So, in 1886, the planchette and the alphabet pointing collided to create the talking board. Someone decided to make a board, take the planchette and not put a pencil in it and just use it as a pointer, and the talking board is born. It was probably done a little before this, but that's when it leaked into popular culture.

Four years later, it's named in Baltimore. There were two gentlemen named Charles Kennard and E.C. Reiche that claimed to invent the board that would become Ouija. Charles Kennard claimed that one day he was sitting in the kitchen of his new house, and his mind was blank. He tipped over his teacup and put it on a breadboard. He realized his hands were moving it around, but he was not consciously telling them to move.

So, he put some letters and numbers on it, and it started spelling out answers. He was amazed, and according to him, he took it to his office mate E.C. Reiche, who was an undertaker and coffin maker, and asked him to make him some of these. He did, and they shared it with the neighbors, and they were very popular. Charles Kennard said, "Let's go into business." Reiche said no, and that he wasn't very interested as he had a lot going on with his own business and didn't see this becoming very successful.

Charles Kennard left for Baltimore in 1890. E.C. Reiche also claimed and proved to this company that Charles Kennard was going to start that it was actually him who started it. We don't know what that proof is as we're going back a long time. But we do know that Charles Kennard went to

Baltimore and met up with a man named Elijah Bond, who was a fellow mason and the future in this talking board. He believed that people would buy a mass-manufactured one instead of a homemade talking board, which was what people were doing up until then.

So, Elijah Bond patented it, and one night in April of 1890, on the corner of Charles Street and Center Street in Baltimore, there was Elijah Bond, Charles Kennard, and Elijah Bond's sister-in-law, who he considered a strong medium, all sitting at this boarding house. Charles Kennard said, "You know we haven't set a name yet. Let's ask it what it wants to be called." So, with Helen Peters at the board, she asked. It answered, "O U I J A." When they asked the board what that meant, the board answered, "Good Luck."

Right after that reading, Helen Peters took off her necklace and showed it to Charles Kennard. It had a figure of a woman, and it said, "Ouija." He said, "Wait a minute. Were you thinking about that while we were asking the board?" She replied, "No, not at all." But if the word was invented when they were asking the board, how was she wearing a locket with the name "Ouija" on it? We don't know because we don't have the locket. We believe that she was wearing a board that actually said, "Ouida." One letter different, but it makes all the difference in the world. "Ouida" was a famous authoress at the time, and in 1890, not everyone agreed that women should read, but Ouida wrote specifically for women. So, we think that maybe she was wearing a locket for Ouida and that "Ouija" was probably a misspelling.

Q. Why do you think talking boards became so popular that they could mass-market them and sell them to the common family back then?

A. You were coming off the Civil War, a time where there was massive, pervasive death in the country that touched us in a way no war or epidemic has. So, everyone lost a father, son, husband, grandfather, or nephew, and they just didn't have to deal with the death. They had to deal with the mystery of what happened because often, many of these people were killed on the battlefield, and no one knew who they were. So, they just went away and never came back.

We also lived in a time back then when epidemics swept pretty quickly and killed a lot more than they do in our modern age of immunization and shots and different things. It wasn't uncommon for someone to have twelve children and lose six of them. Back then, to remember them, you would take photographs of your dead child with your live child, and you would hang that on the wall to remember them.

They also didn't have a lot of electricity. You didn't have phones. You didn't have the things that connect us, and you had a lot of quiet time when the sun went down. So, talking to dead people wasn't uncommon.

Q. There's a lot of people that believe the Ouija is tied to witchcraft or demons. Why is that?

A. Anything mystical, we put those names or symbols on them. If they look mystical and scary, we call them witch things, witching boards, or witching rods. We make up all kinds of names and put them on there.

If you think that Ouija boards are something awful, let's just look at the numbers from 1967 to 2004. 1967 was the first full year that Parker Brothers made the Ouija board. From 1967 to 2004, 13 million Ouija boards were made. Let's stretch that out, 1890 to 2015. Millions and millions and millions. How many really bad stories have you heard from the Ouija board? I bet if we put them statistically next to each other, it would be better than car crashes. It doesn't matter what the facts are because it's what people believe. If people believe these things are bad and evil, they will tell these stories. People will believe them, and they will have those experiences. It's like a cycle.

Q. Today, it's also paranormal television shows. I don't know how many times that

I've been watching one of them, and the investigators on the show will ask the people who are experiencing a haunting, "Did you ever use the Ouija board in the house?" If they answer that they have, it would be told to them that this is probably why they now have a haunting.

A. Then they proceed to walk into the house and pull out their EVP recorders and say, "Is there anyone here? Do you have a message for me? Tell us why you are here?" Wait a minute, isn't that just what they did with the Ouija board?

If we look at the paranormal community as an extension of or an outgrowth of the spiritualist movement—the spiritualist movement were the ones who invented the talking boards, now the very community where they came from—they (Ouija boards) are now a bad thing.

Q. Besides spiritualism, why else was the Ouija board popular?

A. The Ouija board in Victorian times broke Victorian norms in that men and women were not supposed to be in a room together. They weren't supposed to be touching. The Ouija board brought some pretty great date things in the Victorian Era. You would wait until night. You would light some candles because you didn't have any other lights. The Ouija board would lay on your lap so your knees were touching and then your fingers were touching. Why do you think the Ouija board was so popular? It was an amazing date game.

Norman Rockwell captures that in May of 1920 on the cover of the *Saturday Evening Post* that showed a man and a woman playing right on the cover because that's how popular the Ouija board was.

Q. Do you think that some of the backlash toward Ouija boards is because of the competition it gives to the paranormal community?

A. Some of the very first people who came out against the talking board were mediums and other spiritualists who were using them. If you think about why that is – why would someone who was using them be against them? Suddenly, they're being sold to everyone, and before the talking boards hit and were popular, if you wanted to have some type of séance, you had to hire a medium.

After the Ouija board was mass-produced, for $1.50, you got to have this small séance in your house. You could do it over and over again, and you didn't have to pay twice. Suddenly you're hitting an entire industry in the pocketbook really hard. So, you didn't like that if you were a medium. So, some of the first people coming out talking bad about these boards were mediums saying things that were very familiar with today, "Don't use the Ouija board. You don't know what you're dealing with. This is opening doors you can't close. You don't know what you're dealing with. You need someone like me. Someone who has experience dealing with this to guide you through."

Listen to the full interview with Robert Murch on my website:

www.alanrwarren.com/hom-
podcast-episodes/episode/
d4b9e34a/ouija-boards-
robert-murch-2014

Astrology

Astrology is considered another pseudoscience that will use celestial objects such as the planets and stars in order to get information about people and the events that happen throughout their lives.

Stephen Frampton is a psychic medium who practices astrology. Astrology's history goes back to the second century and has been used in several cultures to predict things to come in their lives. Quite often, it was the wealthy and rulers of nations that would have their own Astrologer with them at all times.

In the Astrological field, there are so many different kinds and practices it's hard to know where to go for information. I searched for the most popular and successful in the field. After several interviews, I decided on one that seemed the most honest to me. He wasn't perfect but really lived by astrology in his own life. He also made a living off not only guiding his clients with astrology, but helping businesses use it to be successful and to make the correct operational decisions.

Steven Frampton was on our show two times, and these are the highlights from those interviews. He is still currently running his consulting service, and his website is at www. stevenframpton.consulting

Q. How did astrology enter into your being a psychic medium?

A. Well, I'm very analytical, Al, and I like evidence. When you have a consultation with a medium, for example, you're looking for evidence that your loved one continues to exist on the Astro plane or the spiritual plane. It's mind-blowing when you have a good mediumship counsel.

I'm very fascinated by psychic art. There's a wonderful lady in spirit by the name Coral Polge, and she would basically draw a portrait of somebody in spirit. You can see in documentaries about her that her clients would literally then take out a photograph of the person, and it would be the same as the portrait that Coral Polge had drawn. Exactly the same. Extremely evidential.

Although I'm a psychic medium, and as a child, I used to see my main spirit guide, Arthur, standing in my room talking to me. He would materialize physically as well as telepathically, and I decided that in order to help people, I wanted to be sure that I could validate what I sensed. But also, I'm very mathematical and analytical, as I said. So I'm very interested in systems and tools that enable us to decode or decipher a problem or life more generally.

As I researched Astrology, starting from the age of about nine or ten, I was fascinated by how accurate it is, and I was also fascinated by the fact that good quality Astrology can enable us to understand pretty much anything and everything that's occurring in the world.

Q. What is the difference between the Medieval Astrology that you work in as compared to the stuff people see in their newspapers every morning?

A. That's a brilliant question because when you are looking in the newspaper at a horoscope, there are a number of issues with that. First of all, it's nearly always focused on a person's sun sign. So, it's looking at the sign of the Zodiac the sun was in when a person was born. Now that's an interesting indicator to understand which sign your sun is in is very useful. But it's one very small part of a big and complex picture. The problem really is with modern Astrology, the sort of stuff that you see in the newspapers is, it's very watered down, and often very much, you've got to bear in mind that if you're writing for a newspaper, the newspaper will obviously have guidelines about how they want that column to be, and they might want it quite watered down. They might want it not to be too controversial. It's like entertainment for people, really. So, people read their horoscope, and it's a bit of fun and entertainment. It doesn't really do good quality astrology that's much use in terms of demonstrating how powerful or how useful Astrology is.

The other factor quite simply is looking only at the sun sign is a mistake because we have to look at all parts of the chart. So, to give you an example, Al, the sun in my chart is a weak planet. I don't have a powerful sun. The sun in my chart has no connection to what's called the "ascendant," and it's the ascendant in the chart that describes the individual. My sun is a symbol of my father, and the sun in your chart might be more symbolic of your spiritual teacher or priest. So, you have to be very careful because if we just generalize, we get the wrong end of the stick. So, those columns, in my opinion, are rarely useful and often do a disservice to good astrology.

Q. Where did those horoscopes come from, and why is it that they are what gets run in newspapers?

A. I think it's simple to look at the person's sun sign, and it can provide useful insights because as long as the person's looking at the correct sign, it can be helpful. But it's not comprehensive enough to be particularly useful.

In order to answer your question, we have to go back and say, "What happened to Astrology?" If you go back hundreds if not thousands of years, Astrology was very much part and parcel of life. If you look at India now, Astrologers understanding mythology, etc., is part and parcel of everyday culture. I've done a lot of business there and have a lot of clients there, and corporations, for example, will schedule negotiations on dates that are astrologically advantageous. There are cultures that are still very much aware of Astrology.

If you look back in time, kings and queens had astrologers as advisors. There's no reason for us to think that just because we're in the twentieth-first century, we're really smart and everybody in the past was an idiot. Powerful people who were protecting their realms, their kingdoms, their wealth, and their resources were using Astrology because it was a useful tool. If it wasn't useful or it wasn't accurate, they wouldn't have used it.

You move forward in time, and you think of scientific discovery, and the time where we started to develop our scientific understanding, we really polarized towards science. If you can't prove it scientifically, it has no value. Mixed in with that is the fact the Catholic church outlawed Astrology. There's been a lot, I think, in time, a lot of action in time that has deliberately discredited Astrology. Because Al, it's so damn powerful. It's so useful that if we gave it to everybody, we would all be empowered.

If you think of how the world works, if you couldn't control resources and people, then you lost power. So, if you wanted to hang onto power, you had to keep things to yourself. Note, Freemasons and secret societies are very much about Astrology. Whether Junior Freemasons know it or not, the roles they play in ceremony are astrological roles.

Q. But the rulers and leaders today are not using Astrology, are they?

A. It's difficult to say as I don't have any insights or evidence showing that our leaders are using Astrology. What I know is that it would be quite risky for a leader or president to say, "Yes, I consulted an Astrologer." Astrology has a bad reputation. It shouldn't have. We need to raise awareness of good Astrology.

It's well known that Nancy Reagan used an astrologer, Joan Quigley, very frequently. There was a time when he (Ronald Reagan) was particularly at risk, and he didn't leave the White House for several months because they were told by the Astrologer that he was at risk. There was an assassination attempt, as you probably know. Apparently, even the timing of flights when Airforce One would take off, for example, was determined astrologically, so they say.

But if you look at, for example, the Middle East—and the Middle East is very interesting because Avalonia and other civilizations in the Middle East had an incredible knowledge of the stars and the influence of the planets and the involvement of the planets in our lives, including the life of civilization—there very much used Astrology. Again, there's been so much shift, so much turmoil in the world that things have changed considerably.

But the bottom line is that good Astrology is accurate. Well, interpreted so accurately that you can't argue with it. Anybody that says that Astrology is nonsense doesn't know anything about Astrology. If you challenge them and say, "Excuse me, how many years have you spent studying Astrology?" Invariably, they have not even looked at it. They are just saying it's nonsense.

Q. Why do you think Astrology has such a bad name?

A. I think it's a complicated picture. It's partly a version of anything that's not scientific. Although, I argue that Astrology well understood and well-practiced, is very scientific. It's partly that shift away from spirituality, in faith, etc., towards pure science. But it's also my opinion that there's a deliberate agenda to discredit Astrology. It doesn't mean there's a conflict between Astrology and science. They work well together just fine. But people don't necessarily realize it.

Astrology has sort of lost its popularity because I think a lot of the problem was that it was made illegal. If you were interested in spirituality, let's say in England, you would be executed. So, it wasn't safe to openly state that you were practicing this sacred and marvelous art. So, again dangerous for many people, and we've gone backward, in my opinion, in many ways.

Q. Where did Astrology start?

A. The answer is that we don't know.

Q. How does religion apply to Astrology?

A. It depends on the religion. You know many faiths prohibit Astrology, and again that's partly due to control. If you think of the Catholic Church, for example, people were told the only route to God is through the priest. If you want to speak to God or if you want to hear from God, you go to your priest. So, this intermediary was put into place. That's partly due to control.

I believe that we're speaking to God every day. I'm not convinced that we listen to God every day. We should. But I believe in using Astrology and observing what God put in place for us. I believe that we're listening to God, but religions and different societies are packed with different agendas, and we're not free, really.

I don't believe that we are free to do as we please, really, to practice what we want to practice. We're a product of our history. We're a product of our cultures. We're a product of our society, our leaders, our rulers. We are living in this day and age, and hopefully, we are doing the best we can. But we're subject to so many factors that are beyond our control.

Q. You are a psychic medium. How does that work with Astrology, or does it?

A. There are ancient techniques that enable you to consider previous existences or life beyond or prior to this time. My belief is that we come into this world with a great history. I am not just a product of what's happened in this lifetime. I am a product of everything that's ever occurred for me. I know that we live before we come to the Earth plane, and our physical body is a tool. If you want to have an experience on the physical plane, you need a physical body. You wouldn't be here without one. If you think of yourself, you are far more than a body. Think of the most powerful thing, really: love. Think of how much you love someone. That's not physical. That's a feeling that's within your consciousness. Our conversation is not physical. I'm sharing my ideas. You're asking questions.

This is not a physical thing. If you think of who you are, you're not really physical. You just occupy a body that you manifested in order to be on this plane of existence to have your experience here on the Earth plane. The body expires, and expiry is a reference to exit spirit. Spirit will exit the physical form. Consciousness doesn't die. I wrote a blog recently about a scientist, excuse me for not remembering his name, but he's a really well-known scientist, and he's done the research, and he's saying that consciousness doesn't die. The physical body does, but consciousness doesn't die.

Q. Reincarnation. Is that us choosing to return?

A. I don't know. I think that we get a choice. I believe that there are certain things that we need to learn on the Earth plane, and I believe that if we've failed to learn what we needed to learn in order to grow, then we have to repeat those experiences. You see that a lot with clients. You see a client that has a particular relationship profile in their charts, and you say to the client, "These are some of the dynamics of the relationship you manifest, and until you understand this and evolve beyond it, then you'll create the same thing again and again."

Or you often see people repeating themes between themselves and their parents or repeating that theme with a partner. An abusive parent turns into an abusive partner and things like that. I don't believe we move beyond those things until we've mastered the lessons. So, I think as we transition to spirit, we don't just become perfect. It's another birth. There has to be death for birth. If you think of a mother giving birth, her body dies as it was. It's never going to be the same. Her life is never going to be the same. She now has this child. She's changed something huge in her world and her experience.

Q. What would you as an Astrologer offer to someone that a medium wouldn't?

A. If somebody has a relative, a friend, or a loved one that passed to spirit, they want evidence. They want to know, "Is my person okay? Is my dog okay? Does my dog continue to exist?" They want that evidence. If we can provide that evidence, then we offer a wonderful service. If you have a good consultation with a medium, you just get good evidence from spirit.

After a client has a good reading, they often start to ask questions about themselves. I have a consultation that is purely Astrological in which we are answering certain questions that the client has about themselves. So, they might ask about the boyfriend or the girlfriend and is this the person that I am going to spend my life with. We see all of that astrologically. We see how long it will last. We can see what happens afterward. We can see what happened before. So, we've got many tools at our disposal. My objective is to give the client what they need.

Listen to the full interview with Stephen Frampton on my website:

www.alanrwarren.com/hom-
podcast-episodes/episode/
b43c406d/astrology-stepen-
frampton-encore

Numerology

INTERVIEW WITH ALISON BAUGHMAN

During the early 2000s, there was a lot of talk about how numbers affect our lives. Quite often, I will see paranormal shows on television that had a guest who claimed that every time they looked at a clock or watch, they would see the same series of numbers within the time. Even when they were driving on the road or walking the street, and they looked out somewhere, they would see those numbers again. The claim was that these series of numbers they were spotting could not be a coincidence and that there must be some meaning behind it. Was it a loved one from the other side trying to connect with us? Were they trying to warn us about something bad that was going to happen?

Numerology has been around for a very long time. It often gets tied in with Astrology and horoscopes and therefore is still considered a pseudoscience and more of a belief than anything real. Numerology has developed into something that much more detailed than I thought. It is centered on a divine or mystical belief in the relationship between numbers having a direct meaning to things that are going to or have happened.

I looked for popular Numerologists that were out there talking on radio or television shows and perhaps writing books. One of the most popular Numerologists around who had made plenty of appearances on Coast to Coast—probably the most popular among paranormal radio shows—was Alison Baughman.

Alison Baughman has a website at www.visiblebynumbers.com

This interview took place in the spring of 2015.

Q. So, let's start with the basics. What is numerology?

A. Well, it's an ancient divination tool that dates back ages. It has ties to ancient cultures such as Rome, Egypt, Greece, China, and it's really based upon the teachings of Pythagoras that lived in 560 A.D. So, we are talking knowledge that goes way back. When people think in terms of numerology and numbers, you think of adding and subtracting them. You think of mathematics. But really, what numerology is saying is that numbers are actually energy.

So, each number is representative of a certain energy. Basically, what numerology does is it takes the name that you are given at birth, and your date of birth, then using very specific calculations, you come up with numbers that would identify what your energy is and give indications of why you are here and what your purpose is. For me, numerology is an ancient divination tool. It's really surprisingly accurate.

Q. So, I read that you go by January 1st rather than the birth date. Is that correct?

A. Yes, you're absolutely correct. You're talking about the personal year, I am assuming?

Q. Yes. Can you explain that better?

A. Well, even in astrology, there is not a one hundred percent agreement amongst astrologers. The same thing goes for numerology. There are certain things that not all numerologists agree on. Personal year is just one of them.

Some numerologists would say that it's a birthday-to-birthday vibration for the personal year. While others would say that it's January 1st. It depends on which book you read. But I have found the most respected numerologists with the largest bodies of work, the ones that you would certainly give credence to their work, say January 1st.

I think it takes more than that. It takes more than just somebody saying—I'm a skeptic myself in the sense that if something bothers me, and I can't figure it out, I'm going to do the research. I'm going to do the background on it. I'm going to prove it to myself. I'm not going to take something at face value—even more so, when you have a body of experience doing thousands of readings that I've done. Obviously, I'm going to listen to my clients, and listen to their stories, and listen to what's transpiring in their lives. When you listen to that, there's the validation that comes from that, which really solidifies my opinion on when the personal year starts.

Q. For listeners that know nothing about numerology, how does it work?

A. When you give the numerologist your information, the name on your birth certificate, and your date of birth, that really holds the information for your life. It's kind of like a GPS system to guide you through your life. Each letter represents something. Each number represents something. The numerologist is going to take that information and run calculations on it. There are various different kinds of calculations for coming up with various different aspects of your own personal numerology chart. Once you get the numbers, then it's just a matter of being able to explain what that number is and how that influences you.

If you are looking at your own numerology chart, what can it tell you? Well, it absolutely can tell you what your talents and abilities are. That can be an extremely useful tool as far as guidance and knowing what you'll be good at. It'll tell you what your soul came to do, meaning what is it the soul came to achieve in this lifetime. What is the mission?

It can tell you what your challenges are in life. Everyone, no matter who we are, all have challenges written into our numerology chart. Everyone does. So, when you understand what your challenges are, that can help you overcome them much quicker. Identify them and understand what is needed, and then overcome them. That certainly helps you to be successful.

Numerology, besides the fact that it's identifying who you are as a person, what your talents and abilities are, explains why you feel the way you do, why you decided to do the things you do, why the things that are important to you are important, and why you dreams the dreams you dream. It definitely focuses in on everything that makes you the unique person you are.

Then you can go even further into the numerology chart, and it's also telling you the road that you're on. The pathway. How do you take these talents and abilities, and how do you progress through life? What are your opportunities? Are you going to have opportunities to use these talents?

There's a pathway that's written through the pinnacles. This is one of the reasons why when we all reflect on our lives. We understand that we have shifted, and changed, and evolved. Circumstances have changed in our lives. The pinnacles are very often are the reason for that because the energy has shifted and changed throughout our lives.

If we can understand what the pinnacles are, then we can understand what is being asked of us and how to proceed through that time in our lives and get the best possible results. Then you can look at the energy that applies to the year, such as the essences, the personal year, the personal month, which comes in on a much finer look at a very smaller piece of time. It's like taking a magnifying glass out, and instead of looking at the entire life, you can hone in on one year in the person's life. Then you are able to understand what energy is influencing this person.

Q. How sensitive is this? For example, what if your mother was going to call you one name, then decided to change it to something different? Or, if you change your name later, do any of these make a difference in your numerology chart?

A. Parents play a huge role in naming their child, and a lot of that is done because it feels right. So, I put a huge amount of credit on what the parents have chosen to name the child. That's usually what's on the birth certificate. If the parents later decided to change the name, I would definitely take a look at it. But if we change our name later, that doesn't have as much influence as the names that we were given. That's what we call a minor vibration, and it can add to or take away from the original energy that was found in the name on the birth certificate.

Q. What do the letters in our name actually mean?

A. If you look at the cornerstone, which is the first letter of the name, A, J, and S are all ones. Usually, the cornerstones are speaking about how you approach things. Someone with an A—I'm an A—is direct, straight, and to the point. They have a certain amount of leadership ability as well.

Q. When and why do people come to you to find out their own numerology?

A. People usually call when they're at a crossroads in their life. Or perhaps they have some difficulties in trying to understand. Some people could be in the middle of a divorce, or some people call for compatibility. Is this person right for me?

People usually call because they are trying to understand something that is important to them.

One of the best things about a numerology reading is the sense that we all know who we are. So it's really nice to have a perfect stranger come along—they have never met you and know nothing about you—but using numerology, they can define you and talk about you like they've known you all their lives.

So, getting a numerology reading validates you as a person. It validates your talents and abilities, and sometimes when a person doesn't believe in themselves, doesn't believe in their talents and abilities, maybe they don't have the confidence, you come along as a numerologist and tell them what's in their chart, and this helps them do what they are meant to do.

Q. Do you ever get scary readings from people that come to see you?

A. I've always been true to what I see in the charts, and sometimes I wish I had a magic eraser, and I wish I could erase numbers out of people's charts because I see the difficulties. I wish I could make it go away, but I can't. I wouldn't call it scary because I think that if we're all being realistic in life, we all learn through our experiences, and adversity is a great teacher. I think that we've learned some of our greatest lessons from the times that tried our strengths and resolve. That's where we learn the most.

Q. What about those who claim that numerology is something evil or the devil's tools?

A. I was born and raised a Catholic, and it never resonated with me. Numerology has the single most important tool to connect me with my God because, to me, this embodies Christ. It embodies love. It embodies all of the aspects of spiritual philosophy – all that is good, all that is beautiful, all that is what God is.

Listen to the full interview with Alison Baughman on my website:

www.alanrwarren.com/hom-
podcast-episodes/episode/
77f33765/numerology-alison-
baughman-2015

Tarot Cards

INTERVIEW WITH MICHAEL M. HUGHES

There are a lot of Tarot readers out there, but just like most things when it comes to using divination tools, there can be a lot of those who are not the most trustworthy. I wanted to find out what Tarot was, starting from its history to how it was meant to be used. The questions I think of are: What can you use tarot for? How does it work? Is it real? Where did it come from?

Back in 2014, I interviewed Michael M. Hughes, a popular fiction writer. Looking at his background at that time, I found out that Hughes was interested in magic and Tarot Cards. Years later, when I went to write this book covering the paranormal interviews, the previous interviews I had conducted on Tarot were not complete enough in their information. It seemed that the Tarot reader actually knew very little about the Tarot other than the process of telling someone their future.

This led me to contact Hughes again and ask for his knowledge on the Tarot in order to complete this book. This interview happened at the time of writing in December of 2021.

Q. What is the history of what we call Tarot?

A. To understand the beginning of Tarot, you have to understand the beginning of playing cards because that's where it came from. If you wanted to have cards, you needed paper, and paper originated in China. So, it's in China where we see the very first playing cards, and they were the very first to produce them in large quantities.

Even when we look back at those earliest cards, there were four suits. Throughout history, for hundreds and hundreds of years, there have always been four suits for some reason. Maybe it was just because humans like things divided by four. You know, like the four seasons or the four elements.

As paper started to be made in other countries, one of the first decks we saw was Islamic decks. There's one called the Mamluk deck, which originated around the Mamluk Dynasty around the 13th to the 16th century in what is now known as Egypt. The Mamluk deck also had four suits: there were scimitars, which are like curved swords, coins, polo sticks, and cups.

As those Mamluk cards started spreading and making their way North, those curved swords turned into straight swords because the Europeans used straight swords. The coins, clubs, and cups stayed the same. As they spread through Germany, France, and England, they became more abstract, these suits.

What was originally the scimitar then the sword, by the time the cards made it to

Germany, they became the spades that we know now. The coins became diamonds, the cups became hearts, and the polo clubs became the clover-like clubs we have now.

Q. When was the next change?

A. In Northern Italy, around 1430, we start to see decks of playing cards with these symbols on them. But we see another suit entirely added to these cards. In some cases, it might be different birds or flowers or Greek Gods. Eventually, someone came up with the idea of adding triumphs or trump cards. They came up with some provocative images for them, and some of them have transformed over time. But those are the 22 major arcana cards now. Those are those cards that really grab people like death or the hermit.

So the Tarot cards have come from the playing cards. There has been a lot of people that say that the playing cards come from the Tarot cards, but that's completely untrue. Tarot grew out of playing cards, and it grew out of people playing games with regular playing cards with images on them and then deciding that they wanted some extra cards.

The game that they were playing in Northern Italy was called Tarocchi. We don't know where that name came from or why that name, in particular, became associated with his game. It was a trick-taking game, so you would bet money and things like that. It was mostly played in the royalty courts because there was no mass-printing production back then. So, these early decks from that era were hand-painted individual decks. It was a pastime of the aristocracy.

Q. What was the reason for adding the trump cards?

A. That brings up a myth that the cards were somehow pagan and they were not. If you look at the decks, they are Christian because, at the time, the Roman Church basically ruled Europe. If you look at the images on the cards nowadays, you'll see the high priestess on the card. On the original Tarot, it wasn't a high priestess. It was the papas or female pope.

All the imagery—everything from the last judgment to the sun and the moon, and the way that the celestial objects and symbols are portrayed throughout the Tarot—is Christian iconography. The fact that a lot of people today are scared of the Tarot because it's some weird pagan invention luring people into witchcraft and things like that. It's not.

So, why did they put those cards in there? Because it was just to make the game more fun. Whereas nowadays, if we were designing our own Tarot deck, we might use cultural symbols and images and things like that drawn from our culture. That's why you see so many strange Tarot decks today, like the "Walking Dead Tarot." So, the Tarot, as it was originally created, was a game to be played for fun and for betting money and winning, and the iconography was explicitly Christian.

Q. How did Tarot become more than entertainment like what people use it for today?

A. Tarot was played just as a game as far as we know until about the 18th century. Freemasons are the reason that we have the Tarot as a divination tool. In that era, a lot of freemasons were into esotericism. There's not as much of that today as freemasons are more of a social club than anything. But back then, a lot of men who were aristocracy had a lot of time on their hands because they didn't have to go to work every day. They could sit around and debate esoteric ideas like alchemy or qabalah.

Antoine Court de Gebelin was a French and Swiss Protestant pastor, but he was also a freemason like a lot of the learned gentlemen of the day. He saw this countess playing a Tarot card game, and he was blown away. When he saw the images, he thought that they must have come from ancient Egypt. He wrote a book about the Tarot, claiming that it came from ancient Egypt, and the book caught on fire among the European gentlemen who were freemasons.

One man who really made a difference was Alphonse Louis Constant, who was a kabbalist and freemason, who wrote a book that tied the Qabalah and Tarot together. This influenced a group called the Hermetic Order of the Golden Dawn. If it wasn't for this group, we probably wouldn't be using Tarot cards today. This group became this powerfully influential secret occult order around 1888, when their first temple was established. The bad boy of occultism, Alastair Crowley, was also a part of the Golden Dawn. All modern western magical traditions come from the Golden Dawn.

Q. How did Tarot become something that is considered evil or tied to witchcraft?

A. Out of the Golden Dawn came two individuals, Arthur Edward Waite and Pamela Colman Smith. When most people think of Tarot, they think of the Waite-Smith deck or Rider-Waite deck because Rider was the publisher and Waite was the creator. It's the Tarot decks that you see in movies all the time. Pamela Colman Smith was the artist. This deck was first published in 1910, but it didn't blow up in popularity until the 1960s, when suddenly these decks became mass-produced, and they were available in the U.S.

I think the reason that it's associated with witches is just because people didn't have the facts, so they made up all sorts of stories. A lot of people will say, and they believe this, that the Tarot came from Egypt, and it was carried by the gypsies or appropriately known as the Roma today. Gypsies were associated with fortune-telling and divination. That's where a lot of that bogus history comes from. Most of the Roma used regular playing cards because that's all they had or could afford. So they did use cards, just not Tarot.

So, in the 60s and 70s, there's this sort of occult explosion. It was the age of Aquarius, and people were feeling liberated from traditional religion and wanting to explore alternative spiritual systems and things like that. Occult bookstores started popping up in cities like San Francisco, and it was the birth of what we later called "The New Age."

Now, because the Waite-Smith Tarot deck came out of the Golden Dawn tradition, it had occult symbols in it. Like instead of the coins in the older decks, it had pentagrams. And that immediately triggers a lot of people. So, because the deck had occult symbols in it and it was embraced by this new age occult awakening in the United States, in particular, the cards lent themselves to all sorts of interpretations.

Q. There are also some weird rules or traditions with the Tarot cards.

A. Yes. Some people believe the cards have some sort of energy to them. I don't. I think it's cardboard and ink. But some people go to elaborate ways of cleansing their cards with salt or smoke, and that's cool. It's just not my thing.

Q. How do you think the cards work?

A. It's amazing. I can have a conversation with someone for thirty – forty minutes sometimes and get some really interesting material out of it. That's what blows my mind. I'm a pretty scientific guy, but at the same time, I have to admit that these cards doing this thing we call a Tarot Reading, bringing your intention to the experience to these images and having a conversation with someone, is magic. Really interesting stuff comes out of that, and I don't know how. I don't think I'm particularly psychic or anything. I teach people to do this, and they can do it. It works, and crazy accurate details come from it. That's the fascination we get from reading the Tarot cards.

Q. So the Tarot card reader can use these cards from whatever religious point of view that they have—whether they are Christian, Jewish, or Pagan or not religious at all—and it will still work the same?

A. Exactly. It doesn't matter what your spiritual or religious beliefs are or if you have any at all.

Q. Can you read for yourself?

A. You can read for yourself too. That's another myth that I run into. Of course, you can read for yourself. You ask a question, pull out some cards, and you start seeing patterns. I think it's critical to read for yourself and to get to know the cards and the meaning of those cards.

Listen to the full interview with Michael Hughes on my website:

www.alanrwarren.com/hom-podcast-episodes/episode/b5c50aed/michael-m-hughes-tarot

Haunted Items
INTERVIEW WITH JOHNNY ZAFFIS

There's a large amount of conversation floating around the television paranormal world about evil spirits or demons being able to attach themselves to inanimate objects. In this chapter, I am not talking about spirits attaching themselves to people or to a house, even though a haunted house has been the primary focus of ghost stories for many years now. I wanted my focus to just be on other objects that are supposed to be haunted.

Not surprisingly, the most popular item is probably the possession or spirit attachment to dolls. We have seen this in movies such as *Chucky* or *Annabelle*. Now Chucky's story was a complete fiction created for entertainment first seen in the

1988 movie called *Child's Play*. But the Annabelle story had some real history.

The story of Annabelle became famous after the release of *The Conjuring* and *Annabelle* movies. The real Annabelle doll was apparently a Raggedy Ann doll which was given to a nursing student in the 1970s by her mother. According to this nurse and her roommate, every time they came home from work, the doll would move to a different place in their apartment. They also claimed to have found some handwritten notes from the doll asking for help.

So, what do two helpless college girls in the 1970s do when their Raggedy Ann doll is moving around their apartment and leaving them notes asking them for help? They call in paranormal investigators Ed and Lorraine Warren. What else? As usual, with the Warrens, they took the doll to their Warren's Occult Museum and wrote a book about their experiences with the demonic doll, which later became three movies.

Upon researching the community, the name Johnny Zaffis kept appearing when referencing haunted items. Not only did paranormal investigators know Zaffis, but he had started his own television series in 2011 called *Haunted Collector*. In this television series, Zaffis, who also claims to be a demonologist, and his team would go to reported haunted locations and try to locate the item that Zaffis considered to be the source of the haunting and remove it. Zaffis would then take it to his haunted relic museum located in Connecticut.

Zaffis is also considered to be part of paranormal royalty, as his uncle was Ed Warren, of the Ed & Lorraine Warren paranormal team, who had the famous possessed Annabelle Doll that led to *The Conjuring* movies. His show ran for three seasons, and it was just after his series ended in 2014 that I had the opportunity to interview him about his haunted possessions to try and find out what was going on.

Here are the highlights of the interview with Johnny Zaffis.

Q. Does collecting all of these items that are haunted and taking them back to your place, how does that affect you and living with them?

A. Well, there's a lot of prayers and bindings and different things that are done over the items to contain the energy or to break the energy that's associated with them. I'm a very firm believer that if it's a public type of building or an area where people aren't living, then that's where those items should remain. It keeps it away from people because, again, we deal with energy, and we know energy can't be destroyed. Therefore, a lot of time, when we come into contact with an item that might have something attached to it, it can trigger it and cause paranormal activity to occur in homes. So, I always recommend to people to definitely not keep them there.

Is there activity in the paranormal barn where I house these things? Yes. People have a lot of different experiences, and people tell me continuously about the different items that are down there that I've never talked about or never really brought out into the forefront, sharing some of the information.

It's one of those difficult things, Al. It's like a house or a piece of property that really can't communicate with us. So, therefore, we do everything we can as far as trying to break the activity associated with them.

Q. When people contact you, they don't know that it's a haunted item in their house causing the problems. So, how do you know when someone contacts you that they are dealing with a haunted item?

A. Well, one of the key things with investigating is asking many questions, and one of the questions I ask in every case I get involved with is, "Have you brought anything new into the house?" Believe it or not, a lot of times, that will refresh a person's memory. "Gee, you know what, I just happened to pick up this glass set, and that's just about the timeframe when everything started." So, that's what we will always look for in these circumstances – anything new that was brought in or anything they picked up from a yard sale. These are typical types of questions that I do ask these individuals.

Then, when we're there investigating, again, we check to see if we can get any readings off an item or any EVPs around the items. A lot of times, I recommend to the homeowner to take the item out and put it in your garage or a building outside the house, and we'll see if things calm down. If they feel that it's that particular item and things calm down, that tells me there's a good possibility that we have something associated with that.

Q. When you find items that have an attachment during your investigations, are there certain particular items that you choose for your museum? And certain ones that you don't want in your museum?

A. Usually, the way I look at it is, if I'm having a lot of difficulties and it's a heavy-duty case, and the item is definitely associated, and something is attached to it, I do sometimes make a decision to bury the item or throw it into a body of water. Unless I have clergy with me, or a spiritual person like a Shaman or something, then I will let them make a choice on how they would like to dispose of it.

Breaking or burning an item, you got to be very careful if there is indeed something attached to it. It can gravitate right towards you. So, there are items but not by any particular circumstances as far as an item and whether I will bring it back to the museum or not. You know there are things I definitely have to dispose of.

Q. How do you dispose of them then? Are you saying not to burn it or throw it away?

A. I definitely recommend to people not to burn it or break it. Call somebody to have it removed. There are paranormal groups everywhere today. I would definitely recommend that if somebody is not comfortable, call their clergy to come in and bless it, because if you have a family heirloom, I mean, I'm not really interested in Grandma's five-carat diamond ring. Again, that's a family heirloom. So, I recommend that they have a binding or something. Put it in a safe deposit box, put it in a location, especially if it's not being worn or something, where the energies are not going to intermingle and cause a disturbance to transpire as far as paranormal activity.

Q. Let's talk about the dolls that are possessed?

A. I have many of them in the museum that have either been sent to me directly or that we have removed from a lot of investigations. It's always interesting because you would think of a doll, children play with them, and there are not usually any issues. People are often confused on why would something so innocent have energy attached to it. Because it's again, it's something you wouldn't expect. You wouldn't expect a porcelain doll or Raggedy Ann doll to have something attached to it.

A lot of times, we find there's a lot of intent and purpose with the dolls that the energy is attached to them. It could have belonged to somebody, and it was their favorite toy, or it was their favorite item that they had, and dolls just seem to be a really be a big target for paranormal activity.

Q. Are there ever items that you never expect to be haunted?

A. I think it's religious items of any nature. You know, in the beginning stages, it was something that was very mind-boggling because you wouldn't think that anything from a Synagogue, a church, or a chapel, or any of these places would necessarily have something negative attached to them.

But many items that people have bought at auctions or that have been removed from spiritual locations can trigger a lot of paranormal activity. Again, it's used in a positive attribute, if you will, with these items. They're done with worshipping things on a positive, but when they come into a negative environment or are used in a negative environment, it can trigger paranormal activity when people bring these types of things into their homes. Bibles, candle holders, religious statues, you name it. There are a lot of different things that you would least expect to be having a paranormal issue that really had some major things occurring to it.

Q. Can you share what you would consider the darkest item that you have ever encountered?

A. Yeah, I have what I refer to as an idol. It's a bust. A young man got himself involved with practicing things in the occult on the dark end of that. For several weeks, his personality started to change, and one night, he just came down and started telling his parents that he got himself involved in stuff, and it was wreaking havoc on him. They went on up to his bedroom, where he had an altar set up, and this two-foot statue was there. He said that "Whatever I have conjured up or I brought in is living inside that statue now, and it is telling me to kill myself." It was removed, and now it resides in the museum.

Q. On your investigations, do you ever bring a medium in to analyze items?

A. Absolutely. I've had the opportunity on many investigations, including the T.V. show, to work with several people that are gifted. You have to remember that I've always worked with them. Lorraine Warren, as far as I'm concerned, is a very gifted person. I've watched her walk in cold and get more information than you could ever imagine that would tie in with something.

Q. Do you use a lot of equipment?

A. My entire team does. There's 26 people that work in my group, and the horns, bells, and whistles, as I call it. There are so many different things out there. I still stick with the basics. What I mean by that is, sometimes I do photography work, and I have my tape recorder usually running. It is an extremely important element for most of us. Sometimes when activity spikes, it's really interesting watching all of the equipment go off. It just is because it's verifying that there's something occurring that we can't see or we can't touch, but we're all experiencing.

Q. Is there a certain location that you love to go investigate, even if you've been there before?

A. Gettysburg. I've been going there for as many years as I could possibly remember, and I'm always intrigued each and every time I go down there. It's a unique type of place. Most battlefields are, but Gettysburg is one of those unique kinds of places where it's interesting to watch people have an experience for the very first time. Because if anything's ever going to happen on a paranormal level, it's in Gettysburg, Pennsylvania.

Q. What are your thoughts on Ouija boards?

A. Well, I'm very cautious. The Ouija board is nothing but a game, and it's not the board, and it's not the Planchette that brings the spirit in. It's us, the individuals. We're the catalyst. So, when certain individuals play it, they end up opening up the door to the spirit world to establish communication. Sometimes that energy attaches to these boards just like pendulums, tarot cards, or anything. Energy is going to attach to it. The Ouija has become very popular with being one of

the "Devil's Tools," so to speak. I have
many of them in the museum that has been
removed from investigations. I could
probably have a hundred boards in the
paranormal museum.

Listen to the full interview with Johnny Zaffis on my website:

www.alanrwarren.com/hom-
podcast-episodes/episode/
e3e7866c/johnny-zaffis-
haunted-collector-2015

RELIGION & THE OCCULT

Church of Satan

INTERVIEW WITH MAGUS PETER
GILMORE

All of us have heard about Satan. He is supposedly the "Lord of Evil" found in the Christian bible and a fallen angel who is in our world amongst us with the intention to create death, destruction, and chaos. He is usually portrayed in movies as a man dressed in red, with a long black cape, and sometimes even has horns on his head.

Satan usually gets the blame whenever something awful happens in the world, and the reason why is usually claimed by Christians to be something that people are doing wrong with our behaviors, such as, "We let the Gays marry, and this is why God created AIDS."

In the eighties, Satan also started a Satanic Panic in America where it seemed that every day there would be a murder committed by a Satanist. This became a daily topic among the media, with Geraldo Rivera leading the pack. Unfortunately, this media obsession created such hysteria that several people were arrested and charged, claiming they were Satanists involved in terrible crimes, including baby-killing for rituals. None of these cases ended up being true and ruined people's lives.

I wanted to find out who this Satan guy is, so I thought that I would go to the source and talk with the Church of Satan itself. Only I found out that there was more than one Church of Satan. But if there was only one Satan, why would there be more than one church of Satan. I guess if there can be several types of Christianity, each with its own church, I suppose it could be the same for Satan.

I ended up going to the three largest of the Satanic groups around and approached each of them for answers about who they were and what they believed in. The first was the official Church of Satan that was started on April 30, 1966, by Anton LaVey in San Francisco. LaVey was the

High Priest from its beginning until he died in 1997. In 1969, LaVey wrote and published the *Satanic Bible*, which gave the basic rules to living a Satanic life. Later, in 1972, he also wrote the *Satanic Rituals* to explain how to do a Satanic ritual correctly.

The basic belief of the Church of Satan is that there was no real Devil, and there is no God of any kind, Christian or Islamic. Satan was used as a symbol of a challenge to any of the Abrahamic Gods and came from the Hebrew meaning of adversary. It did not represent any kind of deity or entity.

After LaVey's death, Peter H. Gilmore was named the new High Priest and still holds that position today. After approaching the church and explaining what I wanted to know, they booked me an interview with Gilmore.

I will say that this was by far one of the most informative interviews I have ever had that covered the subject of Satan, witchcraft, or magic. In fact, of well over a thousand interviews I have completed, Gilmore was one of the most charming and well-spoken people I met.

This interview was recorded in the winter of 2014.

Q. What are the fundamentals of the Church of Satan?

A. Essentially, Anton LaVey founded us in 1966. His background was that of a showman. He was basically in carnivals and circuses. He also did police photography, and he was usually shooting crime scenes. He got to see the essential nature of man, which he saw as being a beast. Just like all the rest, but sometimes more vicious, worse than the ones walking on all fours.

So, he felt that humanity had this wonderfully wide range of abilities, from being tragic, awful, and criminal to being heroic, creative, and magnificent. He really didn't find any philosophy that encapsulated mankind in any realistic way. So, he looked to Satan as the symbol of mankind and its potential. So, he adopted that, he created a philosophy called Satanism. Of course, Satan means adversary, opposer, and accuser in Hebrew.

So, he's standing up as the opposer and accuser to all of the spiritual religions of the world and saying enough of that. This is not really germane to our species, and we need something that is going to fit us. So, his philosophy was an atheist philosophy, and Satan was employed as a symbol of pride and liberty, and individualism.

He approached this from a pragmatic, skeptical, and materialist perspective. Not one that has any kind of spirituality at all. In fact, he called Satanism the world's first carnal religion because it rejected spirituality entirely. So, there's no faith in Satanism, and there's no looking to other worlds. It's very much about being in the here and now living fully.

He felt that he needed to create a philosophy too that challenged the people who were in it to take responsibility for themselves. Each Satanist creates his own hierarchy of values, and that's quite a challenge for most people. Most people would rather have that handed to them by some guru of some sort, whether that'd be a spiritual guru, or a political guru, or whatever kind.

A lot of people are directed in many ways by forces around them. But it's the rare individual who says I'm going to take command of my own life and be the captain of my destiny and really take responsibility for my choices and my behaviors because when you do that, and if you fail, it's on your head, and you have to deal with that. That's something that, in this culture especially, I find with younger people, they want to blame everybody else for anything that's not going right in their lives. Not that it's not been part of an earlier culture, but certainly, I think these days, it's even more part of the way that the people act.

Satanism stands against that, so it was a way really about creating a very grounded, materialist approach but being open-minded too. Because the whole point of understanding the world around us is using reason and science but not closing our minds to potentially really fascinating things. There's all kinds of evidence out there, especially when you look at things that we call paranormal – we call them super normal, Satanists, because they're part of the full existence that we have. They are not outside of it, but perhaps just more unusually experienced.

Q. So, Satanists are open to the paranormal, such as past lives, ghosts, and even U.F.O.s?

A. We think that you have to investigate all of that and really be very critical about all of the evidence being presented. Sadly, a lot of it doesn't hold up very well. There are some interesting things with ghosts that come up, and I think for me, what I've noticed that seems to be something that's consistent, is that ghosts seem to play like a residue from somebody's life, but they're not a conscious survival of life.

If people were really having regular interactions with ghosts and conversing with them, the world would be a really different place.

You wouldn't just be hearing some weird phrase here and there, some strange sound that you are trying to interpret as a word. But you could be having conversations with Galileo or Beethoven, and sadly, that's not going on. So, I don't think that's really the way it works. The ghost phenomena might just be a kind of you might call it a psychic residue of some sort. Perhaps some extreme emotional situation has been left. How it left that on the fabric of existence for certain people to get, we don't know yet. We don't understand all of physics. We're still trying to figure things out with quantum entanglement and the idea that things at great distances might be linked. We don't even know how that works yet. We have a lot to learn before we understand the fabric of the universe.

Q. So, when and how did you become part of the church?

A. Essentially, when I was a young fellow, I declared myself an atheist. When I was eight years old, I had read Christian scriptures, and I read some Hindu scriptures, and I read Greek and Roman mythology, and I saw them all as being equivalent and equally fictional. So, the idea that a deity existed and any religion had any validity beyond what it was doing socially, to me, seemed obvious that these things were social constructs.

I was an avid reader of Science Fiction, and I went down to a place called the Book Bar, which was a nice bookstore in the Port Authority bus terminal because I used to take the bus from upstate New York where I lived, to go down to the Museum of Natural History because I was particularly fascinated with dinosaurs.

On the way home, before catching the bus upstate, because this was before I could drive naturally since I was pretty young, I would always go and pick up new science fiction books. Arthur C. Clark and Harlan Ellison and books like that because that was one of my favorite forms of literature. I saw this book on the book rack called, *The Satanic Bible*. I picked it up, looked at it, and turned it over. On the back, there was this picture of a guy with a shaved head and a goatee that's tinted in red and thought that was pretty theatrical and wild, and I thought, who is this guy?

I flipped through a few pages and thought this sounded kind of interesting. I've read Christian scriptures and didn't think much of them. Maybe at some point, I should read this and see what this perspective was. I actually set the book back on the rack and went and got four other books of authors that I love. I was waiting in line to pay, and there was that black book again, sitting on the book rack. I picked it up and said, all right, I'm going to read this. It's inexpensive, and it's maybe intriguing. And that was really it. That was the step.

When I got home, I read that book from cover to cover in one sitting and realized that I was not just an atheist but that I was a Satanist. That was kind of an interesting thing to learn. There was somebody out there that thought many ways similar to the ways I was thinking. I had a new definition for myself and one that actually focused on ways that I found very useful for my life.

That was my conversion, if you will, to Satanism. We don't really feel that you can convert, actually. Satanism is a recognition of yourself in philosophy. We always say that the books, our literature serve as a mirror. Once you read it, and if you see yourself reflected in that, then you're a Satanist. You might not want to be, and on some level, it might alarm you. But you might find that so much of the philosophy is really what you have thought all along, and I think that's the magic of Satanism. That it's not being argued into something, or given some kind of revelation, or you're saved, or that kind of nonsense like that. It's really a very rational evaluation of yourself. Being very self-aware and then reading that literature and saying this really is me in here.

Q. At that time you were still pretty young. So, what was your family's reaction?

A. Well, my family knew I was pretty precocious. I was reading early and doing all kinds of things. Again, running down to the city by myself at a young age to go to museums and such. It didn't bother them. They weren't particularly religious. My mother was technically a Catholic, and my father converted from Episcopalian to Catholic just so they could get married. But she wasn't any kind of real religious person. My mother liked to play music, and she was a pretty carnal lady as it was, and my father was an entrepreneur. He was always starting different businesses, and religion had no part of that.

So, I didn't grow up with any kind of philosophy being imposed on me. I was allowed to observe people around me, and I got a library card as soon as I could and really just began reading tons of things. I would take out stacks of fifteen or twenty books at a time, read them and then bring them back and read the same amount again.

So, when I came out and said this is how I see myself, they weren't surprised. They didn't give me any type of negative feedback. They were really quite nice about it. Most folk's parents often have very different reactions.

Q. I would think that a lot of parents that get told by their children that they are Satanists would get scared. I think it's considered something evil and against Jesus?

A. I think that's the problem with most Christians since Christianity has spent thousands of years trying to oppose anybody else who didn't agree with them. They figure that anybody who doesn't agree with them is going to do the same thing to them. Not that they don't deserve it.

Our philosophy is one of "live and let live," as long as you have a point of view that's giving you a satisfactory way of handling your life. We feel more power to you, but don't try and impose it on us. We find that, of course, today, many religions are trying to find ways of dealing with the government to impose their beliefs on people. We find the Middle Eastern nations, of course, are linking up with all sorts of heavy-duty Islamic beliefs with Sharia law and such, and they want to impose on all of their citizens.

Here we have plenty of laws that are still based on Christian concepts that really have no rational basis, and right now, we have the great civil rights struggle for same-sex marriage going on, and really the opposition to it is solely based on religious ideas. Obviously, it's something that should be swept away, any kind of opposition to that, but knowing how entrenched these things get, it's very hard to do.

Q. I am a gay man, and I really don't care if someone likes it or not.

A. Good, that's how it should be. That's how we Satanists feel too. The whole point of freedom is that people are free not to be offended. If our beliefs bother you, then that's your problem and tough. That's what a free society is all about. You do what you like, and other people are going to do what they like. As long as they are not forcing themselves on you in some way, then that's the consequence of living in a free society.

Q. I agree that's how it should be, but it's not always that way.

A. Well, most of the world and most of human history hasn't been that way. I think that's a kind of remarkable thing about the late twentieth century moving into the twenty-first. That we're really getting to the point where we might have an equitable social contract that could, in time, work globally – that would be truly a part of the evolution of human society, and that's something I think that we could look forward to help evolve.

Q. Is there a fear of not having a religion?

A. I think there's a fear in people because they are really being determined, most of their values, by something outside of themselves. They aren't self-determined, and if they see the source of those values being eroded, in their opinion, then they feel that the rug is being pulled out from under them and that they have no security anymore. That just shows to me that they really didn't have very firm beliefs in the first place. That's where I think it's definitely coming from a social and psychological sense that the framework of their understanding of the universe around them is one that is not so sturdy. That alarms them and makes them terrified.

Religions have spent so much time telling people their lives are just transitory times, so if your life is just crap, don't worry about it. Because if you do the right things, you are going to go to heaven. Whatever that means, too, because if you look in the texts of Christianity and such, heaven is a pretty boring place.

It's all about pleasing God for eternity which sounds like serving a megalomaniac, and I personally don't find that something I'm looking forward to. At least the Islamic folks feel you're going to have virgins to have sex with or something. That's something that's better for them probably than what they're getting. That other alternative sounds pretty awful. That's what you're supposed to be hoping to achieve?

There have been preachers that have tried to do things where they say, "Grab onto life." There was a guy named Reverend Ike, who would say, "Why have your pie, by and by, when you can have it right now and with ice cream on top." And he was a Christian, and we're going, "Well, that's Satanism." He found our philosophy and tried to throw Jesus in there somehow.

Q. Sell it any way that they can, right?

A. And they do, and I think that is a problem with things. Since God doesn't come down and actually talk to people, aside from the people in the asylums that tell you he does or running other crazy pretentious organizations. Again, people are very insecure mostly and that they can doubt things leads to fear. I think that's a change.

Satanism offers strength in that we doubt everything. We question everything. We're skeptics, and that doesn't give us fear. It actually provides interest and stimulus for us. I think on a certain level that people who do always look for some sort of outside authority figure to control their lives are a different kind of person than the people who look to themselves for the framework to live.

It doesn't matter what culture you come from either. You can really come from anywhere. People come from all over the world and become interested in Satanism because they feel alienated from this basic concept of having an authority tell you what to do, and they are feeling comfortable with that. When they see Satanism, they say wait a minute. That perspective says be yourself and take responsibility for yourself. They are not frightened by that. They are excited by that. But I think that's a rare kind of person, a sort of niche. That's why I think Satanism will always be a niche philosophy for those sorts of people.

Q. It's really hard for people to go away from the religion that has been in their family for generations.

A. Well it is. It's very hard, especially when you look over the past when those religions have been linked with governmental states, and were therefore free to impose their ideas on everybody under them. You know, when you look back at The Inquisition, when people were being burned at the stake, first being tortured, and then their property, lands, and their beholdings, whatever they had, was confiscated by the church. Of course, the right bribes were paid to the right governmental officials, and they were profiting off anybody they didn't like, condemning them with witchcraft, whether they were actually trying to practice anything that might be defined as sorcery or not. That's a scary thing when religion has that kind of hand-in-glove control over the populous with the governmental force. It's all throughout human history, though, and it really doesn't matter what culture you look at. That's generally been the state of being for the human species.

Q. What do you think about the Hollywood perspective in their use of films in portraying Satanism?

A. There's actually been very little in the way of films that have actually defined

Satanism in a way that's consistent with the reality of it. They're usually horror films, and there's some kind of devil worship going on, where there's somebody going to be sacrificed to the Prince of Darkness or one of his assorted infernal minions. They are meant to just frighten people because Satan, of course, has always served as an easy boogeyman. Satan has been the best friend the church has ever had because he's kept it in business for all of these years. That's certainly true for Hollywood as well.

Of course, there are always interesting exceptions. If you saw *The Devil's Advocate*, with Al Pacino playing Satan, some of his ideas, even though he's playing a real Satan and we don't believe such a thing exists, his philosophy was actually kind of carnal and realistic and pragmatic and refreshingly Satanic.

If you even go back to the old Roger Corman *Mask of the Red Death* film, starring Vincent Price, he plays Prince Prospero, who is essentially a devil worshiper. But there are parts of his speeches that were before the Church of Satan was founded. It's really spot-on Satanism. It's really kind of fun. I also suggest to people that watching an old Vincent Price movie is a good thing to do for Halloween.

Q. So, is Hollywood not a positive thing for Satanism?

A. Most Hollywood films are really just meant to frighten people when they bring Satanism up. We'd really love to see something where a Satanist was an actual character and was the skeptical, intelligent person who maybe solved the situation, who kept clear-headed, and was somebody that you went to. Maybe not the hero because that would be way too much for the general audience to accept?

When you watch these contemporary superhero films, Loki is the devil in Norse mythology, and he's certainly getting lots of love from the audience. And you'd have to say that in *The Avengers*, Tony Stark, he's a total Satanist in his philosophy in the way he behaves. We've got some. They're not explicitly Satanists, but we've got some very Satanic people out there in films who are quite popular now.

Q. So, what kind of music do you like? Typical heavy metal? I had to throw that in.

A. That's always fun. Metal decided that the Devil was going to be a staple of the genre, and it became widespread. Of course, there are Satanists who are metal musicians. King Diamond is quite open about his membership in the Church of Satan. But then there are different people like Marc Almond of Soft Cell, and he's a member too, as he's admitted. I can't tell you anyone who is not open. We are very confidential about our membership, but a number of our folks have been quite open about being members. Marilyn Manson, too, was given a priesthood in our church, and he understands the philosophy quite well; even though the music that he does is his own artwork, it's not trying to present Satanism.

For me, I am a classically trained musician. I have a bachelor's and master's degree in music composition from NYU. The kind of music that I listen to really is Mozart and Beethoven, and up to contemporary film composers or contemporary orchestral music composers. But favorite composers would be Mahler, Bruckner, and Shostakovich.

Q. What are your thoughts on how the media portrays Satanism? It seems that every time there's an awful murder or something sinister that has happened, the media will always say that the culprit was a Satanist.

A. That's been an issue for us. Back in the eighties and nineties, there was a thing called the "Satanic Panic." At that time, Christians Evangelists decided that a way of getting people under their control was to tell the world that there had been former members of evil cults that were literally in communication with the Devil himself, and of course, they were all high priests and high priestesses. These were often people with IQs of seventy-six or something talking, so you might think that Satan's got pretty low standards where that's concerned.

The idea was that from kids spraying graffiti pentagrams under highway overpasses up to Generals of leading armies and corporate heads, everybody was tied together in this grand conspiracy ruled by Satan himself from the underworld to subvert Christianity and the word of Jesus.

Newscasters, particularly Geraldo Rivera, ran with that. They found it a great way of entertaining people and getting attention, and they promoted these people saying this nonsensical garbage. I spent a lot of time on shows with these folks debunking them. The F.B.I. naturally spent time researching this because all of it was alleged criminal behavior, and they don't take that lying down. So, when they looked into it, they really found no evidence of any of it. What was sad, though, was that we found that kind of journalism actually got people to imitate the sort of villainous portrayal that they were making. We would call those people "Geraldo Satanists." They were a bunch of kids who would take drugs, put a pentagram on a tree, and they would go out and decide to sacrifice a cat. They thought, "Hey, I am being a Satanist and this is cool. I am evil, and rebellious."

Q. Where do you think people get these ideas to sacrifice a cat or goat?

A. It was every day if you were watching these talk shows. People were telling you that these things were going on. There were Satanists out there with portable crematoriums, and that women were breeding babies for Satan that were being sacrificed. We had that McMartin trial, which was, I still think, the most expensive trial in all of the American jurisprudence.

That was all about child abuse and sacrifice at a daycare center, and none of it was true. It went on for years. It ruined people's lives. It cost millions of dollars, and it was all nonsense. This kind of hysteria is something that seems to grip the public easily, and you have folks who basically had a P.T. Barnum attitude of whatever the show is. It can make us a few nickels, so let's run with it. Journalism is putting on the kind of horse and pony show, and then, of course, Hollywood follows suit too.

Q. Journalism seems to have gone to hell lately. Excuse the pun. Journalism is just entertainment.

A. It's utterly entertainment. The worst part of contemporary journalism is that nobody does any research. You could issue a press release that says, "A giant spaceship landed in Cameroun, and elephant-like aliens came out and waved and invited Jesus down for tea." It would just be reported. They would repeat it, and they wouldn't spend any time examining it. There are plenty of folks who take advantage of this naturally. Why would they? It's an easy way to get some attention. If you can get attention, you could probably get some money off people. When I was growing up, I used to read newspapers that actually had fact-checking, and if something was in error, they would print retractions.

Q. What is your life like as a Satanist? What kind of relationship do you have with the church?

A. Most interestingly, the Church of Satan is a concept. It's an idea. It's the people in it. It's not a building, and we don't gather for meetings or services. Essentially, the Church of Satan is people who share the philosophy of Satanism.

Since the basic idea of our philosophy is individualism, everybody determines their own personal values and tastes and pursues them. Satanists might deal with each other if they can meet each other by knowing that they are Satanists. They really only ever interact on a deeper level if they share other things beyond Satanism. Because again, Satanism is only a tool for getting the most out of your life.

Rather than a devotion, there's no worship in Satanism. There's no faith in Satanism. We do have rituals. But ritual is basically a form of psychology that we employ. Lesser magic is a form of magic that is the manipulation of people around you. It's learning how to be charming, learning how to be glamorous, speaking to people so that they will do things that you would like them to do. It's old school charm that so many people seem to have lost these days because they simply think that because they exist, everything should be theirs. Which I think older folks like us find tedious.

Greater magic, which is ritual magic, is the idea of having an emotional decompression chamber. It's an intellectual decompression table, as Anton LaVey called it specifically. The idea was to set up a framework of ritual where you express emotions and release them which are hindering you from pursuing your regular pursuits by getting that out of your system. It's a form of self-therapy, very cathartic. You can use transformational psychodrama if you want to use fancy words. But essentially, it's a way of making yourself feel better. You can deal with grief, lust, or anger. All of these things, any kind of emotion that you have, but one that's become obsessive in your life, and the idea is to let it go. And then you can go out and do things that you want.

Rituals have a dramatic format, and it's very personal because you're dealing with these deep emotions and not a worship service. It's not you get a whole bunch of people together and pray and jump up and down and all that kind of stuff. LaVey gave a basic format for ritual in the *Satanic Bible*, and that can be altered at will because, again, rituals are meant to be something that's personally affecting. It's not something that we need to have other people for. Rituals can be solely something that you do yourself. It can be done all in your mind too, in your imagination. It doesn't need ritual tools like candles and bells and all of that, which is fun. It's theatrical. I think people enjoy being the center of attention during a ritual. But you can be your own celebrant in your own ritual, so you run the show, and you don't have an audience in the ritual.

When you go to a lot of worship services for spiritual religions, there's some kind of priest of some sort, and he's interceding with the supernatural entity that the folks believe in, and the congregation is generally repeating things, and standing up, and sitting down, and praying, and doing all that kind of stuff. But in many instances, it's not something that they are really participating in in a way that's significant emotionally. Some of them are. It's all what you get out of that kind of rite.

Q Is there anything after we die?

A. We think that there is no afterlife in Satanism. We really don't believe in such things. You only live on in the memories of others or by anything that you have left that you created during your life.

Q. So when you die, it's over?

A. Yes, that's it. Life is so damn precious to us. Don't waste a minute because you are not getting that minute back. You can't tell when you're going to go, and for us, we try to live life as it's going to be like a lovely party that you don't want to leave. Most religions tell people that the good stuff is going to happen after death.

Q. No reincarnation?

A. No, we think there's no evidence of that. It's just people living pipe dreams. I think all of those ideas were invented by folks who wanted to control people.

Listen to the full interview with Magus Peter Gilford on my website:

www.alanrwarren.com/hom-podcast-episodes/episode/ba55e438/magus-peter-gilmore-church-of-satan-2014

Witch of Sleepy Hollow

INTERVIEW WITH KRYSTAL MADISON

Witchcraft has held the attention of people for many generations. In most cultures, it has been seen as something evil where the person that uses witchcraft is out to harm others and to gain something that they want for themselves. A witch is supposed to use their studies of magic and spells, along with having some supernatural power, to perform their craft.

In both medieval and nineteenth-century Europe, where the witchcraft term became used a lot whenever something bad had happened to the community, they sought out the person who was causing the misfortune on the town and banished them. Witches were thought of as immoral and people who were into the occult and should be avoided. In the twentieth century, they were attached to Satan and devil-worshipping.

Even with such bad press, witches were considered healers as well. People were generally terrified of witches, but if someone became sick in their family and the doctors were unable to cure them, they would go see their local witch for help.

In more modern times, a lot of society has softened their feelings on witches. Popular culture and movies have brought forward a more positive light on witches by presenting them as more natural homeopathic people. They live on the Earth, from the Earth, and use natural resources, such as wind and the sun, to make their lives better. The term "White Witch" emerged as a person who only uses witchcraft for positive things.

One of the most popular historical times for witches was the "Salem Witch Trials" that occurred in 1692 and 1693 Massachusetts, when more than 200 people were accused of practicing witchcraft in the community. Thirty people were found guilty, with fourteen women and five men being executed for their crimes.

I figured it would be a good time to find an actual witch and ask them some questions. I wanted to find out how they live in today's society, if such a negative history of witches affects their day-to-day lives, and do they have a different understanding of what actually happened to people who were living as witches in the past. The person we found was Krystal Madison, also known as the "Witch of Sleepy Hollow." She was a delightful and friendly person to talk with, very open and honest. I think the biggest thing that you will take away from her interview is that she lives her life just like everyone else does.

We interviewed her twice, and these are the highlights of both interviews. According to Krystal's website, she is ordained in the Temple of Diana and a member of the Cabot Kent Hermetic Temple in Salem, Massachusetts. Krystal is also a member of the Wiccan Family Temple in Brooklyn, New York, and has lived her life in the service of spirits and using magical and occult arts.

Krystal Madison can be found online at http://www.sleepyhollowwitch.com/

Q. Let's tell the listeners all of the things that you do. According to your website, you're a medium, you're a witch, and you talk about Paganism. You clearly support people with communicating with those that have passed over, and you are also a psychic. For those who usually don't use a psychic, tell us a little bit about that?

A. I think that when most people think of psychics, they think of that shop along the street that has the flashing neon palm. They think of things they've seen in movies and the craziness going on. My approach is very different from that. I'm very down to Earth. I'm very direct. I don't hold back the messages that I get and the things that I see. I always have plenty of tissues for the readings. I'm a hugger too. I mean, I've been known to, even at festivals, get up from my chair and go over and hug the person because I can actually feel the energy coming off them, and they're about ready to cry.

It's not always how much do you charge for a reading? Some people have said, "I don't have money, but I can make you a pie." And I've said, "Fine." I'm not the psychic most people would think. There's no crystal ball. There's nothing crazy going on when someone comes to see me. It's a very relaxed atmosphere. My office is all Earth tones. No skulls, nothing like that. That's in my house, not my office.

Q. When you do a reading, how do you receive the information? Many mediums would describe this in a very different way. I describe it as a thought that comes in, and you then make sense of it. How do you describe it?

A. Oftentimes, it comes as a thought. You're absolutely right. The easiest way for spirit to communicate is telepathically. So, a lot of times, it'll come in as a thought, and sometimes they are symbols. I'm also a physical medium. So if the person sitting in front of me has an ailment or the person who has passed that's communicating passed away from some type of condition, I'll actually begin to feel it. With emphysema, I'll start coughing and have a hard time breathing. If there was impact trauma to the head, I'd feel it.

It's all about interpretation, too, when you're being shown symbols. For example, I had another client in front of me, and I kept seeing the castle for Disney. In front of the castle, you know how in the Disney movies, there's that Disney font, and I kept seeing the name "Walt" in it. So, I assumed Disney World, and she's insisting that she had never been to Disney and no connection to Mickey Mouse. But this is exactly what I'm seeing. I'm seeing the castle for Disney and seeing someone write the name "Walt" in Disney font. Then she says, "My husband's name was Walt."

So, if they're not giving to you telepathically, you have to interpret that energy. Sometimes it's not personal to you. You're just the messenger. So you're trying to relay this message, and you don't know what it means. It's personal to the person in front of you.

Q. Have you always been open to doing readings for people?

A. There was a time in my life where I completely denied the gift that I had. I didn't want it. Oftentimes, they don't stop whether you want it or not. If they know that you can hear them or if you're sensitive, they are going to keep coming. It would be in the most awkward situations or inappropriate times. I finally just said that it's not going to leave me alone, and I need to do something about this, and embrace who I am.

Q. I read on your website that you are an Ordained Minister. So what does that mean? Tell me about that.

A. I am an Ordained Minister with the Ternacion Church in Massachusetts. I am legally allowed to perform weddings, naming ceremonies—that's the equivalent of Baptism—it's a non-denominational church. I also make visits to the local hospitals for those who are sick.

Q. What does the title of High Priestess mean? You talk about being a High Priestess of the Order of Corban.

A. I am the High Priestess of—it's actually a family order—it's the House of Corban. I am the head of the House of Corban. I was also initiated High Priestess into Raven Wing's Coven in upstate New York. A High Priestess is somebody who leads a coven or leads a type of religious or spiritual order or group. It's basically a calling. If you are called to service, and you answer it, the purpose is to serve.

So, a High Priestess is a teacher. High Priestess is a counselor. High Priestess is a Minister. There is a bit of a difference between being a Minister and a High Priestess, only in that a Minister is recognized by the State, but essentially it's the same thing.

Q. What is your earliest experience that you can remember that you think influenced who you are today?

A. Well, I was born into a family of witches. Actually, not just witches but Native Americans. My mother, my grandmother, and my aunt were all Santeras, which they practiced Santeria. My grandfather was Native Mohegan, and my grandmother on my father's side was Hungarian gypsy. I was also made to go to church. I was baptized, made communion, and actually almost became a nun. All I knew was that I wanted to serve.

There were things I would see and things that I would experience when I was a child that I was confused about, and instead of going to my family, I went to the church to try and find the explanations. And the answers were often things like, let's bless you with Holy Water. It wasn't really an answer.

What ended up happening was, I don't know how old I was, I fell asleep one night in the Summer, and there was no fan in the room. It was really hot, so I had the window cracked open and was sleeping above the covers.

I hated going to bed at night because as soon as the lights went out in my room and when everyone went to sleep, the house came alive. This happened as far back as I remember. Even as a small child. This one particular night, I had just started falling asleep, and my feet were hanging off the bed. I could feel something in the room, but I chose to ignore it and decided to go to sleep instead. I was just on the borderline of sleep, and I could actually feel the fingers wrap around my ankles. Something grabbed my ankles and yanked me halfway off my bed.

Q. How scary.

A. It was terrifying. To this day, I cannot sleep without my feet covered. I can't sleep without a comforter. There's always some sort of light on. So, I would say that's probably my earliest experience that brought me to where I am now.

I mean, when I was nine, I was studying Parapsychology while my friends were outside playing. I was doing my research because there were things that I was seeing that I couldn't explain, and I was too scared to talk about. I took it into my own hands and tried to find the answers myself when I realized I was able to see things that other people weren't able to see, feel things that other people couldn't feel, and hear things other people couldn't hear.

In my own spiritual journey between the church and what I was learning at home, I felt more comfortable with just embracing all of it as opposed to having to choose just one. The work I do today, I'm not just a psychic for people who don't usually go to psychics. I'm not your typical witch either. There are many in the Pagan community who are angry, especially when it comes to Christianity or Catholicism, because of the history between those three religions. Where I choose to embrace people for who they are and not for what they believe religiously. In my house, I have gatherings where others who are not part of my order are welcome to come. They don't have to participate. I also get along very well with many Satanists and Wiccans.

Q. How do you handle being a witch with your own children? Your neighbors?

A. I don't turn it off. I mean, I am a witch every day. I'm not running around town with a black hat. I do typically wear nothing but black, but I just incorporate everything. My mother is actually horrified that I'm a public witch because she's 73 years old, and she's of the belief that you hide what you are. I say to her that it's not that way anymore, and it's really important that others are not afraid to come out and be who they are. That's why I do what I do.

My children think it's really cool. They see some things happen, and they go, "I didn't know you could do that." They participate in the gatherings, the festivals that I host or attend, they usually come. I don't force anything on them. I let them make their own decisions. I have two children that have decided to be Catholic.

I have exposed them to many religions and cultures. There's a Buddhist Monastery not that far from me that I have taken them to. I've taken them to Baptist churches and to Catholic churches. I've taken them to Pagan festivals. They've seen every type of culture that I can expose them to. At the end of the day, if you're not true to yourself, you're going to come into a lot of problems.

Q. Do you think spirit has prepared your children for this type of life?

A. My two older children are extremely psychic. Sometimes they scare me with how good they are. A good example, one time my son was 12 years old, and he used to love Power Rangers. One day when he was at school, my mother called and said that she had got him the Power Ranger that he wanted and not to tell him because she wanted it to be a surprise. My son comes home, and the next morning, he gets up, comes down the stairs with a smile on his face, almost like he was up to no good, and says that he knows what Grandma got him for his birthday.

So, I asked him what she got him, and he rattled off the name of the Power Ranger. My mouth just dropped, and I asked him how he knew. He told me that her father and mother told him. My grandparents have been deceased for years. He never even met them. So, I asked him what they looked like. He said, "Sometimes they speak in English, and sometimes I can't understand them because I think they speak in Spanish. Your grandfather likes to smoke cigars, and my room stinks." He couldn't have known.

Q. Recently, there has been a lot of controversy around witches and some killings and the blaming of witches in America. How is that affecting things that you are trying to do? As well as the witch's balls and festivals?

A. We had a thing happen here recently where there was a triple murder that happened on a blue moon. The blue moon is the second moon in a month and only happens ever so often. One of the suspects happens to be or claims to be, allegedly

Wiccan, so the police department automatically assumed that it was a ritual killing by Wiccans. Because of the way that the bodies were placed and because it was on a full moon, a blue moon, it had to have been a ritual killing.

A lot of people with voices, figures in the community spoke up, and I was among them. They said that this is not the act of Wiccan. This is the act of somebody who is crazy. It's easy to blame something that you don't know. That's where fear comes from, the unknown. It's our job to negate that.

Q. Has it had an impact on the events?

A. It hasn't impacted them at all.

Q. If somebody did something to you that was adverse and had an impact, you may well cast a hex or a spell. That gives quite a negative connotation of a witch. So it can be fairly understandable, in some ways, why one would jump to those conclusions about a Wiccan. Would you agree?

A. I do. I agree with that. There's a lot of confusion out there. I had someone from Darkness Radio ask me if witches do hexes, and I unapologetically said, "Yes, we do." I fully expected to get backlash from that, and instead, I got a lot of feedback from people thanking me for being honest.

We do, but here's the thing. This goes back to that thing about Hollywood before. Let's just paint a picture. You have a witch hiding out in the woods, and there's a young couple walking down a sidewalk that is madly in love, and just because she (the witch) is going to put a hex on them, and one of them dies. This is quite the extreme Hollywood portrayal. But that's the idea of witches that people have in their minds. I'm not going to throw that proverbial banana peel in someone's path because I don't like the way that they looked at me or because they have something bad to say.

That's another thing people don't know: not all Wiccans are witches. Some of them just worship the female deity, that's it. They don't cast. Wiccans teach love. They teach a free flow love. That means that whatever you put out to the world is going to come back to you three times. They also have a rule that you can do whatever you want as long as you are not harming anybody while you're doing it.

I think it's a really good way to live if you're starting out and you don't have a mentor. I was not raised that way, and that's not how my family taught, or my family practiced. I was raised "an eye for an eye," however, there has to be balance. If I make a money sale and I receive that money, I am then going to, the first chance I get, do something good, whether it's to donate money to a charity or give of myself and volunteer somewhere because it's about balance.

If you go back to hexing or cursing, I'm not saying that there aren't people out there who will if they get their knickers in a twist and will put something out there to harm whoever made them angry. But the majority of witches won't do that. They really have to be justified, and because that does take a lot of energy to do, the repercussions can be severe, especially if there is no balance and they're not giving back in some way for what they're sending out.

I can certainly appreciate the fear people have, but it really isn't common practice. If somebody came and harmed someone I loved, would I do it? Absolutely. It's also in the interpretation of a curse. You celebrate your birthday, right? You have a cake? You put candles on that cake? Do you make a wish before you blow out the candles? Yes. Well, then you just cast.

Listen to the full interview with Krystal Madison on my website:

www.alanrwarren.com/hom-
podcast-episodes/episode/
b3fc315c/krystal-madison-
last-witch-of-sleepy-hollow

Luciferins

INTERVIEW WITH WINTER (JOHN) LAAKE

After speaking with the best well-known Church of Satan's Magus Peter Gilmore and learning a lot about the Satanists that follow the *Satanic Bible* created by Anton LaVey, I realized that there were others out there that actually did believe in an entity that is the Devil, but they weren't these people.

In this search, I found those that call themselves "Luciferins" and heard all sorts of rumors about these people. They were definitely devil worshippers and liked to live a life of excess. But what do they really believe? Did they really live those wild sex orgy lifestyles that get portrayed in those B-movies about Satan?

The person I found who was an admitted Luciferin Satanist that would agree to be interviewed was Winter Laake. His real name is John Lake, and he had written eight books by the time of our interview, all about living as a Luciferin Satanist. So, I couldn't ask for a better man to speak with about their lifestyles and what is real and not real from everything I've ever been told.

Laake was kind enough to sit with me in the spring of 2013 and tolerate my very basic and sometimes silly questions over two interviews and several hours, and these are the highlights of the interviews.

Q. Your name, Winter Laake, is a cool name. I'm guessing that you were not born with that. So, why did you change your real name to that?

A. It's just my writing dialogue name. I have a real name. Winter Laake was just something with me and part of my poetry and music. So, it was something that I just evolved with. It wasn't anything that I was born with. I really don't care about names, ironically. Names really don't mean a whole lot. I like the pronunciation of my last name, Laake, which is really my last name, ironically admitting that. It has Nordic roots. It has Germanic roots. There's a lot of things, with the double-A in it, and it brings out all of the old ancestries that my heritage is. It's kind of gloomy which I am at one with. I am kind of a gloomy person. Don't mean to be. I mean, I'm generally in a happy gloom, but it's a weird place. But the dynamic of the name fits who I am as a persona. I'm very dark comedy'ish. I have a dark sense of humor. I really don't care about ego. I have nothing to prove. Quite often, I'll meet someone with some grandiose name, and they have the ego to match it. And it's just so annoying. You have nothing going on. It's just someone home in your mother's basement, and you call yourself "Count something."

Q. Take me back to the time in your life where you got initiated into the Satanic Black Magic? Was there some sort of event or happening for you?

A. Well, I wasn't born into it myself, so I just found it. Most people in my family aren't this way, but I embraced it. It happened at a really young age. I would say about five years old. I got a real strong interest towards the dark side, or whatever you want to call it. Even that's kind of a cliché. It just grew in me.

I have had supernatural events my whole life, and that proclivity led me, and you get into seeing things. Mostly, these things are on vibrations. Then I saw signs and synchronicity in life. I had experiences with weird creatures like bats. It just was a natural progression, and then I got into it stronger in my teenage years.

I started reading a little more. I started educating myself a little more, and I found that other people shared the same kind of proclivity. And I just went with it. Then I began to realize, truly, that I garnered power, and things were happening for me. Doors were opening for me.

I began, in a witchcraft sense, to mold reality to my will, and ever since that time,

I have perfected it, in my opinion. When you venture down the road in Black Magic, which is not understood by 90 percent of the populous, it's a very solitary path. And usually, a lot of practitioners are solitary anyway. But in this regard, it really takes you to another level of oneness and to manifest and make things occur. For me, it just drew down to a philosophy of inherent evil and acceptance of my true nature.

Q. In essence, do you think that you are inherently evil?

A. Absolutely. I think all of mankind is inherently evil. We are all created evil.

Q. With that in mind, why do we do anything good?

A. Good is a part of the altruistic aspects of a lesser evil. It's just a very subtle instinct within us all as we look at our cordoned and conditioned reality, especially from slave religions. It seeks to control and keep us in our order. My grand question from my philosophy was, "If we remove the boundaries of the law, why are we at each other's throats, and why do we kill each other off?" Therein lies the whole aspect of my philosophy, and I realized that man is evil. Because if we launch and release these codes of law which we created around ourselves, we're just automatically these barbaric monsters. We just unleash our will, and we just go at it, and even if you're altruistic and choose to try and have a lesser path, it becomes very reactionary. So, you could be a person who plays with flowers and sits under a tree while others would comfort you, so you will react to this action, reaction evil on evil kind of force. I think that mankind is leading itself from a civilized evil, which it is in currently, into a more perfected evil. The more perfected evil will probably not occur until after a grand holocaust, because after we overpopulate ourselves out of existence, things will begin to run out, mankind's tension will become more intense, and then we'll be at each other's throats more, which will lead to nuclear war, which is inevitable, It will occur, and then it'll just become this experiment. From that experiment, in my super consciousness and others of that nature, would rise to a more perfected evil.

Q. How is Satanism brought into this?

A. Satanism, by its fundamental nature, is that aspect of evil. Now there are different philosophies on Satanism from self-worship, theistic, and so on, all of these other types. But my definition of what Satanism is includes the embracing of the evil nature for the selfish intent of the user, who intends to have his own result occur in society.

Now, I just call a spade a spade. Satanism is God. It's power. It's all-encompassing. It's a reflection of a creator. But in my opinion, we are all one in the dark spirit. We are already murderers throughout the universe with this ever-flowing Satanic consciousness that there was never a severance from. We were always one with it; hence we are one with whatever created us, an inherently evil God, or whatever you want to call it.

That God could be called Satan. It's not necessarily something that you would worship. You are already at one with it. There has never been separation with or even a need. Now, there are intonement, incantations, and powers that may manifest in this current society, in this current state and time.

Quite simply, Satan is a power. It's a name. It's a manifestation of what I would call the force of the Satanic consciousness throughout the universe, that is evil and that we are with one with. You can call it any name that you want. These are just things that men do, to give labels to things in order to understand certain things.

However, on the other side of it, about 80–90 percent of society, on the whole, rejects the evil nature of themselves. They aspire to a lesser evil, and they will term themselves as good creatures. So, it is a denial of that Satan or that Satanic consciousness or that energy. It's an odd conundrum of humanity because it's really death-orientated as well.

People don't realize that in this current state of existence, it's very finite. That we are living in a very finite existence and that death, in even itself, is in denial. As well, they're inherently evil, and in that, they do not understand.

Q. So, let me try to understand what you are saying. Satanic would not necessarily refer to a religion. So, it wouldn't be Luciferin, would it?

A. These labels are very interesting: Luciferianism, Satanism, Black Magic, or even Paganism or witchcraft, or whatever you want to call it – anything that is tapping into this force. These different people believe in different forces, but in my opinion, the force is always the same, and the labels are all the same. It's essentially the evil nature in ourselves that we are tapping into.

Q. I am trying to put it into terms such as when people believe in Jesus Christ or some sort of a God, and therefore the opposite is Lucifer, who is their devil or evil entity. So, you are saying that it's all-inclusive and really one force?

A. Everything is one force. The dynamics of messiahs have come and gone. Anton LaVey – you look into the life that he lived – he was into Atheistic Satanism which is basically death worship and self-worship. Everything is in the here and now and materialism, and that's all you need to have.

Now that's a great way to live, too, as it's very fatalistic. I'm fatalistic myself, and then you live every day to your highest potential. But you will also get into the dynamic like Liz Lamont's thing where we believe in truth, and everyone else she doesn't believe is under the hammer of death. So, that is a threat. When you get into that kind of thing, that is a problem. It's where someone seeks to take away Luciferin liberation or just freedom in general.

I am a freedom-loving individual. I'm talking about how certain of these kinds of religions, like this Muslim thing, like this whole ISIS nonsense, where either you believe, or you are an infidel. If you are labeled an infidel, that gives us the right to enslave or crucify you, mangle you, destroy you, molest you, rape you, and so on.

So, in their own belief system, they are giving themselves permitted access to commit great forces of evil on others. That is not anywhere near what Satanism or Luciferianism is. I don't seek to convert anyone. I don't seek to destroy anyone who I would deem, "You don't believe in what I believe; therefore, cut your head off." But that is the grand threat that is happening in this society or in this world. And that is something to be watched. It definitely has to be eradicated from the Earth, in my opinion, because freedom is we have the choice to do what we want to do as long as we don't move outside of the boundaries of our law.

I'm am looking at it from my perspective as I have accepted that I am inherently evil, and from that, I can understand why certain things are in place. And I think in the conundrum of society as a whole, they don't realize that. Also, to have a conjugal of death brought down on anyone who is deemed an infidel, where I have the right to go into a village and take all of the girls and kill all the children and so on. This kind of thing is nonsense and horrible. It needs to be stopped, and I hope it will.

Q. Do you think that the whole ISIS thing in itself proves your theory that we are all evil by nature, and even if we do wipe that part of it out from humanity, another evil will just come along? There will always be this kind of evil?

A. Yes. There is a demonic pecking order, and there are higher up levels of evil. I kind of look at myself as a sophisticated evil or civilized evil in the current country that I live in and the boundaries I give myself. There's a lot of philosophies that say that evil has no boundaries, and in a lot of ways, it does not unless you put yourself in the boundaries.

Q. Now, you also have a different side to you. According to your website, you remote view and do readings on people. Is that correct? How did that start for you?

A. Well, it's really odd how it occurred. Again, there are labels: you can call it clairvoyant, clairaudient, but I like to use the remote viewing tag because it was created by black operatives and different people that were involved in the experiment and creating what remote viewing was.

It was a natural progression. I started looking at things, streaming into the future using divination tools, using Tarot cards. Then I started looking and seeing into the past, and I arrived at what I believe was quantum thinking. I do think that everything has happened before, even our deaths. I had to look into why people like myself were able to look forward and backward and have clarity because it had to have already occurred.

But how it happened was when I was a teenager, I would get interested in certain things like missing persons. I would see articles where I would look at it, read it, and then start to experience certain supernatural vibrations. I would see a street sign or clothes. I was just able to find those people.

It can get really spooky. It can get really accurate. I do not do these things anymore. I remote view just for myself now. I solve crimes for myself. I don't involve myself with law enforcement anymore because you just get deemed as a suspect.

Q. In the remote viewing that you do, do you actually go places?

A. Correct. Have you ever tried remote viewing before?

Q. No, I have never tried it before.

A. I think you could. I have an intuition that you could. I think anybody can learn this. They just have to have the desire to. It begins in simple ways where you see objects. But then you begin to pick up on vibrations, and you run with them. I think it's the evolution of mankind striving to become more psychic and utilize more of its mind.

Q. Black Magic. Where does it come from, and how do we use it?

A. "Black magic" is a term that I use for my own personal advancement. It could be "witchcraft" to somebody else. It could be "white light projection" to somebody else. I choose to call it for what I feel it is. It's harnessed from a projection from within the will of society, the will of nature, to manipulate it to your own personal adventures. I just call it that. "Black Magic."

It's the form of magic that I practice, and it's brought about the evoking elements within the universe. It's revoking or breaking the reality that you exist in. You call unto yourself just anything really that you want to manifest or desire.

It's something that is not for everyone because they typically want to have a watered-down version of it. No one wants to be that direct, and they are very terrified of it. And they should be. With Black Magic, you are accepting your nature of evil. You wish and want results. Like you want to be a millionaire, or you want this certain girl, you want to have certain things happen in the political spectrum, or you want to manipulate your enemy, these kinds of things are all fascinations with certain people. With Black Magic, you can make these things happen.

Evil is that core force in the galaxy, in the nature of things. Now others won't call it that. They'll call it something else, or they are coming from a different point. But I feel that I am at one with it. That is where Black Magic will come in—its lust for results. It's incantations. It's casting curses. It's releasing people from curses, which I can do. It's telling them their future. It's setting a course out for their whole world.

Q. Can you use Black Magic to hurt other people?

A. Well, you can in climbing the corporate ladder. You can hurt others and get them out of your way, or you can help yourself and manifest your account to have thousands of dollars, if not millions. You have to combine these things with action. I'll meet a lot of different practitioners, and they'll ask me why I am successful with this. It's so dangerous, and they supposedly believe in repercussions, which I do not. I do not believe in Karma. I think Karma is a conditioned herd lie that is told to the sheep to control them. If Karma was real, then mankind would have been annihilated a long time ago.

Q. Do you know a lot of other people such as yourself with these same beliefs?

A. Very few. It's rare to meet a really strong practitioner. A lot of times, these characters have egos that are just way out there. They think that they are just empowered with some kind of supernatural energy, which they probably are, but they let it go to their head. So, really they're not fun to hang out with. They do not have a sense of humor. They are not social.

Q. How do you live your life? I mean that as in, do you live like the majority of people, get married, have kids, work a job, etc.?

A. Well, I mean, it's not for everybody. I have nothing against anybody being in a relationship with one person. I don't have anything against anyone who wants to have children. For me, personally, it's not for me. Just like I won't put on some paint and pretend I'm some death metal person. I mean, I'm not putting on a show. If you saw me on the streets, you probably wouldn't realize what I'm into.

But I live a pretty normal life. I'm pretty down-to-earth. I live clean, and I don't really have any drama. So it's pretty status quo.

Q. So you don't actually put your faith into a Lucifer-God Construct?

A. I run into a lot of people who are stuck in the Lucifer-God Construct, or they're putting their faith into some Bible, or a book, or something. Or they're into Islam or Allah. I don't think that you should put your faith into anything, especially a book or a messiah. I think that you need to just believe in yourself.

Despite what my philosophy or anybody's philosophy is, Luciferin is liberation and having the power of choice, having the power to go into and do whatever you want to do. It's when you get into these other things like labels of us versus them, or we are the pure, and you are the hated. There will always be these kinds of things in human nature.

Q. Is there anybody that you pray to?

A. I don't really pray to anything. I'm already at one. I am more into evocation. I pray to the Satanic force in the universe if you were to say it like that. But I'm at one with this. It's not something I worship. I worship myself, and I worship the world that's been given to me, if I were to ever use that word. Technically, I don't worship anything, and I'm just kind of at one.

Q. You don't really belong to a church, then?

A. No. I don't really belong to an organization. I'm a solitary practitioner, and I'm on my own path. I'm more of a philosopher myself. I sit and think. But I'm not really into being a teacher. I am sort of selfish, and so is my journey. But I think we are all selfish, as is this philosophy. We are still evolving as a Satanic species.

Listen to the full interview with Winter Laake on my website:

www.alanrwarren.com/hom-podcast-episodes/episode/debbed5b/winter-john-laake-lucerferin-2015

Traditional Church of Satan

INTERVIEW WITH REVEREND DR. ROBERT FRAIZE

There are so many variations of Satanism that it's hard to keep track of which one is which. There are not nearly as many versions of Satanism as Christianity, but it only started just over 60 years ago. With the way that people become political in groups, and everyone wants to have control, I'm sure they'll get there one day.

Not only is Robert Fraize the self-declared Creator and Head of the Traditional Church of Satan, but he he has also given himself the titles of Doctor, Reverend, and even Pope. He wrote the main doctrine for the church that he calls the *Satanic Bible* that sets the rules or way of life for members.

Fraize created the church as a break-off from the Church of Satan that was originally created by Anton LaVey and is now run by Magus Peter Gilmore. Fraize believed that Gilmore had taken the church in the wrong direction, and he wanted the church to go back to more like how LaVey ran it. As he explains in this interview, he wanted the church to be more philosophical.

He also says that his church is for free-thinking Satanists. Since Fraize has a strong belief in the afterlife, including the paranormal, such as ghosts and spirits and extraterrestrial alien life, which is not accepted in the current LaVey Church of Satan, these could be the main reasons for calling it that.

On the writing of this book, I was no longer able to find the Traditional Church of Satan's website and only able to find Robert Fraize's blog page, which was last posted on in 2020. It can be found at www.occultflower.com. But he still seems active on Facebook at www.facebook.com/popefraize

This interview took place early in 2015.

Q. The Traditional Church of Satan. Where did it start, and what are their policies?

A. I started the Traditional Church of Satan because lately, we see a lot of Satanic groups basically acting too fundamentally. I don't believe Satanism is about that. I believe that Satanism is a philosophy and a religion based on individual freedom and expression. So, I want to take Satanism back to its roots and really emphasize the individual.

Q. You are not following a "devil" per se, as the Christian religion would call it?

A. Correct. The word Satan itself is defined as an adversary. Now I am a theistic Satanist, and I recognize an adversarial deity. Her name is Tiamat, which is a Babylonian Goddess creator. Now, other Satanists may view Satan as an actual external force. They view it as a symbol of rebellion against tyrannical systems in society.

Q. Now you are the creator of the church, correct?

A. Yes. The Traditional Church of Satan.

Q. What made you start it and not just join one of the other existing Satanic Churches?

A. I started this church last year on June 6th. (2015) I did not affiliate with the Church of Satan anymore because they no longer, in my opinion, go by the philosophy of LaVey. They changed the whole structure around. Not only that, they charge people $200 for a red card that basically you cannot even use to go to meetings or anything. They no longer really have meetings or group interactions. It's more like a fan club.

I really didn't want to become a part of that. I wanted to bring Satanism back towards a religious structure because there are so many groups out there, and that's fine, politically active, and just basically activists. I do belong to a couple of them, but I do not see any groups out there that are religious.

Q. How does a member of the Traditional Church of Satan member live their life?

A. This would depend because Satanism is an individual philosophy based on freedom, so it would really depend on that individual's way of life. I can only speak for myself. Basically, I wake up every day, and I take care of my son. I'm a basic regular guy. I don't go out there and stalk people or look for animals to sacrifice or anything like that. I live like a typical person.

Q. How often would you go to meetings or get together with others from the church?

A. Our church, which is the main office, which I run, meets a few times a month, and the various chapter houses throughout the United States, Canada, and England hold their own meetings. We try to keep things monthly or at least bi-monthly.

Q. What goes on in the meetings?

A. Basically, the members will interact and have a meal or a drink or two together. We celebrate life. We talk about our goals and achievements and how we can reach these goals.

Q. So, it's really more of a support system.

A. Yes. We're not teaching any set doctrines. Everyone has their own belief system. We're not going to be saying that you can't follow this or you can't develop your own system. We encourage everybody within the church to develop their own system and path.

Q You don't exclude anybody because of their race or sex or anything like that?

A. No. The only type of people we don't allow within the church are sex offenders. Sex offenders, rapists, or wife beaters, things like that, because we believe those actions are very counterproductive to what we're about.

Q. You have written two books, *The Satanic Bible* and *The Black Book of the Abyss*. What can people expect to get out of this book?

A. *The Black Book of the Abyss,* I wrote during the time that my mother was dying of cancer. I had to fill the time to take my mind off that. Basically, I see it as the starter point for Satanists. It's how to do rituals and that kind of basic thing.

The Satanic Bible is more so of a traditional sense, a bible. It has mythology. It has its rituals, songs, all that kind of stuff. Then, it has some written notes near the end of it. So, I think people will get a lot out of both of those books.

Q. So, just to get this straight, this is not a church that worships and promotes Lucifer or the Christian's idea of the devil, per se?

A. No. Many of us are not Luciferins. Although, there are a couple of Luciferins in the church, by which definition would sit under adversarial theistic Satanism. We really don't have many of them. But there are no devil worshippers in our church. The Luciferin concept you can kind of bring back prior to Christianity.

Q. Now, you believe in the afterlife or ghosts, which LaVey didn't. Tell me about that and why you don't agree with them?

A. Personal experience I've had all throughout my life. I think people should research it, and it's okay for people to be skeptical. As you said, the Church of Satan does not recognize that stuff. LaVey, when he first started, was a deist. So, he recognized an actual external force. Peter Gilmore has basically changed the structure of that church around to make it into an atheistic kind of religion which, in my opinion, is an oxymoron. I just think the paranormal exists, and people should really look into it.

Q. What was your first experience?

A. The night I was born, there were UFOs over the hospital. My mother told me about that. Then, when I was four or five, and I had an urge to look up to the window while in the basement, and I saw what looked like a cross between that vampire Nosferatu and a great alien. Ever since then, I have been having experiences with shadow people. It's not just an illusion in my mind because other people in my family have seen them as well.

Q. Why do you think that there's certain people like yourself who have these experiences with shadow people, which seems to be a popular phenomenon lately?

A. I'm still researching the phenomenon of shadow people, but I believe that they are inter-dimensional beings. And I don't know why they choose certain people to avail to, or why some people can see them while others cannot. I really don't know if they are good or evil because there have been many descriptions by many people who have said that they have done good things and others that have said that they've done bad things to them. But I really don't know yet, and it is something that I am still researching.

It's kind of what got me into the occult in the first place. Since I began to experience paranormal activities in our homes, I began to read about it to try and find out what was going on. Eventually, I got into demonology and then into occult practice.

Q. Where do you think that these beings come from?

A. I do not know yet, but I believe that they are from another dimension.

Q. You mentioned U.F.O.s. So you believe in aliens or people from other planets?

A. Definitely.

Q. How does this belief connect with your Satanism?

A. I believe that there are different alien races, and each race has its own agenda. Just like in the human race, there are good ones, and there are bad ones. Again, good, and bad is subjective depending on how you yourself view them. Basically, these aliens come here, and some want to help the human race, and others don't. Some use us as test subjects and things like that. They have their own motives, but basically, I think it's about resources now. These aliens come here for resources. They recycle energy-matter.

Q. Is there a future for us, the human race, with these aliens?

A. I think they are already involved in our day-to-day life. I think within twenty years, they are going to reveal themselves to the general public. But they definitely have influenced human beings in the past.

Q. So, when bad events happen, such as the recent ISIS attacks, do you think the aliens are behind these events by creating them or are they just watching us?

A. I think some of them have influenced it, and the others let it happen. If you think about it, all of these religions that started all believe their gods came from the sky. So, automatically those gods are aliens. They're not from this Earth.

Q. So, they let people believe in these Gods on purpose?

A. Yes. They do it to separate people too, and they do it, so the people are not going to be one unit. They have created different colors of skin and all the different things just to create separation, and it's working right now.

Q. So, does that mean that the aliens are the real God?

A. The reptilians, I believe, represent the Sumerian divinities. And so, I believe it's also the actual true God. I try to keep it as simple as that and basically focus on that.

Q. Who can join the church and become a member?

A. Anybody can, except for sex offenders. You can easily go to the website and sign up for free.

Q. When someone joins, is there some sort of regulations or rules? Are there things that they have to do, like attend meetings? What happens?

A. No. I don't believe people have to go through all that kind of stuff because that's like dictation towards others and to tell them what to do. That's very unsatanic and against our religion.

Q. We have to clear up the thing about sacrificing humans or animals for the church. Do you guys do it?

A. No, we don't do anything like that.

Q. You don't support anything like that either?

A. No, we don't.

Q. When the aliens decide to expose themselves to the general population, will that end all religions then?

A. I don't think it's going to totally end. I think it's going to heighten at that point because that's when the Gods reveal themselves to the people. Then it's going to become more difficult from there.

Q. What happens to us after we die?

A. I believe that we are made out of energy, and our soul is energy. So it goes back into the universe, and it can go back into other things. Everything is made out of the same energy, and we're all connected to one thing. So, when we die, I think sometimes our energy and consciousness can separate from the body without recycling into the universe. Other times, we will go back into the universe and be recycled into something else.

Q. Do we come back as human beings, or animals, or something else?

A. I'm not exactly sure yet. But as I see it now, I think we can go back as anything like trees, the sun, water, humans, and at all times, this energy is constantly being filtered and recycled and put back into anything else. That's how everything keeps going.

Listen to the full interview with Reverend Dr. Robert Fraize on my website:

Exorcist

INTERVIEW WITH JEFFREY SEELMAN

Some of the major religions of the world believe that a negative or evil supernatural being, such as a demon, can possess a living human being. Each of these religions claims that only a holy man who is trained and practiced in their religion can cast out or exorcise this evil entity from the possessed human being. In today's world, there are also those who are spiritual, such as a shaman, psychic, or someone else like that, who can also do this procedure and release someone from this ailment as well.

Another popular thing that it seems only psychics can do is to "clear" a house of building from negative spirits who have decided to reside there along with their human counterparts. This has become a popular thing to see on many paranormal television shows. But like most things that are supposed to be based on reality and that are on television, it's usually scripted or formulated, and you are not going to find out anything real about the occurrence.

I decided that I would seek out at least one person who conducts house clearings and calls themselves a demonologist or an exorcist. The major problem in this area is, like several others that are in the paranormal community, there are no regulatory agencies or places that people go to be certified. It's not that I am saying that somebody couldn't do such things unless they've been to a school. It's just that there are no real standards in what to expect from such healers.

Everywhere you go and talk to people in the paranormal community, you will get a different answer. Every paranormal show is much the same. Or, if anything, they all claim the same things but without any real documented proof.

After meeting with several of each type of person in the field of house clearing, demonology, and exorcism, there was only one that I thought spoke from the heart. There is no doubt in my mind that this guy was wholeheartedly out there trying to do his best to help others with these issues. This is Jeffrey Seelman.

Seelman became a professional house clearer, psychic, author, and exorcist after being in the air force. He took several courses and studied in the areas of metaphysical thought, as well as philosophy. Seelman started working in the house clearing field by clearing negative spirits from both people and the places where they lived or worked. He also gave these people what he called tools to protect themselves from other attacks.

Seelman's website is www.starclear.com

I interviewed Seelman three times during my ten years on the air with the *House of Mystery* and also once while producing another paranormal radio show. He is one of the nicest men that I have ever met, very honest, and easy to talk with. As with the other interviews in this book, I have included the highlights from all of these interviews, but they are all available to listen to on the website.

Q. As I ask everyone in the paranormal field, where did this start for you?

A. The day I was born. I was born with psychic abilities. I was able to see spirits when I was a child and also had premonitions of things that were going to happen, which came true. They were small things within my family and it kind of startled my parents. When I talked about seeing spirits around my classmates in the first few years of my school, it greatly disturbed the teachers. So, I lost friends before I could ever make them. I learned to shut up very early on in my life.

I was born in 1959, so we're talking about 1965 or so. It just wasn't all that popular of a subject. In certain circles, it might have been, but in the general population of where I lived, you don't tell your teachers that there are semi-visible people in the classroom.

My parents had brought me into a hospital for testing to see what was going on. What happened out of that was the hospital kept me overnight for one of the tests and put some electrodes on my head, and I was awake for the whole night. They just said that I had the equivalent of ESP or whatever they called it at the time. They didn't ever tell me anything as I was so young. My mother didn't really fill me in on any of that until long after I started my business.

When I went to high school, I always knew when trouble was coming, so if people were outside doing something they weren't supposed to do, I always had this little bell go off inside my head. It really wasn't a bell. It was a warning thing that the teacher, principal, or the police would be coming around within the next 15 minutes or so. I always got away with stuff, so people learned to bring me along when they were doing things, and they could use me to know when to run.

After I got out of the air force, I studied metaphysical concepts including spirit communication, good and evil, the nature spirit for about ten years. I sort of fell into a group of people who were doing some

Ouija boards, and I didn't have much interest in it at the time. But since one of the people, the leader of the group, was my new girlfriend, I decided to attend. During this, a lot of the people started having problems happen in their homes and stuff, and it actually came through the board that they should have Jeffrey take a look at it.

So, I went over to the first apartment, and it just came to me out of the blue what to do. I saw something move around in this apartment, and I threw some energy at it. It took off and never came back again. It happened a second time and they were quite startled, this group because some of them were adept at dealing with metaphysical issues. This would be about 1990. I had it recommended to me to bring this to the public, so I put a small ad in a very small newspaper in the city I was living in, which pretty much brought no attention except from the newspaper itself. So, I didn't really get any jobs. As a matter of fact, the first job I got, they didn't pay me. It didn't deter me, but it really wasn't a great moment for the first time.

The newspaper did write an article about me doing this, and that led to a national television spot on the show called *Sightings* back in the mid-nineties. It would eventually end up on the SyFy network. It was about three girls having a terrible time in their condo. Somebody was watching them take a shower. They saw the shadow outside of the shower curtain. They would wake up with indentations on their bed. They had called me, and the show got involved somehow. *Sightings* put the girls in a hotel and separated them from me so that we could have no dialogue. So, I went out there for the shooting, and it was successful. I got rid of the problem, and the problem never came back. That led to more work for me in television and radio.

Q. Back in the sixties, it was considered kind of an evil thing if you were talking to the dead. People, especially if they were religious, would think you were some sort of evil person.

A. That's a good point. I was brought up in a home that was not religious in any way.

They attended church but said they left for political reasons. As far as they thought, the church was getting political. It was not an extremist church or anything like that. It was just a regular church. It (religion) just wasn't talked about at all.

Q. How does religion fit into your life now because of what you are doing with negative spirit clearings and exorcists?

A. Kind of a fine line. I try to say nice things about religions because the people who belong to religions, very often a good percentage, tend to be very nice people. Most religions, to me, pretty much believe in the same thing generally. It's the fine print where they have differences – how to get there, that kind of thing. Many religions say there's only one path. I walk between the religions so that I can help everybody. I'm not prejudiced towards anybody for their religion or sexual orientation or gender or anything else in between. I knew that if I joined any kind of religion, even a new age religion, that only people from that religion would call me. I wanted everybody to call me.

If somebody would call, let's say a Catholic priest, but in order to have a Catholic priest come into your home and do any kind of work, just sprinkle holy water, which is really pretty much what they do unless they know there's something more serious going on, you would have to be Catholic. There's a lot of people out there who just couldn't get help because they weren't members of a particular religion.

They also ran into the problem of the pastors or priests going in there and essentially not doing anything that would actually get rid of the problem. Too many of my clients have reported to me that leaders of their religion who were supposed to help them would actually become frightened and would just make up excuses and leave. That did my clients no good, and they would call me.

Q. Does everybody have this ability to connect?

A. I think we're all connected, and I believe that we each have two levels to our system: the physical and the non-psychical. The non-physical is all telepathic and is kind of like a river that is running in between each and every one of us, and it's happening right now. So, we all have psychic abilities.

It's my belief that spirits have no physical attributes, meaning they have no eyes, or no ears, no mouths, or anything like that, so they communicate telepathically, essentially mind to mind. They can create eyes and ears by visualization, creating their form and image, and clothing not through cloth, but something that looks like it but it's just energy.

We all have that happening, but we're not necessarily attuned as much to it as we could be because we are so focused on the physical world. And because our eyes and ears are geared toward the physical universe.

Q. What do we need to protect ourselves against in our homes?

A. The most common problem that I find is negative emotional energy. Anger and fear, unhappiness, and depression all have corresponding energies to them, and most people live in places where other people have lived before many times. A hundred people have lived there if your building or house is very old and people have lived there.

We all generate good and bad energies, emotional energies, which are non-physical energies. And those energies have a tendency to accumulate in our living and working environment and also in our body's own energy fields, also known as the aura. That can be problematic because we're now living with other people's energies that might have lived in our homes fifty years ago.

We might replace the windows or carpets and all of that stuff, but one thing that we don't do is we don't replace the atmosphere of the living or working environment, and we don't clear our own body's personal energy.

We work on our physical system to strengthen our physical bodies, but we do not do anything about our non-physical bodies. Now that's not true of everybody. I am generalizing. But for the most part, we are not taught that we pick up emotional energy from other people and also from environments that we come into contact with. And that it can build up inside of our bodies and cause all sorts of problems.

Q. So, are we all leaving energy in the places where we live? So, when I was in college, and I lived in an apartment for a few years while studying, then moved away when I graduated, did I leave some energy behind?

A. Yes. We generate emotional energy as easily as we generate sweat. Even people who visit the place where you live are releasing emotional energy into the atmosphere. So, there's a very large accumulation, and so you can imagine how much emotional energy can be trapped and left behind in our living environments.

Q. I can imagine the workplace that had hundreds of people working in them, such as a warehouse, would be pretty wild then?

A. Yeah, and even smaller amounts too. Say that you are working in a restaurant, and maybe there have been two restaurants, ten restaurants, or even 20 restaurants there before that. Those restaurants eventually failed, were sold, or something. But there's usually some kind of failure, and with that, there's going to come a lot of anger, depression, and hopelessness.

So, here, the new owners come in, and they spend lots of money on the renovations—maybe they put in a new kitchen, and new tables, and new chairs—but what they forgot to do was clear the atmosphere. So, people come in, and everything looks great, but it doesn't feel great. And people don't like eating in restaurants that don't feel right.

I think everybody has gone into a restaurant or shop or even somebody's home, saying this place doesn't feel really good. It feels kind of weird. It feels uncomfortable. What they are picking up on is emotional energy.

Q. When you are in a place that has had severe emotional energy, like a murder or something, would that be a harder place to clear?

A. No, not really. There are some misconceptions about that. Those are negative events that happened. What the real danger is, is the build-up of emotional energy. Now when real negative events happen in a certain place, it can attract negative spirits because there is negative energy. And also, some negative spirits consider it to be kind of like a shrine. This negative event happened there, just like we might consider certain places where good events happened, or bad events have happened in history, sort of like a shrine or negative place. Negative spirits can be attracted to places where negative things have happened. If there's a lot of emotional energy in that environment from an event, it can make them (spirits) feel stronger. It's kind of like the thickening of soup, and it makes it easier to transmit emotional energy when there's a lot of emotional energy in the environment. If a negative spirit is going to attack a person or a family, it's much easier to do in an atmosphere where there's a lot of emotional energy.

Q. How does that work when we get places like the 911 Towers or the London Towers, where people were beheaded? And let's say you go and clear those places, but then afterward, you now have thousands of visitors going to these places every year, and they are going with the memory of what happened there in their minds. Won't they be putting that negative energy back into those places?

A. That would be true, but with something like 911, that happened actually very quickly. So there was not a lot of time to leave a lot of negative emotional energy, and many of the victims didn't even know what was happening. They just knew the building was on fire and didn't know why, and then, of course, they collapsed, so it happened rather quickly.

Maybe a better example would be maybe a concentration camp or a prison where there's long-term abuse of humans or animals or anything else. Animals also have souls and so do insects. These things happen over a long period of time, over a number of years, and you have a much greater build-up of negative emotional energy than an event that happens very quickly.

In an event like 911, you would have more fear energy created because most of the people who were victims didn't really know what was happening. The visitors who go to that usually have an outpouring of sadness, and maybe some anger as well, and certainly if it's directed towards a certain spot, then it can build up in that area, or it can dissipate as well. It all depends on what they are focusing upon.

Q. How can you tell the difference between a spirit and residual energy?

A. A spirit is essentially a soul that is not really any different than a living person, whether they are from this planet or another planet, and it's happening right now. Residual energy is not alive and has no consciousness to it. But it is actually an energy and a different kind of energy. Spirits move from place to place where negative emotional energy tends to go. It's supposed to navigate towards the Earth, which naturally takes in negative energy. I'm not saying the Earth is alive. I don't really believe the Earth has a consciousness to it, but it certainly has a lot of beings that have the consciousness to them. So residual energy looks just like the energy that does not belong, and spirits look pretty much something like you and I do. They don't look any different, really. They just generate a form like we do.

Q. Now, your website says that you perform exorcisms. Do you actually get a lot of cases that need an exorcism?

A. Well, yes. People get attacked all the time, and negative spirits try to get people to do negative things. That would be under the category of spiritual or psychic attack. An exorcism is a separation of two spirits that are intertwined—where a spirit has actually entered into the energy field of a living person on the level of their spirit or soul and is affecting them. And in the worst-case scenarios, even in control of them, but that is far less common.

How these things usually happen is extreme amounts of anger, depression, also substance abuse. I want to make it really clear that when I'm talking about substance abuse, not use, sometimes when people use too much of a certain chemical, they sort of check out, and something else checks in temporarily. Temporary possession is what it is.

If they are completely possessed and being directed and controlled by a spirit, the last person they are going to call is somebody like me. I mean, they are not going to let the person call me. If they are in complete control, they are not going to call an exorcist that's going to evict them from a person or a home.

Usually, what I run into most often is people under attack, and they are either being affected by negative emotional energies that are in their living environment or at work, or they are coming from somebody around them, or there's a spirit that is in their home.

Another misconception is that spirits live in people's homes. Spirits don't need shelter, and they don't really need to live in people's homes. If they want to go around and cause trouble throughout the day or throughout the night, they can hit a hundred homes. They don't have to stay in one particular home. They can just go from one home to another, and they very often do that.

They can travel instantly, as they don't have a physical body. They can just visualize where they want to go, and with a little bit of belief and impulse, they actually make that happen. Visualization and imagination and belief can act very differently scientifically on the non-physical level than they do on the physical level. So, all of this is essentially science, and I make it quite clear on my website. I've been doing this for twenty-three years professionally, and I have no problem with physical science. It's real.

As we progress and become more preceptive, then physical science will run into non-physical science because it's completely interconnected, and there's just no opposition or problems between these two sciences.

Q. You say that you can teach Astro-traveling. What is that?

A. We do Astro-traveling every night. Whenever we sleep, we actually leave our bodies. Part of our consciousness leaves our body and goes out and interacts with other people who are dreaming and also spirits who are fully conscious. So, we do Astro-traveling naturally every night.

I teach people how to do it when they are fully conscious. I don't really teach remote viewing. I really don't believe in it. Actually, it can be done, I just don't think it's a very good idea, and I think it's an invasion of privacy. So, I don't teach people how to do that. What I teach them is how to get in contact with their spirit guides and how to take their consciousness and actually look at other realms. Essentially, what some people might call heaven, or other people might call the other side.

Q. Would that also be a way of connecting with a passed loved one?

A. It is, but also it's a great way to strengthen the mind and to see what the other side looks like, which is really not so much different than what it looks like with what the physical looks like to us. Now there are no physical objects or people on the other side. That does not mean that spirits do not create clothing because they like to look nice. They don't have any sexual organs, but they like to look nice. They also create houses and homes and even towns and cities on a collective conscious level.

Listen to the full interview with Jeffrey Seelman on my website:

www.alanrwarren.com/hom-
podcast-episodes/episode/
dc673110/exorcist-jeffrey-
seelman

Cryptozoology
INTERVIEW WITH NICK REDFERN

What exactly is cryptozoology? The first time I heard that word talked about with some paranormal television people, I pretended to know what they were talking about. But I didn't have a clue. It ranks up there with ufology. Both words have been created from the paranormal community to cover the study of certain subjects within that community.

Even though both words sound official and even scientific, they are not. Cryptozoology and ufology are both pseudosciences trying to sound like they are based on real and studied science accepted by the world of academia, but neither of them is.

I am not trying to put both categories of research down, but only conveying how it really is. One of the biggest problems with having a group of people who believe that a certain phenomenon or creature is alive and walking the face of the Earth without any science experience is they usually don't know the proper steps to study it correctly.

The cryptozoology name is meant to prove the existence of beings that have come from old tales and stories over the years which started with "Bigfoot" or "Sasquatch" in the 1970s, brought on by the popularity of the Patterson Gimlin film from 1967. Today, cryptozoology covers all things and creatures that are supposed to be out in the world we live in, such as the "Yeti," "Chupacabra," "Dog Man," and more. It also covers the history of monsters such as the Loch Ness in the U.K.

Over the years, we talked with quite a few different people covering both categories, and probably the most reliable person I was able to find was Nick Redfern. He was reliable mostly because he has written well over 30 books, and during his research in strange creatures, he was the only person that I could find who actually traveled to the location of the spotting and actually spent time talking with the witnesses.

Redfern is a best-selling author of books covering the areas of both cryptozoology and ufology. He has made several television appearances on both aliens and the many unknown creatures of the world. I was able to talk with him for an interview back in 2015. The only place I could find Nick Redfern on the internet is at his blog page at www.nickredfern.wordpress.com or on Facebook at www.facebook.com/nick.redfern.73

Q. So, while doing your research into these subjects, you actually traveled to the locations where the creature was supposed to have been seen, correct?

A. Yes, the internet is a really good resource tool for background information, but what the internet doesn't necessarily provide you with is firsthand case files. For example, I've been on an expedition to Puerto Rico in search of the Chupacabra, while I've been out there and this is across 2004 and 2014, I've interviewed literally dozens and dozens of people that have seen the Chupacabra that has never put their stories on the internet. They were happy to share their reports privately, but they just didn't want to be bothered by everybody.

When you go out to these locations, you hang out with the local people, and they realize that you are doing this research for solid reasons. You gain their trust and vice versa, and then they open up. On the internet, you're not able to do that. You can find articles on the Chupacabra, but that's a far cry from sitting in someone's front room and in a village in the rain forest. I try to take the journalistic approach of following the facts and the witness testimony, even though I'm dealing with strange and unusual topics.

Q. Now, the Chupacabra has only been around twenty to thirty years?

A. It's twenty years this very year when the term "Chupacabra" was first used in 1995, and where all things really began with reports of attacks on farm animals and livestock, etc., on a number of Puerto Rican small ranches and little farms.

The term "Chupacabra" is a Spanish term that means "goat sucker," and the reason it was given the name was a lot of animals that were attacked were small goats. Reportedly, there were two puncture marks on the neck and sometimes another puncture wound on the stomach. In the initial wave of attacks, although the animals were found dead, nobody had seen the predator itself.

But that changed shortly afterward when a number of people saw this thing that they described as having a body, not unlike that of a chimpanzee in size, build, and speed, but he was hairless and had a row of spikes down its head, and a reptilian color to its skin. There were a few odd, unusual reports where people had said it had large bat-like wings, which gave it an almost gargoyle kind of imagery. It caused hysteria for months with major media coverage.

Q. How were the people you questioned about the Chupacabra? Were they scared to talk about it?

A. When I first got to go to Puerto Rico, I was with the SyFy network for a T.V. program called *Proof Positive*. The thing was that because it was with the SyFy channel, they contracted a woman who was a translator who also found all the witnesses for us to interview. So we were able to interview two or three people a day. We got a good solid body of material.

One of the very first interviews we did was a rancher named Mayal, and he told us how he bred chickens, and he got chickens in cages in the sort of backyard area of his ranch. When I say ranch, you know it's not like a huge ranch. Over here, a lot of the people are unfortunately quite poor, so it's farm area sort of about 70 or 80 square foot area of his backyard.

But he told us how he woke up one morning to find all the cages sort of open, but obviously with something that had strength because some of the cages were bent, and they were all dead inside the cages. Now what was weird was the area where they were kept backed onto his back door. You would imagine that in the middle of the night, if there'd been all these attacks going on, the chickens would have been making a lot of noise. They would have woken up not just him but the whole neighborhood in this little village in the rain forest.

But that didn't happen. It was only when he woke up the next morning that he would find them all dead and with these weird puncture wounds. That was the very first case that really plunged us into the heart of the mystery, if you like.

Q. That would be quite odd.

A. Yes, everything about that case was odd: the puncture wounds, the reported blood loss of the animals, the animals hadn't been touched, you know, or partially eaten with the wounds. That was kind of odd because if it would have been a predator attacking in somewhere like Puerto Rico, it's going to need a food supply, particularly in the rainforest. It's not just like a wild dog attacking, wildly attacking a few sheep in a field. In Puerto Rico, the predators are looking for food, not to just kill an animal and leave it there.

Unfortunately, we weren't able to get somebody to do an autopsy of the chickens because this was a couple of years earlier. Had that happened, we might have been able to tell if there was, as reported, a significant blood loss through the wounds or not. That certainly quickly became the staple part of the mystery, like a vampire angle to it.

Q. When you first got to this ranch and heard this story about the chickens, what was your first thought on what could have happened?

A. Well, my first thought, and probably the correct thought, was that I was thrown into this surreal world that was even more bizarre and surreal than things I had been doing for the last ten years. But the interesting thing was that they all came across as very lucid, credible, and down to Earth. They just wanted answers for what had happened because this wasn't a rich guy, and it was his livelihood. He wasn't so much telling me this story for the sake of telling it. He was more concerned at the time for his family's livelihood and just putting food on his family's table.

So, in other words, he was looking at it from that angle. From my angle, I was trying to figure out what kind of animal has the ability to be so stealthy that it could kill one chicken after another systematically, without the others even knowing it before the creatures upon them. There was nothing indigenous to Puerto Rico that I could think of to do that.

There are no large predators in Puerto Rico. There's nothing like big cats or bears, nothing at all. The largest animals in Puerto Rico are the imported ones like pigs, cows, cattle, that kind of thing. But there really isn't anything that would have the ability to race around the island of Puerto Rico and slaughter animals, draining blood or not.

Whatever the animal is was either suddenly something new to Puerto Rico, or it was something that had been stealthy all along, but it took until 1995 for people to realize that there was actually something there.

Q. What would this creature's motives be? If it wasn't there to eat the animals or feed their young with, why were they killing? Were the dead animals completely drained of all their blood?

A. Well, that's a good question. The whole issue of blood draining, blood-sucking, blood-drinking, etc., is a very controversial one because, as I said, with the ranchers, a lot of them being very poor, figuring out what the Chupacabra was, wasn't on the forefront of their minds. They were just interested in putting food on their family's table.

The ranchers rarely even bother to keep the animals we're talking about in an environment where the summer temperature goes up to the low hundreds, so for that reason, they just don't leave the corpses lying around rotting and stinking out the environment. So they just get rid of them.

In terms of trying to figure out what the motivation is if they are not eating the creatures, then to systematically take time to kill them doesn't really make sense. So, this is why the scenario of the blood-drinking, in part at least, came forward. A number of witnesses did actually say that they saw the creature not so much sucking the blood but almost lapping it, like a cat lapping milk out of a saucer, that sort of thing. Although I heard several stories of blood-sucking or blood-drinking, I have never been able to prove that blood-sucking actually did go on.

Q. Why do you think the stories only started in the mid-nineties?

A. A lot of people ask me why these stories just started in 1995. There are some reports that sound, in hindsight, like the Chupacabra attacks that occurred many years earlier. For example, in the 1980s, there were reports of a creature that became known as the "Devil Bird." This creature reportedly attacked animals in similar fashions as the Chupacabra. But it died away fairly quickly, so it was forgotten.

The same thing happened in 1975 with a creature known as the "Moca Vampire." Moca is an area in Puerto Rico, and the creature acted in a very similar fashion to the whole Devil Bird and the Chupacabra scenario.

In other words, we have this sort of a very weird situation of animal attacks going on decades ago, long before the term Chupacabra was created. In hindsight, it could have been the creature.

Q. As your investigation continued, you actually say that you interviewed somebody who actually had a face-to-face meeting with the beast?

A. Yes. I think that was the third day we were on the island. We met a lady named Norca, who actually lived in a house in the high forest. In order to access it, you would have to go around this windy road. Norca told us how that in 1975, she was driving home, and it was sort of dusk. So it wasn't dark, but the sun was starting to set. She was driving slowly, which is the only way that you can do it in that area because the roads are so twisting and winding. She saw this creature or thing on the righthand side of the road. She was only doing about 15 miles an hour, so she was easily able to slow down before she got too close.

She said it was like 5 feet high, and it almost looked like a cloak over its head, and it was shuffling slowly from right to left. She couldn't figure out what it was. It looked like a little old person shuffling across the road. She said that she just sat there and watched it, kind of puzzled. She got terrified when it turned towards her, and she saw these bright red fiery eyes, and suddenly, what she assumed was a cloak opened up into two very large bat-like wings. It didn't take to the skies or anything like that, but she felt that possibly, in hindsight, that he opened his wings as a sort of a form of intimidation.

This thing looked at her for about five or six seconds, then folded its wings back up and vanished to the other side of the thick, dense rainforest environment. She told us that she did remember that there were some animal attacks in the area in that same period.

What she described sounds like a giant bat. So, the theory has developed that the Moca Vampire, the Devil Bird, and the Chupacabra could be some sort of huge mutant type of vampire bat. In the fossil record, we do see evidence of large bats that did exist in the distant past. So, it's not impossible.

Q. How many stories did you come across?

A. I probably now have somewhere in the range of 30 or 40 witness reports, and the vast majority of them, apart from maybe one or two, talk about a creature that apparently has the ability to move on two limbs or four limbs. There are a number of known animals that will do that, like the baboon. They can skillfully do that. The bear will stand up on its hind legs, but its main form of walking is on four limbs.

I would say a good 50 or 60 percent of the reports describe a row of spikes down its head or down the back of its neck. I would say about 7 or 8 percent of the people talk about the wings. Now admittedly, some of the witnesses said that they didn't see wings until the thing actually opened its wings. There could have been more wing-based reports had the people not just seen the creature fleetingly and just from the front.

The other important thing to remember, of course, is that although the ranchers tend to find their animals attacked when they get up in the morning, most of the attacks occur during the night. Most of the sightings occur late at night, so in other words, when you're in an environment where, here in the U.S., we're bombarded by light pollution. In Puerto Rico, when you get out of the main city of San Juan, where you are out in the little towns and villages, there aren't any streetlights, and for the most part its very dark. The only illumination is from the homes. When you get out into the rural countryside, it's sort of pitch black. So, for the witnesses, that can make it doubly hard to get a full positive description when they might have a fleeting view of it for about five or ten seconds in an area where the only illumination is merely car headlights, or if they got a flashlight.

Q. Have there been any humans that have been attacked or had the blood sucked from them?

A. That's an interesting question, and I'll tell you why it's so interesting. Every time I've been to Puerto Rico, I've heard these stories of Chupacabra attacks on people. There literally has not been a time when I haven't been to Puerto Rico that I have not heard these stories. But I have to admit that these have been the most dangerous ones to chase down, and as far as I got with these stories is somebody that says, well I got it from this person, they got it from that person, you know. Sort of a friend-of-a-friend story. It doesn't necessarily mean that the stories are just urban legend or folklore. What I do think is that if there have been human attacks and human killings, that would, without doubt, be the one area that the local authorities on the island would want to keep under wraps. So, it doesn't surprise me that so many of these stories are shrouded in secrecy.

Q. I have also heard about some rumors of the military having captured some of these creatures and taken them to the mainland. Is that true?

A. That's something again that I have heard several times. It relates to a military base on Puerto Rico called Roosevelt Road, which closed down in 2004, and it was the largest U.S. naval base in the area. I am sure that everybody has sort of heard these stories of the U.S. government having dead alien's bodies in bunkers where they are sort of cryogenically preserved and were recovered from UFO crashes several years ago. They have people come in every so often to autopsy or study them to figure out what they are.

There are kind of similar stories to that with the Chupacabra in Puerto Rico. I'll probably get about 5 or 6 stories of people who claimed to know that the U.S. military from Roosevelt Road reportedly was able to capture some pretty vicious living Chupacabra and also kill some others. They were reportedly flown in like steel cages, and they sedated the ones that weren't dead and transferred them to the U.S. with some unknown destination. Sort of a military installation, on the lines of something like Area 51.

The stories were quite detailed about the living ones and how the military knew where they had their lair, which was a particular cave system. What's interesting is that Puerto Rico has a vast, literally massive number of caves, caverns, and cave networks that go not just along the island but deep down. Some of these cave systems are out of bounds to the public and against the law to go into, which adds to the conspiracy.

Q. Do you associate this creature with what has been called "Dog Man" on the mainland of America?

A. Well, all of these creatures, whether it's Bigfoot, Loch Ness Monster, Chupacabra, are collectively all known as cryptids, and the name comes from the subject of cryptozoology – the study of unknown animals or unacknowledged animals.

As in terms of associations and connections, the main similarity that we have between the Chupacabra and the so-called Dog Man is this ability to sort of run and walk on two legs and four. The Dog Man sort of provokes imagery of werewolves, and whenever you mention werewolves, you have this picture in mind of somebody bursting out of their clothes on a full moon and changing into this killer werewolf that can only be stopped with a silver bullet or whatever.

If you look at the reports that people have done like Linda Godfrey, who more than anybody else has done a massive amount of research and written 5 or 6 books on this topic, Linda hardly has a case on somebody claiming to have literally morphed and transformed from human form to a werewolf. Most of the reports, although they have a werewolf quality to them, they actually don't involve this traditional shape-shifting, as it's called. Most of the reports that Linda has are of creatures that seem to be wolf-like.

But the fact of both of them being able to walk on both two and four legs is where the similarity ends. There are a lot of articles of the Dogman sort of scavenging food and things like that, whereas the Puerto Rican creature just seems to kill the animals unless it really is the blood aspect.

Q. How do you answer that there are no bodies found of these creatures?

A. Well, you know that's an extremely good question, and it's one I get all the time. The one answer that has a degree of plausibility but cannot explain everything is the fact that when something dies in the woods, the other animals just don't let it lay there. Nature has a way of getting rid of these things. It doesn't take long when a bear dies in the wood before other animals move in, and it's dinner, breakfast, and lunch for the next few days. That could certainly explain a large number of reports of why we don't have a body of Bigfoot, for example.

The other theories that have been put forward do offer an explanation, but they do so by offering even bigger layers of mystery. You have the idea that Bigfoot is sort of a paranormal creature, a spirit God of the woods, that sort of thing, rather than physical flesh and blood animal. If it was something like that, of course, it requires us to explain what a spirit God of the woods is.

Then you have the theories that what if Bigfoot is more of an evolved creature that looks primitive but actually isn't. That being the case, suggestions are being made that they have sort of burial rites even. We actually think that we are the only ones that mourn; however, with elephants, for example, when one of the herd dies, they mourn quite as we do.

The only downside I have with all of this is even I find it difficult to believe that we could never get a body. I could understand how about 90 percent of the time, if these things do bury their dead that we couldn't find them. But for us to never get a body is troubling.

Q. Are animals still being killed in Puerto Rico by this elusive Chupacabra, or has it stopped now?

A. Well, that's a good question because every time I've been to Puerto Rico, I've gotten new reports. But the reason I've got them is that I've been out there, and I took the time and energy to track people down and find them and interview them. In other words, reports are going on, but only because other people are going out and looking for them. It's not like back in 1995 with the hysteria. Today, people aren't just coming forward to say, "Oh, I saw this creature," because all of the hysteria has died down.

Listen to the full interview with Nick Redfern on my website:

www.alanrwarren.com/hom-
podcast-episodes/episode/
ae875bc0/nick-redfern-
cryptozoology-2015

References

1. Ciaran O' Keefe – https://shows.acast.
   com/houseofmysteryradio/episodes/
   ciaran-o-keefe-parapsychology-2014
2. Steve Parsons Interviews – 1) https://
   shows.acast.com/houseofmysteryradio/
   episodes/5b7eeeb736bf3f4166bc8c30 2)
   https://shows.acast.com/
   houseofmysteryradio/episodes/
   5b7eeeb736bf3f4166bc8c5b 3) https://
   shows.acast.com/houseofmysteryradio/
   episodes/5b7eeeb736bf3f4166bc8c5a
3. Lloyd Auerbach Interview – https://
   shows.acast.com/houseofmysteryradio/
   episodes/lloyd-aberauch-parapsychology

4. David Wells Interview – https://shows.
   acast.com/houseofmysteryradio/
   episodes/5b7eeeb836bf3f4166bc8cb8
5. Derek Acorah Interview – https://shows.
   acast.com/houseofmysteryradio/
   episodes/5b7eeeb736bf3f4166bc8c64
6. James Van Praagh Interview – https://
   shows.acast.com/houseofmysteryradio/
   episodes/5b7eeeb736bf3f4166bc8c61
7. Jackie Dennison Interview – https://
   shows.acast.com/houseofmysteryradio/
   episodes/5b7eeeb736bf3f4166bc8c62
8. Mark Allan Frost Interview – https://
   shows.acast.com/houseofmysteryradio/
   episodes/mark-allan-frost-channeling-
   seth
9. Gary Mannion Interview – https://shows.
   acast.com/houseofmysteryradio/
   episodes/psychic-surgeon-gary-mannion-
   2014
10. Rob Gutro Interviews – 1) https://shows.
    acast.com/houseofmysteryradio/
    episodes/rob-gutro-pets-in-the-afterlife-3
    2) https://shows.acast.com/
    houseofmysteryradio/episodes/rob-gutro-
    kindred-spirit 3) https://shows.acast.

com/houseofmysteryradio/
episodes/5b7eeeb736bf3f4166bc8c66

11. Diane Corcoran Interview – https://
    shows.acast.com/houseofmysteryradio/
    episodes/near-death-experiences-diane-
    corcoran-2015

12. Robert Waggoner Interview – https://
    shows.acast.com/houseofmysteryradio/
    episodes/lucid-dreaming-robert-
    waggoner-2015

13. Lyn Buchanan Interview – https://shows.
    acast.com/houseofmysteryradio/
    episodes/remote-viewing-lyn-buchanan

14. Uri Geller Interview – https://shows.
    acast.com/houseofmysteryradio/
    episodes/uri-geller

15. Robert Murch Interview – https://shows.
    acast.com/houseofmysteryradio/
    episodes/ouija-boards-robert-murch-2014

16. Steven Frampton Interview – https://
    shows.acast.com/houseofmysteryradio/
    episodes/5b7eeeb736bf3f4166bc8c8a

17. Alison Baughman Interview – https://
    shows.acast.com/houseofmysteryradio/
    episodes/numerology-alison-baughman-
    2015

18. Tarot Interview –
19. Johnny Zaffis Interview – https://shows.
    acast.com/houseofmysteryradio/
    episodes/johnny-zaffis-haunted-collector-
    2015
20. Peter Gilmore Interview – https://shows.
    acast.com/houseofmysteryradio/
    episodes/magus-peter-gilmore-church-
    of-satan-201
21. Krystal Madison Interview – https://
    shows.acast.com/houseofmysteryradio/
    episodes/5b7eeeb736bf3f4166bc8c5c
22. Winter (John) Laake Interview – https://
    shows.acast.com/houseofmysteryradio/
    episodes/winter-john-laake-lucerferin-
    2015
23. Robert Fraize Interview – https://shows.
    acast.com/houseofmysteryradio/
    episodes/reverend-dr-robert-fraize-
    traditional-church-of-satan-2015
24. Jeffrey Seelman Interview – https://
    shows.acast.com/houseofmysteryradio/
    episodes/exorcist-jeffrey-selman
25. Nick Redfern Interview – https://shows.
    acast.com/houseofmysteryradio/
    episodes/nick-redfern-cryptozoology-
    2015

26. Michael Hughes Interview – https://www.alanrwarren.com/hom-podcast-episodes/episode/b5c50aed/michael-m-hughes-tarot

About the Author

Alan R. Warren has written several bestselling True Crime books and has been one of the hosts and producers of the popular NBC news talk radio show the *House of Mystery,* which reviews True Crime, History, Science, Religion, Paranormal mysteries that  we live with every day. From a darker, comedic, and logical perspective, he has interviewed guests such as Robert Kennedy Jr., F. Lee Bailey, Aphrodite Jones, Marcia Clark, Nancy Grace, Dan Abrams, and Jesse Ventura. The show is based in Seattle on KKNW 1150 AM and syndicated on the NBC network throughout the United States, including on KCAA 106.5 FM Los Angeles/Riverside/Palm Springs, as well in Utah, New Mexico, and Arizona.

Read more about Alan on his website:
alanrwarren.com

Also in The House of Mystery Interviews Series

The *House of Mystery Radio Show* has been on the air for ten years, broadcasting in over a dozen cities in the U.S. It started as a way to interview guests knowledgeable in many of the world's mysteries involving crime, science, religion, history, paranormal, conspiracies, etc. The *House of Mystery Interview Series* is a curated collection of interviews from the show. Each volume focuses on one of the mysteries, providing the background and reproducing the main points discussed in the interviews. There will be no committed answer at the end, as the Interviews series does not attempt to solve the case. Instead, it provides the most compelling aspects of each theory held by different experts. This series is an excellent reference for researchers and a good overview for those unfamiliar with the case. Online links to the actual interviews are included.

VOLUME 1: JACK THE RIPPER: THE INTERVIEWS

Volume 1 of the Interview Series, "Jack the Ripper," covers the ultimate "who-done-it" mystery of 1888 London. Scotland Yard's "Whitechapel Murder File," in which Jack the Ripper had a starring role, went cold before it could be solved. One hundred thirty-two years later, and the fascination with this cold case mystery continues. Ripperologists passionately debate suspects, opinions, research methods, and theories. Even which murder victims to include in the case is widely debated. Astonishingly, work continues, and today Ripperologists still find new clues that bring us closer to solving the mystery.

the HOUSE OF MYSTERY RADIOSHOW presents

JACK *the* RIPPER

THE INTERVIEWS: VOLUME 1

ALAN R. WARREN
MICHAEL L. HAWLEY

The mix of credible and diverse thinkers interviewed includes world-renowned historian Neil Storey, the Godfather of Ripper Research, Paul Begg, Ripperologists: Paul Williams, Tom Wescott, Adam Wood, and Steve Blomer. Michael Hawley contributes his unprecedented scientific approach to the case. Suspect Ripperologists Jeff Mudgett, whose great-great-grandfather was serial killer H.H. Holmes, weighs in, as does Russell Edwards, who believes he solved the mystery through DNA.

VOLUME 2: JFK ASSASSINATION: THE INTERVIEWS

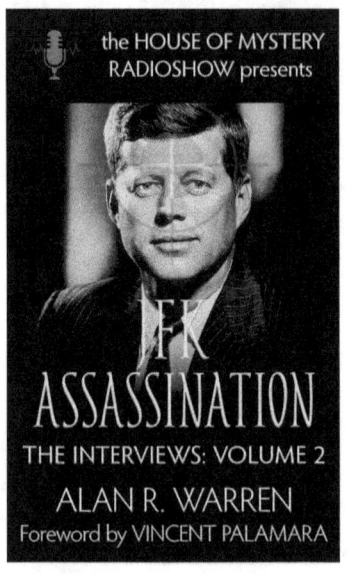

the HOUSE OF MYSTERY
RADIOSHOW presents

JFK
ASSASSINATION
THE INTERVIEWS: VOLUME 2
ALAN R. WARREN
Foreword by VINCENT PALAMARA

Volume 2 of the Interview Series, "JFK Assassination," covers *the* unrivaled historical mystery of historical mysteries. The JFK assassination is the grandfather of all conspiracies in America and arguably where they all started. A highly popular President with movie star looks and charisma, effecting significant changes in society, was brutally cut down in his prime. The official story was that JFK was killed by a sole assassin, Lee Harvey Oswald. However, many conspiracy theorists believe in an assassination plot involving the FBI, CIA, U.S. military, VP LBJ, Cuba's Fidel Castro, Russia's KGB, the Mafia, or some combination of those entities.

The research and interviewing of the JFK assassination experts lasted for over six years. Arguments and counter-arguments from a diverse mix of bestselling authors make for some interesting discussions. And some of the authors interviewed are considered just as controversial as the mystery itself. Most authors focused on who they believe was responsible for the assassination. Others narrowed their focus on certain related aspects, such as the Zapruder film, Nix film, Garrison Tapes, etc. All information collected from each expert adds value to the overall mystery.

VOLUME 3: ZODIAC KILLER: THE INTERVIEWS

Volume 3 of the Interview Series, "Zodiac Killer," covers another serial killer who has stayed in the spotlight for years after their case has gone cold. It's been over 40 years now, and fascination with the Zodiac is still going strong. Experts passionately debate Zodiac suspects, Zodiac"s letters/ciphers, opinions, and theories. Even which murder victims to include in the case is widely debated.

the HOUSE OF MYSTERY RADIOSHOW presents

WANTED

SAN FRANCISCO POLICE DEPARTMENT

ZODIAC KILLER

THE INTERVIEWS: VOLUME 3

ALAN R. WARREN
MICHAEL BUTTERFIELD

The diverse mix of authors interviewed includes cryptologist and cipher expert David Oranchak, authors who propose their suspects are already convicted serial killers, authors who claim the Zodiac was their father, authors who offer new or already considered suspects, and an author who argues the Zodiac killer didn't exist at all and that Zodiac was a hoax.

VOLUME 4: MYSTERIOUS CELEBRITY DEATHS: THE INTERVIEWS

Volume 4 of the Interview Series, "Mysterious Celebrity Deaths," covers interviews relating to the mysterious deaths of the influential rock band Nirvana's frontman Kurt Cobain, the 1960s mega-icon Marilyn Monroe, T.V.'s *Hogan's Heroes* lead actor Bob Crane, the talented and multi-award-winning actress Natalie Wood, and the people's princess, Princess Diana.

VOLUME 5: CONSPIRACY THEORY CULTURE: THE INTERVIEWS

Volume 5 of the *House of Mystery Interviews Series* will focus on theories that go against the scientific facts that we have learned over many generations of the human race. There is something uniquely intriguing about a good conspiracy theory. They tell tales of heroes, villains, and alternative realities. Conspiracy theories represent secret knowledge: real or not, and there is something very pleasing about having supposed insider knowledge.

Because of their entertainment value, you can find conspiracy theories everywhere. Implausibility doesn't make conspiracy theories less entertaining. What if the moon landing was faked? Who would have been involved? How could they have pulled it off, and why? What if the earth is encapsulated by a celestial lid? What if the infamous leader of the Third Reich escaped Germany? What if President Franklin Roosevelt had allowed the Pearl Harbor attacks to happen?

These are a few of the conspiracy theories discussed in this volume. As with the others in this series, this book will cover the most popular conspiracies – the ones that have gained lots of ground in the media and on the internet. Some of them even have celebrity followers. During the interviews, guests were shown the utmost respect, as we tried to find out their reasoning for believing what they do and how they developed their beliefs.